William Cleaver Wilkinson

Classic Latin Course in English

William Cleaver Wilkinson

Classic Latin Course in English

ISBN/EAN: 9783337177553

Printed in Europe, USA, Canada, Australia, Japan

Cover: Foto ©Paul-Georg Meister /pixelio.de

More available books at **www.hansebooks.com**

Chautauqua Reading Circle Literature

CLASSIC LATIN COURSE

IN ENGLISH

BY

WILLIAM CLEAVER WILKINSON

FLOOD AND VINCENT
The Chautauqua-Century Press
MEADVILLE PENNA
150 FIFTH AVE. NEW YORK
1893

The Chautauqua-Century Press, Meadville, Pa., U. S. A.
Electrotyped, Printed, and Bound by Flood & Vincent.

PREFACE.

SINCE publishing, ten years ago, the beginning volume of the "After-School" series of books—the volume then entitled "Preparatory Greek Course in English"—the author has, in successive editions, subjected his work to many revisions and changes. The most important of these have had for their object increasing compression of the matter presented. The present volume may be taken as the final form of that part of the whole work which relates to Latin literature. The series is now complete in four volumes, uniform in plan, in form, in size, in title, and in price, devoted respectively to Greek, to Latin, to French, and to German, literature.

It is proper to add that the original fuller volumes, four in number, treating Greek literature and Latin, are still kept in print for the benefit of those readers who may desire either to see more copiously exhibited the ancient authors embraced in our revised list of immortals, or to see additional names of such brought under review—names that, in the process of abridgment, were unavoidably excluded. The things left out would probably in most cases be by the majority of readers, as they are by the author, accounted not less interesting and not less valuable than the things retained. The problem of compression was not so much to make the pages better, as simply to make them fewer.

The author gratifies himself by renewing here his acknowledgment of debt to his honored friend of many years,

Bishop JOHN H. VINCENT, for the fruitful *idea* which, under that stimulating friend's constant council and encouragement, he has done his best fitly to realize in this series of volumes.

CONTENTS.

CHAPTER. PAGE.

I. THE LITERATURE OF ROME 7

II. SALLUST 13

III. OVID 21

IV. CÆSAR 28

V. CICERO 51

VI. VIRGIL 91

VII. LIVY 143

VIII. TACITUS 175

IX. PLAUTUS AND TERENCE 217

X. LUCRETIUS 245

XI. HORACE 259

XII. JUVENAL 281

XIII. EPILOGUE 296

INDEX 297

CLASSIC LATIN COURSE IN ENGLISH.

CHAPTER I.

THE LITERATURE OF ROME.

OVER everything pertaining to Rome, except her language and her literature, the name Roman lords it exclusively. We say, Roman power, Roman conquest, Roman law, Roman architecture, Roman art, Roman history. It is curious that the language always, and the literature generally, of Rome should be called, not Roman, but Latin. The circumstance may be taken to indicate, what is indeed the fact in reference to Rome, that literature was for her a subordinate interest. Unlike Greece, Rome is less remarkable for what she wrote than for what she wrought. But if Rome wrote as it were with her left hand, while she wrought with her right, that left hand of hers was yet an instrument of marvelous cunning and power. We are to study here in specimen the literature it produced. We confine ourselves to that section of the literature conventionally called classic.

The period during which classic Latin literature, strictly so-called, came into existence was, in comparison to the whole life of the Roman people, very short. The classic period may fairly enough be considered as extending from about 80 B. C. to 108 A. D., and as thus covering one hundred and eighty-eight years—a little less than the space of six generations.

Cicero begins and Tacitus (Tass′i-tus) ends this period. All before is ante-classic; all after, post-classic. Literature with the Romans is thus seen to have been both late to spring into life and early to fall into decay. The names of Roman writers familiar now to the popular ear are few in number, and they are clustered together in time, like the stars of a constellation in the sky.

Liv′i-us An-dro-ni′cus (ante-classic, about 280 B. C.) may be regarded as the beginner of Latin literature. He was an Italian Greek, made prisoner at the Roman capture of Tarentum—prisoner, and by natural consequence, slave. He became a freedman and a writer of tragedy. It is historically significant that Roman literature should have been begun by a Greek. Rome conquered Greece, but as Horace says, "Captive Greece took captive her rude conqueror." What Livius Andronicus wrote in Latin was no doubt mainly translation from the writer's native Greek. Of his indifferent verse a few fragments only remain.

Nævius is another mere name in Latin literature. He wrote a sort of epic on the first Punic war, esteemed by scholars one of the chief lost things in Latin literature. It contained notices of previous Roman history, which nothing survives to replace. Cicero, who had a capacity for appreciating, as great as was his capacity for creating, expresses strongly the delight he experienced in reading the epic of Nævius.

The next great name in Latin literature is still to us little more than a name. It is Ennius. Ennius is praised by Cicero, by Lu-cre′ti-us; Virgil does not praise him, but he copies him; while Horace, too, does not altogether disdain to acknowledge merit in his verse. It is tantalizing to think that Ennius was lost to the world only so long ago as the thirteenth century.

We may skip other names after Ennius, until we come

to names as familiar as those of Plau'tus and Ter'ence. These two were the great Roman writers of comedy. Nævius had done something in the line of the comic drama, but the truly indigenous literary product, like that which Nævius attempted to furnish, seemed somehow never to thrive in Rome. Plautus and Terence won their triumphs by boldly importing their intellectual wares from Greece. Of Terence, Julius Cæsar, in a celebrated epigram, spoke slightingly, as but " a half-Menander." The epigrammatist named thus the Greek (Menan'der) from whom the Roman, if Roman indeed this writer is to be called—for Terence was a native of Carthage—purveyed his comedies. The works of these two writers, Plautus and Terence, represent to us, and represent alone, the literature of the Roman theater. The two men were partly contemporary, but Plautus was Terence's senior. Roman life and manners, beginning, through superfluous wealth and, one grieves to say it, through corrupting influence and example imported from Greece, to show deterioration from their ancient simplicity and comparative virtue, are vividly portrayed in the comedies of Plautus and of Terence.

Another important source of knowledge respecting the everyday life and morality of the ancient Romans is to be found in the satires which their writers produced. The satire may be said to be a form of composition in verse original with Rome. In satire more naturally by far than in comedy, the Roman genius could unbend from its habitual and characteristic severity. Perhaps Roman satire was hardly, to the Romans, an unbending from severity ; say, rather, it was with them a way of giving loose to severity. At all events, satire is a kind of verse in which the Romans distance all competitors. The great Roman masters in this literary form are Horace and Juvenal. But the spirit of satire is a very pervasive spirit throughout Roman literature.

To Cato, famous always and everywhere as Cato the Censor,

may be attributed the merit of being the founder or former of Latin prose. For this service to Latin literature, Cato's merit is as distinctive and as indisputable, as is the merit of Ennius for a corresponding influence exercised in fixing the mold of Latin verse. But while Ennius hellenized, that is, followed Greek models, Cato, in principle and in practice, was stanchly Roman. There is something whimsical in the fact that one of the great creators of Roman literature should have been, as Cato undoubtedly was, quite sincerely and cordially a despiser of literature. Cato wrote to decry writing, as Carlyle lately deafened us all to recommend silence. Unhappily, Cato is now mainly but a tradition in Latin letters. He wrote an important historical work, the loss of which leaves an irreparable breach in the continuity of primitive Roman story. Cato is also named for praise by Cicero as the first Roman orator worthy of that title.

Oratory, from early times down to the establishment of the empire—true oratory the empire extinguished—was a favorite form of intellectual activity among the Romans. It has happened, however, and this from the nature of things, that of the immense volume of an eloquence hardly perhaps, in the aggregate, equaled by that of any other nation, ancient or modern, comparatively little remains to justify the fame which Roman oratory traditionally enjoys. The orator's triumph, as it is the most intense, is likewise the most momentary of all intellectual victories. Cicero, among Romans, reigns alone, in glorious companionship with Demosthenes among Greeks, as one of the two undisputedly greatest masters of human speech that have ever appeared on the planet. Æschines (Es′ki-neez) survives, in equivocal renown, as foil to Demosthenes—Hortensius enjoying a similar privilege of continued remembrance in connection with Cicero. While of Æschines, however, we still have the really brilliant speech which provoked from his victorious rival that " bright consummate flower" of eloquence, the Oration on the Crown, nothing remains of Hortensius but the splendid tradition of his fame. For other Roman orators, there are the brothers Gracchi (Grak'ki), Crassus, and that universal man, not less capable of great words than of great deeds, Julius Cæsar.

Cato, as founder of history for Rome, had a following not less distinguished than that which, as has been seen, he drew after him as founder of oratory. After we have mentioned, first, Cæsar, that name appearing so often, and always among the foremost, when you recall the glories of Rome in different spheres of achievement; next, Sallust, emulating but hardly rivaling Thucydides in force and in point; then, Livy, of the " pictured page," with his lost books, perhaps the chief theme of hopeless deploring for the lovers of classical literature and the students of Roman antiquity; and, fourth, Tacitus, grave, severe, pathetic—but loftily, indignantly pathetic, with pathos made bitter and virile by sarcasm—illustrating in his practice that definition of history which calls it philosophy teaching by example, and so placing himself chronologically second in the line, in which Thucydides stands first, of philosophical historians—when, we say, we have mentioned these four names, we have not, indeed, exhausted, but we have adequately suggested, the list of Roman historical writers. Cornelius Nepos—and the same is true of Suetonius—was a biographer rather than a historian. Suetonius deserves higher regard; but the pretensions of Nepos, as a man of letters, are humble, and what survives of his work is rather tame reading.

It was reserved for the age of Augustus to produce the great epic of Rome, the Æne'id of Virgil. Whatever the merits of the poem, the Æneid has had a fortune of fame and of influence that pairs it, in unchallenged pre-eminence, with the Iliad of Homer. With Virgil was matched and contrasted, in a lifelong friendship equally honorable to both, a very different poet—by eminence the Roman poet of society and manners—Horace, of a fame fulfilling his own celebrated boast and prediction concerning himself: "I have reared for myself a monument more enduring than brass." Horace has a peculiar persisting modernness of manner that keeps him perhaps the most read and the most quoted of all ancient poets.

In connection with Virgil and Horace, let us make mention, in one word, of a man who, producing, indeed, no valuable literature himself, became, nevertheless, alike by his initiative, by his taste, and by his munificence, to such an extent the cause to others of their producing of literature, that his very name is now an immortal synonym for enlightened and generous patronage of culture. If you wish to dignify by a name some wise and liberal encourager of intellectual activity you call him a Mæ-ce'nas. Augustus himself surpassed his minister Mæcenas in patronizing genius, only as the sovereign may always surpass the subject. Ovid, however, a poet in this important respect less happy than his contemporaries, Virgil and Horace, felt the weight of imperial displeasure. Banished from Rome by Augustus, he became as famous to all time for his unmanly tears in exile, as he had been before for his much-appreciated verse.

Ovid in Pontus, puling for his Rome,

is the merciless line in which Mr. Lowell, in his "Cathedral," pillories him for the contempt of mankind.

We must not close this rapid and summary survey of Latin literature without remarking that it was proper of the Roman genius to produce a copious literature about literature, in the form of grammatical, rhetorical, and critical treatises, which, however, we are compelled, though they include such works of imperishable value as Quintilian's, to pass with this mere note of their existence.

CHAPTER II.

IT IS the idea of the present volume, as of its companion volume for Greek, to follow somewhat in order the course of study customarily adopted in school and college. Usually, Cæsar is the first important author to whom continuous study is devoted; and after Cæsar follows Virgil. Not unfrequently, however, a substitution is made, Sallust taking the place of Cæsar for prose, and Ovid of Virgil for verse.

In consideration of this latter fact, we introduce Sallust and Ovid into these pages. At the same time, in view of the predominance on the whole accorded to Cæsar and Virgil, we dispose of the substitute authors first and in less space, as comparatively subordinate in rank and importance.

Sallust wrote three historical works, the "Conspiracy of Catiline," the "Jugurthine War," and a "History of Rome from the Death of Sulla [Sylla] to the Mithridatic War." This last, the most important of the three, has, with the exception of a few fragments, perished. The other two—historical monographs, or even politico-historical pamphlets, we might almost call them, rather than histories—remain to us entire. We shall let Sallust appear in his "Jugurthine War." This will bring the celebrated Caius Marius before us, as delineated by one of the great ancient masters of historical composition. And Jugurtha himself is a striking and commanding figure, set in temporary lurid relief against the threatened, but finally victorious, greatness of Rome.

13

Caius—or to adopt the latest vogue in Latin scholarship, Gaius or Gajus—Sallustius Crispus, more familiar as simply Sallust, the historian, was born 86 B. C. We know little of the beginning of his life. He became senator early enough to be, ostensibly for his profligate manners, expelled from the senate when he was thirty-six years old. He got his seat again three years afterwards. He was lucky enough to choose his side with Cæsar in the civil war, and for this was made governor of Numidia. His Numidian experience, perhaps, qualified him the better to treat the subject of his " Jugurthine War." It at least gave him the opportunity to amass immense riches, with which to retire from public life and devote himself to literature. He died, however, at the comparatively early age of fifty-two. The residence he occupied in Rome was in the midst of grounds laid out and beautified by him with the most lavish magnificence. These grounds became subsequently the chosen resort of the Roman emperors. They still bear the name of the Gardens of Sallust. Sallust moralized with much virtue in his histories, but his actual life was said to be deformed with nearly every vice and excess.

The war against Jugurtha, a usurper of the throne of Numidia, had been prosecuted by Rome with various fortune, inclining to be favorable to Jugurtha. Caius Marius, a lieutenant of patrician Metellus the Roman general in command, goes to Rome, where he is elected consul. Metellus on the field was advised from Rome that Marius had been appointed his successor in the war. The proud spirit broke at this humiliation. Metellus wept.

Sallust had previously, with a few graphic and powerful strokes, thus painted Caius Marius into his canvas :

About the same time, as Caius Marius, who happened to be at Utica [in Africa], was sacrificing to the gods, an augur told him that great and wonderful things were presaged to him ; that he might therefore pursue whatever designs he had formed, trusting to the gods for success; and that he might try fortune as often as he pleased, for that all his undertakings would prosper. Previously to this period, an ardent longing for the consulship had possessed him; and he had, indeed, every qualification for obtaining it, except antiquity of family; he had industry, integrity, great knowledge of war, and a spirit undaunted in the field; he was temperate in private life, superior to pleasure and riches, and ambitious only of glory. Having been born at Arpinum and brought up there during his boyhood, he employed himself, as soon as he was of age to bear arms, not in the study of Greek eloquence nor in learning the refinements of the city, but in military service; and thus, amid the strictest discipline, his excellent genius soon attained full vigor. When he solicited the people, therefore, for the military tribuneship, he was well known by name, though most were strangers to his face, and unanimously elected by the tribes. After this office he attained others in succession, and conducted himself so well in his public duties that he was always deemed worthy of a higher station than he had reached. Yet, though such had been his character hitherto (for he was afterwards carried away by ambition), he had not ventured to stand for the consulship. The people, at that time, still disposed of other civil offices, but the nobility transmitted the consulship from hand to hand among themselves. Nor had any commoner appeared, however famous or distinguished by his achievements, who would not have been thought unworthy of that honor, and, as it were, a disgrace to it.

Marius, still in Rome, was drunk with natural wild temperament and with success. He carried everything before him. The haughty senate was at the feet of this humble commoner, this son of the people. He spurned them in a popular harangue which Sallust constructs for him. We give a few characteristic sentences:

"My speech, they say, is inelegant, but . . . I have gained other accomplishments, such as are of the utmost benefit to a state; I have learned to strike down an enemy; to be vigilant at my post; to fear nothing but dishonor; to bear cold and heat with equal endurance; to sleep on the ground, and to sustain at the same time hunger and fatigue. And with such rules of conduct I shall stimulate my soldiers, not treating them with rigor and myself with indulgence, nor making their toils my glory. Such a mode of commanding is at once useful to the state and becoming to a citizen. For to coerce your troops with severity, while you yourself live at ease, is to be a tyrant, not a general."

Marius easily raised a great army. Everybody was eager to be a soldier under the idolized hero of the hour. He began by whetting the appetite of his troops with maddening tastes of plunder. He captured places and gave up the booty to his men. He rapidly made for himself an army after his own heart—as fierce as brave, and as greedy as fierce. The effect of dazzling immediate success on the part of Marius was to make him almost a god in the eyes of both friends and foes. Thenceforward, a fine saying of Virgil's, by him applied to a comparatively trivial occasion, will be true in this war for Marius. He will be able, for he will seem to be able.

Another celebrated character soon enters upon the scene of Sallust's story, to play a brilliant, though a subordinate part. The player of a second part now, this man is destined in the sequel to drive Marius himself off the stage. It is no other than Lucius Sylla, the future dictator of Rome. Sallust is not reluctant to illustrate his page with a strong portrait in words of this remarkable man. Our readers must see the delineation, unchanged except as translated. And here it is:

Sylla, then, was of patrician descent, but of a family almost sunk in obscurity by the degeneracy of his forefathers. He was skilled, equally and profoundly, in Greek and Roman literature. He was a man of large mind, fond of pleasure, but fonder of glory. His leisure was spent in luxurious gratifications, but pleasure never kept him from his duties, except that he might have acted more for his honor with regard to his wife. He was eloquent and subtle, and lived on the easiest terms with his friends. His depth of thought in disguising his intentions was incredible. He was liberal of most things, but especially of money. And though he was the most fortunate of all men before his victory in the civil war, yet his fortune was never beyond his desert; and many have expressed a doubt whether his success or his merit were the greater. As to his subsequent acts, I know not whether more of shame or of regret must be felt at the recital of them.

When Sylla came with his cavalry into Africa, as has just been stated, and arrived at the camp of Marius, though he had

hitherto been unskilled and undisciplined in the art of war, he
became, in a short time, the most expert of the whole army.
He was, besides, affable to the soldiers ; he conferred favors on
many at their request, and on others of his own accord, and
was reluctant to receive any in return. But he repaid other obliga-
tions more readily than those of a pecuniary nature ; he himself
demanded repayment from no one, but rather made it his object
that as many as possible should be indebted to him. He conversed, jocosely as well as seriously, with the humblest of the
soldiers ; he was their frequent companion at their works, on
the march, and on guard. Nor did he ever, as is usual with de-
praved ambition, attempt to injure the character of the consul or of
any deserving person. His sole aim, whether in the council or the
field, was to suffer none to excel him ; to most he was superior.
By such conduct he soon became a favorite both with Marius
and with the army.

Marius was marching to winter quarters, when one day, just
before dark, the combined armies of the two kings, Jugurtha
and Bocchus (an ally of Jugurtha, and his father-in-law),
suddenly fell upon him. It was a complete surprise. What
happened illustrates so well the accounts given by historians
of the discipline and valor of Roman legionaries, that we
present the narrative in Sallust's own words, simply making a
few silent omissions necessary for economy of space :

Before the troops could either form themselves or collect the baggage, before they could receive even a signal or an order, the
Moorish and Getulian horse, not in line or any regular array of
battle, but in separate bodies, as chance had united them,
rushed furiously on our men ; who, though all struck with a panic,
yet, calling to mind what they had done on former occasions,
either seized their arms or protected those who were looking for
theirs, while some, springing on their horses, advanced against the
enemy. But the whole conflict was more like a rencounter
with robbers than a battle; the horse and foot of the enemy,
mingled together without standards or order, wounded some of our
men and cut down others and surprised many in the rear while
fighting stoutly with those in front ; neither valor nor arms were a
sufficient defense, the enemy being superior in numbers and
covering the field on all sides. At last the Roman veterans,
who were necessarily well experienced in war, formed themselves, wherever the nature of the ground or chance allowed
them to unite, in circular bodies, and, thus secured on every

side and regularly drawn up, withstood the attacks of the enemy. Marius, in this desperate emergency, was not more alarmed or disheartened than on any previous occasion, but rode about with his troop of cavalry, which he had formed of his bravest soldiers rather than his nearest friends, in every quarter of the field, sometimes supporting his own men when giving way, sometimes charging the enemy where they were thickest, and doing service to his troops with his sword, since, in the general confusion, he was unable to command with his voice.

The day had now closed. . . . Marius, that his men might have a place of retreat, took possession of two hills contiguous to each other. . . . The kings, obliged by the strength of the Roman position, were deterred from continuing the combat. . . . Having then lighted numerous fires, the barbarians, after their custom, spent most of the night in merriment, exultation, and tumultuous clamor, the kings, elated at having kept their ground, conducting themselves as conquerors. This scene, plainly visible to the Romans, under cover of the night and on the higher ground, afforded great encouragement to them.

Marius kept his army perfectly still, let the poor Africans have their riot out, let them sink into exhausted sleep, and then, falling upon them at daybreak, slaughtered them as if they had been sheep.

Marius now again takes up his march to winter quarters. A few touches added to the portrait of Marius are as full of the artist's power as they are of the subject's character:

Marius himself too, as if no other were placed in charge, attended to everything, went through the whole of the troops, and praised or blamed them according to their desert. He was always armed and on the alert, and obliged his men to imitate his example. He fortified his camp with the same caution with which he marched; stationing cohorts of the legions to watch the gates, and the auxiliary cavalry in front, and others upon the ramparts and lines. He went round the posts in person, not from suspicion that his orders would not be observed, but that the labor of the soldiers, shared equally by their general, might be endured by them with cheerfulness. Indeed, Marius, as well at this as at other periods of the war, kept his men to their duty rather by the dread of shame than of severity; a course which many said was adopted from a desire of popularity; but some thought it was because he took pleasure in toils to which he had been accustomed from his youth, and in exertions which other men call perfect miseries. The public interest, however, was served with as much efficiency and honor as it could have been under the most rigorous command.

The caution of Marius was wise. On the fourth day following, the indefatigable, the unconquerable spirit of Jugurtha brought him again to the attack. He almost won the day, but once more those invincible Romans snatched victory out of the very jaws of defeat. The battlefield, as it appeared at this moment, is described by Sallust in a celebrated sentence :

The spectacle on the open plains was then frightful; some were pursuing, others fleeing; some were being slain, others captured; men and horses were dashed to the earth; many, who were wounded, could neither flee nor remain at rest, attempting to rise and instantly falling back; and the whole field, as far as the eye could reach, was strewed with arms and dead bodies, and the intermediate spaces saturated with blood.

Five days after suffering this defeat, Jugurtha's confederate, King Bocchus, desires Marius to send him two trusted ambassadors for a conference. Sylla is one of the two sent. With much artful preface, this adroit Roman diplomatist told Bocchus that it lay in his, Bocchus's, power to put Rome under real obligation. He could betray Jugurtha to her. Bocchus started back. Why, there was the kindred tie, the solemn league, between himself and Jugurtha. Besides, Jugurtha was beloved, and the Romans were hated, by his, Bocchus's, subjects. Sylla pressed, and Bocchus—yielded. An ambush was laid, and the father-in-law delivered up the son-in-law to Sylla. It was a proud feather in young Sylla's cap. But it was before the chariot wheels of Marius that, afterwards, Jugurtha, with his two sons, was driven in triumph at Rome.

Sallust's history stops abruptly with Jugurtha's capture. From other sources we learn that the proud captive lost his senses under the dreadful humiliation of the triumph ; also that soon after, with much contumelious violence, he was flung naked into the chill underground dungeon at Rome called the Tullianum, where after six days he perished of cold and starvation. (One authority says he was strangled.) He is said to have exclaimed shudderingly, as he fell, "Heavens, a cold bath this of yours!"

Jugurtha is painted black in Sallust's picture. But the artist that painted him, remember, is a foe and a Roman. Jugurtha must have been, indeed, a false and bloody man. Still he had followers that clave to him. Nay, Jugurtha was to all Africans the most beloved of men. He was universally hailed as deliverer of the nation from Rome. His name long continued a spell of power to his countrymen. It was twenty years after his death—and already his kingdom was in large part a province of Rome—when a son of his, recognized in the force opposed to the Romans, raised such sentiments in the breasts of a Numidian corps attached to the Roman army, that the whole body had to be immediately sent home to Africa.

Jugurtha's bravery, his talent, his endurance, redeem him to our admiration, as do his misfortunes to our sympathy. Supposing Jugurtha had been the conqueror, and some Numidian partisan of his, instead of a Roman partisan of Cæsar's, had given us the history!

CHAPTER III.

OVID (Publius Ovidius Naso is the full Roman name) was born in Northern Italy. It is striking how few, comparatively, of the great Roman writers were natives of Rome. Ovid came of a good family, and he liked to have this known. "In my family," he says, "you will find knights up through an endless line of ancestry." He was born just when the republic died ; that is, he and the imperial order came twins into the world together, in 43 B. C. The boy was a natural versifier. Like Pope, he "lisped in numbers, for the numbers came." His youth coincided either with the full maturity or with the declining age of the great Augustan writers, Virgil, Livy, Horace, Sallust. Unhappily for himself, he did not come under the sunshine that streamed on literature and art from the face of Augustus's great minister, Mæ-ce'nas. The emperor never extended his favor to Ovid ; and in the end, as our readers know, the poet was sent into exile.

Ovid was a man of loose character, and his looseness of character leaked into his verse. In fact, much of what he wrote is now unreadable for rank impurity. One of his poems in particular scandalized the moral sense of even his own age and became the ostensible occasion of his banishment. His Metamorphoses must be considered his chief work. The title means, literally, changes of form. Ovid's idea in the poem is to tell in his own way such legends of the teeming Greek mythology as deal with the transformations of men and

women into animals, plants, or inanimate things. The invent-
ive ingenuity of the poet is displayed in connecting these
separate stories into something like coherence and unity.
This poem has been a great treasury of material to subsequent
poets. Even Milton has condescended to be not a little indebted to Ovid for images and allusions, which he dignified by
adopting them, with noble metamorphosis, into his own
loftier verse.

Our one specimen of Ovid's Metamorphoses shall be a condensation of his story of Pha'e-ton. This we can give in a
version which, if it is not quite so closely literal as would be
desirable, is excellent art of its kind, and is at any rate, a classic
too in English, for it is from the hand of Joseph Addison.

Our readers will like, by way of introduction to our exem-
plification of Ovid's Metamorphoses, to see what the poet himself—in one of his most delightfully buoyant moods surely it
must have been—thought of his own work as a whole. We
give, accordingly, the conclusion of the Metamorphoses in
literal prose translation :

And now I have completed a work, which neither the anger of
Jove, nor fire, nor steel, nor consuming time will be able to destroy! Let that day, which has no power but over this body of
mine, put an end to the time of my uncertain life when it will.
Yet, in my better part, I shall be raised immortal above the lofty
stars, and indelible shall be my name. And wherever the Roman
power is extended throughout the vanquished earth, I shall be
read by the lips of nations, and (if the presages of the poets have
aught of truth) throughout all ages shall I survive in fame.

There is, perhaps, no part of Ovid's work that constitutes
upon the whole a better warrant to the poet for his cheerful
anticipation of enduring fame, than that which we now in
specimen present. Phœbus (Apollo) is god of the sun. He is
applied to by his not universally acknowledged son, Phaeton,
with a startling request. We omit the brilliant opening
which describes the dazzling palace and the richly dec-
orated enthronement of the god. Phaeton has arrived and

presents himself. To Phœbus's gracious welcome of his son,

> " Light of the world," the trembling youth replies,
> "Illustrious parent! since you don't despise
> The parent's name, some certain token give,
> That I may Clymene's proud boast believe,
> Nor longer under false reproaches grieve."
>
> The tender sire was touched with what he said,
> And flung the blaze of glories from his head,
> And bade the youth advance. " My son," said he,
> "Come to thy father's arms! for Clymene
> Has told thee true: a parent's name I own,
> And deem thee worthy to be called my son.
> As a sure proof make some request, and I,
> Whate'er it be, with that request comply:
> By Styx I swear, whose waves are hid in night,
> And roll impervious to my piercing sight."
>
> The youth, transported, asks without delay
> To guide the sun's bright chariot for a day.

Phœbus is distressed. He begs Phaeton to reconsider and choose more wisely for himself. This at considerable length and with much poetical eloquence. But Phaeton was not to be dissuaded, and the reluctant father has his chariot brought out. Then at daybreak,

> He bids the nimble Hours, without delay,
> Bring forth the steeds: the nimble Hours obey.
> From their full racks the generous steeds retire,
> Dropping ambrosial foams, and snorting fire.
> Still anxious for his son, the god of day,
> To make him proof against the burning ray,
> His temples with celestial ointment wet,
> Of sovereign virtue, to repel the heat;
> Then fixed the beamy circle on his head,
> And fetched a deep foreboding sigh, and said:
> " Take this at least, this last advice, my son:
> Keep a stiff rein, and move but gently on:
> The coursers of themselves will run too fast;
> Your art must be to moderate their haste.
> Drive them not on directly through the skies,
> But where the zodiac's winding circle lies,
> Along the midmost zone; but sally forth,
> Nor to the distant south, nor stormy north.

> The horses' hoofs a beaten track will show;
> But neither mount too high, nor sink too low.
> That no new fires or heaven or earth infest.
> Keep the mid way; the middle way is best:
> Nor where, in radiant folds, the serpent twines,
> Direct your course, nor where the altar shines.
> Shun both extremes; the rest let Fortune guide,
> And better for thee than thyself provide!"
> Meanwhile the restless horses neighed aloud,
> Breathing out fire, and pawing where they stood.
> Tethys, not knowing what had passed, gave way,
> And all the waste of heaven before them lay.
> They spring together out, and swiftly bear
> The flying youth through clouds and yielding air;
> With wingy speed outstrip the eastern wind,
> And leave the breezes of the morn behind.
> The youth was light, nor could he fill the seat,
> Or poise the chariot with its wonted weight:
> But as at sea the unballasted vessel rides,
> Cast to and fro, the sport of winds and tides,
> So in the bounding chariot, tossed on high,
> The youth is hurried headlong through the sky.
> Soon as the steeds perceive it, they forsake
> Their stated course, and leave the beaten track.
> The youth was in a maze, nor did he know
> Which way to turn the reins, or where to go:
> Nor would the horses, had he known, obey.
> Then the seven stars first felt Apollo's ray,
> And wished to dip in the forbidden sea.
> The folded serpent, next the frozen pole,
> Stiff and benumbed before, began to roll,
> And raged with inward heat, and threatened war,
> And shot a redder light from every star;
> Nay, and 'tis said, Boötes, too, that fain
> Thou wouldst have fled, though cumbered with thy wain.

The bewildered charioteer is racked with emotions which Ovid feels himself at leisure enough to describe with great particularity. Then follows a very detailed account, with many geographical names, of the progressive effects of that unguided drive. We omit and resume:

> The astonished youth, where'er his eyes could turn,
> Beheld the universe around him burn;

The world was in a blaze; nor could he bear
The sultry vapors and the scorching air,
Which from below, as from a furnace, flowed:
And now the axletree beneath him glowed.
Lost in the whirling clouds that round him broke
And white with ashes, hovering in the smoke,
He flew where'er the horses drove, nor knew
Whither the horses drove or where he flew.

'Twas then, they say, the swarthy Moor begun
To change his hue, and blacken in the sun;
Then Libya first, of all her moisture drained,
Became a barren waste, a wild of sand; .
The water nymphs lament their empty urns;
Bœotia, robbed of silver Dirce, mourns,
Corinth Pyrene's wasted spring bewails;
And Argos grieves while Amymone fails.

The floods are drained from every distant coast;
Ev'n Tanais, though fixed in ice, was lost;
Enraged Caicus and Lycormas roar,
And Xanthus, fated to be burnt once more.
The famed Mæander, that unwearied strays
Through many windings, smokes in every maze:
From his loved Babylon Euphrates flies:
The big-swollen Ganges and the Danube rise
In thicken'ng fumes, and darken half the skies:
In flames Ismenos and the Phasis rolled,
And Tagus, floating in his melted gold:
The swans, that on Cayster often tried
Their tuneful songs, now sung their last, and died.
The frighted Nile ran off, and under ground
Concealed his head, nor can it yet be found;
His seven divided currents all are dry, .
And, where they rolled, seven gaping trenches lie:
No more the Rhine or Rhone their course maintain,
Nor Tiber, of his promised empire vain.
The ground, deep cleft, admits the dazzling ray,
And startles Pluto with the flash of day:
The seas shrink in, and to the sight disc'ose
Wide naked plains, where once their billows rose;
Their rocks are all discovered and increase
The number of the scattered Cyclades;
The fish in shoals about the bottom creep;
Nor longer dares the crooked dolphin leap:
Gasping for breath, the unshapen Phocœ die,

And on the boiling wave extended lie :
Nereus, and Doris, with her virgin train,
Seek out the last recesses of the main :
Beneath unfathomable depths they faint,
And secret in their gloomy caverns pant :
Stern Neptune thrice above the waves upheld
His face, and thrice was by the flames repelled.
The earth at length, on every side embraced
With scalding seas, that floated round her waist,
When now she felt the springs and rivers come,
And crowd within the hollow of her womb,
Uplifted to the heavens her blasted head,
And clappèd her hand upon her brows, and said
(But first, impatient of the sultry heat,
Sunk deeper down, and sought a cooler seat) :
" If you, great king of gods, my death approve,
And I deserve it, let me die by Jove :
If I must perish by the force of fire,
Let me transfixed with thunderbolts expire."

    .   .   .   .

Jove called to witness every power above,
And even the god whose son the chariot drove,
That what he acts he is compelled to do,
Or universal ruin must ensue.
Straight he ascends the high ethereal throne,
From whence he used to dart his thunder down,
From whence his showers and storms he used to pour,
But now could meet with neither storm or shower :
Then aiming at the youth, with lifted hand,
Full at his head he hurled the forky brand
In dreadful thunderings.   Thus the almighty sire
Suppressed the raging of the fires—with fire.
At once from life and from the chariot driven,
The ambitious boy fell thunderstruck from heaven ;
The horses started with a sudden bound,
And flung the reins and chariot to the ground :
The studded harness from their necks they broke,
Here fell a wheel, and here a silver spoke,
Here were the beam and axle torn away,
And scattered o'er the earth the shining fragments lay.
The breathless Phaeton, with flaming hair,
Shot from the chariot like a falling star,
That in a summer's evening from the top
Of heaven drops down, or seems, at least, to drop,

> Till on the Po his blasted corpse was hurled,
> Far from his country, in the western world.

A "long bright river" of verse it is, in the original, and in the translation as well. We have been sorry to break the current with omissions. Nothing essential, however, is lost. One simply fails to receive a full due impression of the melodious prolixity, the "linked sweetness long drawn out," which is characteristic of Ovid.

Some monuments of architecture there are, which, besides being composed of choice stones exquisitely wrought, are great wholes whose aggregate mass and proportion impress you with an effect of grandeur or beauty infinitely surpassing the sum of the effects due to all the component parts taken together. Of such a structure a few stones by themselves would give a very inadequate idea. But the Metamorphoses of Ovid form an edifice from which even a single shapely and polished precious block brought away will serve to suggest all the beauty that belongs to the building. You have merely to say, There are a great many lovely pieces like this. You could not truly say, The glory of the whole is greater than that of the sum of all the parts.

Ovid had predecessors in the treatment of his subject. To these predecessors how much he was indebted, we have no means of judging. The earlier works have perished, and no critics who knew them have transmitted to us their estimate of Ovid's obligation. We need hardly say that Ovid's forerunners were Greek.

Of Ovid we thus now take leave to go on in the following chapter with an author who, to a character of social dilettanteism in which he might have rivaled Ovid himself, joined a character of stern and strenuous practical force, for affairs of war and of state, in which he scarcely admitted any rival, ancient or modern—we mean, Julius Cæsar.

CHAPTER IV.

THE present writer himself holds a more moderate view in the case, but there is with many judges, presumptively competent to pronounce opinion, a strong disposition to accord to Julius Cæsar a place of lonely pre-eminence, as, upon the whole, in amplitude of natural endowment, and in splendor of historic achievement, perhaps the very first among the sons of men.

It undoubtedly requires much comprehensive and comparative knowledge of the heroes of history, to appreciate the large-molded, many-sided character of such a man as Cæsar. Julius Cæsar is great in an order of greatness like that, for instance, of Mont Blanc or of Niagara among the works of nature ; of St. Peter's or of the Milan Cathedral among the works of human hands. You have to study him to measure him. You have to put other great men alongside of him, to perceive how he dwarfs them by the contrast of his easy and symmetrical magnitude.

In the present volume, we are to let Cæsar, in large part, make his own impression of himself by one of his literary works. This work is the account which he wrote of his campaigns in Gaul. " Commentaries " is the name by which the account is technically known. The word " commentaries " in this title is not, of course, to be understood as signifying remarks in criticism and explanation. These have somewhat the character of journals of camp and march and fight.

They are, for all that, much admired for the style in which they are written. Clear, straightforward, simple, manly records they are, of great achievements, hardly, but triumphantly, performed. Cæsar writes constantly in the third person, never, save in some three or four, perhaps inadvertent, certainly unimportant, cases of exception, in the first. That is, when he means Cæsar he says "Cæsar," not "I," or "me."

There are two quite different ways in which we may read Cæsar's Gallic Commentaries. Either we may regard them as telling the story of the thorough and masterful manner in which he accomplished an important share of certain serious work that it fell to his lot to do for Rome and for the world; or we may regard them as giving an account of a piece of canvassing, on his part, for place and power in the Roman state, canvassing conceived and executed on a scale of largeness and enterprise beyond the reach of any but the most magnificent political as well as military genius. But whichever of these two views we take, it still remains true that this history is vitally related to the whole subsequent history of mankind.

We might in reading Cæsar's story, seem to be reading only how consummate skill and discipline in war, supported by boundless resources, overwhelmed brave, but helpless, barbarism, with the irresistible mass and weight of an equally brave, but also a splendidly equipped, civilization. But let us correct our very natural misconception of the case. The truth is, the Gauls were by no means a wholly uncivilized people, and they were a really formidable foe to Rome. For good reason, Rome dreaded them with immemorial dread. One of the saddest and most shameful of the early traditions of Roman history was the taking and sacking of the city by Gauls. A vast, dense, black cloud of ever-threatened irruption hung, growing, in the quarter of the Roman sky toward Gaul and Germany, ready to break on Italy and pour a flood of devastation against Rome that should even sweep the city from the face of the globe. Cæsar's bold plan was to open the cloud and disperse its gathering danger. He perhaps saved Europe to civilization and to Christianity. Four hundred years later, the barbarians pressed again against the barriers of the Roman empire. This time the barriers gave way, and the floods came in. But meantime, and this as the result of Cæsar's work, Gaul itself, indeed all Europe, west and south, with Africa, too, had been permanently Romanized ; and there was moreover now a Christian church prepared to welcome the inrushing barbarians to her bosom, and make them, retaining much, no doubt, of their native fierceness still, yet strangely gentle pupils in the school of Christ. Such, whatever may, or may not, have been Cæsar's own wisdom and will in his work, was the providential purpose that this colossal military and political genius subserved.

Caius Julius Cæsar was of an ancient patrician family of Rome, who claimed derivation from Iulus, son of Trojan Æneas. He was politician from a boy. He was married (or perhaps only betrothed) early enough to get himself divorced at seventeen, for the purpose of allying himself to Cinna through a second marriage with that democratic leader's daughter. This wife, too, the aristocratic dictator, Sylla, now omnipotent at Rome, advised young Cæsar to put away. Cæsar had the spirit to refuse compliance, but he had also the prudence to flee from Rome to escape the dictator's resentment.

In due time, the tide of Roman public sentiment turned strongly in favor of the people and against the aristocracy. Into this powerful movement, Cæsar threw himself and his fortunes. He went rapidly through a succession of public offices: as quæstor, bidding for popularity by pronouncing a eulogy on his aunt Julia, wife of the redoubtable democrat Marius ; as ædile, still further courting the favor of the common people by entertainments provided on a scale of unmatched magnificence, and of course at correspondingly enormous expense. The result was to plunge him millions on millions of dollars in debt. Now occurred the conspiracy of Catiline, in which Cæsar himself was implicated, in the suspicion of some. The mere existence of the suspicion tends to show how active and how unscrupulous in politics Cæsar was held to be. Mommsen, the German historian of Rome, a warm eulogist of Cæsar, holds it for tolerably certain that his hero was in fact a fellow-conspirator with Catiline ; nor does he on that account (or on any other account) at all abate the great man's praise.

Cæsar wanted to be pontifex maximus, that is, chief priest of the Roman religion. He was a thorough-paced skeptic, and his aim in this matter was worldly-minded in the extreme : he needed the office as a refuge from his creditors. Without it he would have to flee from Rome. He was triumphantly elected. The next year saw him prætor. At the close of the year's prætorship, he was, in due course of Roman custom, given a province to squeeze. Spain was his lot. From Spain, at the end of his term of office in that province, this masterful spirit hastened back to Rome to run for the consulship. The consulship was the top round in the ladder of Roman political ambition. Cæsar saw all things possible to himself once chosen consul. He was chosen. Cæsar's consulship, in its bearing on his own personal fortunes, was an overflowing success. Cæsar's consulship expired, he went to Gaul as proconsul. It was as proconsul in Gaul that he did the memorable things of which we are now to study in specimen his own masterly account.

Cæsar's Gallic Commentaries are divided into eight books. Each book recounts the events and incidents, these and no more, of one campaign, covering a military year of time. The first book, after a bit of geography to begin with, occupies itself with two series of military operations on Cæsar's part, one directed against the Helvetians (Swiss), and one against a body of Germans who had invaded Gaul. Of these two military movements, that against the Helvetians resulted in the death or reduction to slavery of a quarter of a million of souls—men, women, and children ; for Cæsar fell upon the Helvetians engaged in the act of a national migration to other places of abode. It is a ghastly modern commentary on this achievement of Cæsar's that excavations made under the munificent auspices of Napoleon III., uncovered, in some of the localities identified as scenes of Cæsar's Gallic slaughters, vast deposits of human remains, in which could be distinguished the skeletons of men, women, and children.

So ended the Helvetian war—war, to indulge Cæsar in his own non-descriptive word. The future dictator had begun prosperously in Gaul. Already he had made up his score to one quarter of the full million of human lives that he must take in Gaul, to prepare himself for by and by crossing the Rubicon, on his way to empire and to bloody death.

The crowded first Gallic campaign of Cæsar is to be closed with a series of operations better deserving, than did the slaughter of the pilgrim Helvetians, to be styled a war. A certain Ar'i-o-vis'tus, German prince and conqueror, invoked at first as ally by one of the Gallic tribes at war among themselves, has turned intolerable oppressor and usurper, menacing especially the prosperity and power of the Æduans, who were allies of the Romans. Cæsar of course interferes, and, to sum up all in a word, annihilates the army of Ariovistus. Of the fugitive Germans, a few escaped, among them, their leader. All the rest, dryly observes Cæsar, "our cavalry slew." But the historian meantime has made an interesting note of the German military method, which we may show in the writer's own words :

They had about six thousand horse, who chose a like number out of the foot, each his man, and all remarkable for strength and agility. These continually accompanied them in battle, and served them as a rear guard, to which, when hard pressed, they might retire; if the action became dangerous, they advanced to their relief; if any horseman was considerably wounded and fell from his horse, they gathered round to defend him; if speed was required, either for a hasty pursuit or sudden retreat, they were become so nimble and alert by continual exercise, that, laying hold of the manes of their horses, they could run as fast as they.

In his grand way, Cæsar closes the first book of his Commentaries as follows:

Cæsar, having in one campaign put an end to two very considerable wars, went into winter quarters somewhat sooner than the season of the year required. He distributed his army among the Seq'uani, left Labienus to command in his absence, and set out himself for Cisalpine Gaul (Northern Italy) to preside in the assembly of the states.

Cæsar's winter in Northern Italy is disturbed, perhaps not disagreeably to himself, by reports brought to him that the Belgians are "conspiring" against the Roman people. But the Remi are, like the Æduans, after Cæsar's own heart. He gets the following statistics of numbers from these forward informants—we give them in Cæsar's own summary:

He found the Sues-si-o'nes had within their territories twelve fortified towns, and promised to bring into the field fifty thousand men: the like number had been stipulated by the Nervians, who, inhabiting the remotest provinces of Gaul, were esteemed the most fierce and warlike of all the Belgian nations: that the At're-ba'-tians were to furnish fifteen thousand, the Am'bi-a'ni ten thousand, the Mor'i-ni twenty-five thousand, the Men-a'pians nine thousand, the Cal'e-tes ten thousand, the Vel'o-cas'sians and Ver'o-man'duans the like number; the At'u-at'i-ci twenty-nine thousand; and the Con-dru'sians, Eb'u-ro'nes, Cæ-rœ'sians, and Pae-ma'ni, all comprehended under the common name of Germans, forty thousand.

The battle that soon was pitched between the Romans and the Belgians had its vicissitudes, but there was a foregone conclusion of them all. The Belgians, worsted, resolved on returning to their respective homes. They broke up their camp in the night. The noise was like that of a rout. At daybreak, Cæsar started in pursuit.

All day long the Roman dogs of war fed on the helpless Belgians as if they had been sheep. Read Cæsar's business-like statement, and consider that it is of hunted men, not of beasts, that he is speaking :

Thus, without any risk to themselves, our men killed as great a number of them as the length of the day allowed.

This was not cruelty ; it was simply cold blood. Cold blood was Cæsar's strength, and Rome's. Cæsar was Rome.

Cæsar's struggle with the Nervii was one of the sharpest crises that he encountered in the whole course of his Gallic experience. His report of their national character is interesting. He says :

That they suffered no resort of merchants into their cities, nor would allow of the importation of wine or other commodities tending to luxury ; as imagining that thereby the minds of men were enfeebled, and their martial fire and courage extinguished ; that they were men of a warlike spirit, but altogether unacquainted with the refinements of life ; that they continually inveighed against the rest of the Belgians for ignominiously submitting to the Roman yoke and abandoning the steady bravery of their ancestors. In fine, that they had openly declared their resolution of neither sending ambassadors to Cæsar, nor accepting any terms of peace.

The Nervians were beforehand with the Romans in attacking. In truth, this time the Romans were taken by surprise. They had not a moment to put themselves in proper order of battle. Nay, the men could not even arm themselves as usual. It was not so much one battle, as it was a confusion of separate battles, that ensued. Cæsar for once found himself in imminent peril. His officers were slain or disabled. He had himself to hasten from point to point as he could. There was one moment when all seemed to be over with him and his army. A body of his own auxiliary horse actually fled head-long home bearing that news to their countrymen.

But Cæsar was the man for emergencies. He soon made it the turn of the Nervii to be dismayed. Dismayed, however,

as they might be, they fought with desperate valor. When a
soldier among them fell, his comrade behind advancing would
stand on the corpse and thence continue to fight. He falling
in turn, and another, and another, still the indomitable
Nervii would only make mounds of their slain from which to
discharge their weapons on the foe. There was no flight, no
surrender, no giving way. The Nervii fought till they died.
But they died almost to a man. The nation and the name
were well-nigh annihilated.

It is time our readers had another taste of Cæsar's own
quality in narration. We give his account of his transactions,
in arms and in diplomacy, with the Atuatici, a tribe of Ner-
vian allies. This tribe had been coming up to assist the
Nervii. On their way, they heard of the battle just described,
and turned back. They threw themselves into a town of
theirs, which Cæsar proceeded to attack.

Cæsar says :

When we had now finished our approaches, cast up a mount, and
were preparing a tower of assault behind the works, they began at
first to deride us from the battlements, and in reproachful language ask the meaning of that prodigious engine raised at such a
distance! With what hands or strength, men of our size and make
(for the Gauls, who are for the most part very tall, despise the
small stature of the Romans), could hope to bring forward so
unwieldy a machine against their walls?
But when they saw it removed and approaching near the
town, astonished at the new and unusual appearance, they sent
ambassadors to Cæsar to sue for peace. These being accordingly
introduced, told him : "That they doubted not but the Romans
were aided in their wars by the gods themselves, it seeming to
them a more than human task to transport with such facility an
engine of that amazing height, by which they were brought upon a
level with their enemies, and enabled to engage them in close
fight. That they therefore put themselves and their fortunes
into his hands, requesting only, that if his clemency and goodness,
of which they had heard so much from others, had determined
him to spare the Atuatici [Aduatuci] he would not deprive them of
their arms." . . . To this Cæsar replied : "That no surrender
would be accepted unless they agreed to deliver up their

arms." . . . They accepted in appearance the conditions offered them by Cæsar, and threw so vast a quantity of arms into the ditch before the town, that the heap almost reached to the top of the wall. Nevertheless, as was afterwards known, they retained about a third part and concealed them privately within the town. The gates being thrown open, they enjoyed peace for the remaining part of that day.

In the evening, Cæsar ordered the gates to be shut, and the soldiers to quit the town, that no injury might be offered to the inhabitants during the night. Whereupon, the Atuatici, in consequence of a design they had before concerted, imagining that the Romans, after a surrender of the place, would either set no guard at all or at least keep watch with less precaution; partly arming themselves with such weapons as they had privately retained, partly with targets made of bark or wicker, and covered over hastily with hides, made a furious sally about midnight with all their forces and charged our works on that side where they seemed to be of easiest access.

The alarm being immediately given by lighting fires, as Cæsar before commanded, the soldiers ran to the attack from the neighboring forts. A very sharp conflict ensued, for the enemy, now driven to despair, and having no hope but in their valor, fought with all possible bravery, though the Romans had the advantage of the ground, and poured their javelins upon them both from the towers and the top of the rampart. About four thousand were slain upon the spot and the rest obliged to retire into the town. Next day the gates were forced, no one offering to make the least resistance, and, the army having taken possession of the place, the inhabitants, to the number of fifty-three thousand, were sold for slaves.

What sum of money the sale of these people brought Cæsar, he does not descend enough into particulars to name. Numbers of speculators from Rome were no doubt in attendance on the progress of conquests so important as these of Cæsar in Gaul. The bidding, we may presume, was spirited, and the prices realized were probably satisfactory. How cold-blooded it all seems ! What a different spirit Christianity has infused even into business so unchristian as war !

Cæsar, having quartered his legions for the winter near the scene of their recent exploits, repairs himself, as in the year previous, to Italy. And so ends book second.

The third book, as dealing with transactions of less magnitude than those already narrated, we may somewhat summarily dismiss. It seems to be dedicated, in large measure, to a skillfully conducted laudation of young Crassus, son of Cæsar's wealthy political partner. One can hardly help suspecting Cæsar's object to have been in part a thrifty one, that of giving pleasure to the father, for the sake of the benefit that might thence accrue to himself. Young Crassus was a lieutenant of the great commander.

Three things especially, in the fourth book of Cæsar's Commentaries, are of commanding interest. The first is the case of alleged perfidy, with enormous undoubted cruelty, practiced by Cæsar against his German enemies. The second is Cæsar's famous feat in throwing a bridge across the river Rhine. The third is his invasion of Great Britain.

Far northward toward the mouth of that river, two more tribes of Germans had just crossed the Rhine. Men, women, and children, they reached the number of near half a million. This immense migration could not be permitted. Cæsar marched against the Germans.

As he came near, ambassadors from the Germans met him, desiring terms of peace. But Cæsar would make no terms with the Germans, as long as they remained in Gaul. There was no land there to be given away. However, if they liked to do so, they might settle among the U'-bi-i.

The German ambassadors were at a stand. They would carry back Cæsar's reply. But would Cæsar stay where he then was, and give them a day or two in which to go and return? (The two armies were still some days' march apart.) Cæsar would not consent. He assumed that what the Germans wanted was to gain time for recalling their cavalry from a distant foraging expedition.

The Roman army, which the Germans could no more stop by entreating, than by entreating they could have stopped the circuit of the earth about the sun, had now come to within twelve miles of the enemy, when the German ambassadors returned to Cæsar. They begged Cæsar to halt. The earth kept moving and—so did Cæsar. "Pray, then," besought the ambassadors, "pray at least send orders in advance to the Roman vanguard not to engage in battle; and permit us meantime to send ambassadors to the Ubii. If the Ubii will engage under oath with us, we will do anything you say. But let us have a day or two in which to negotiate."

Cæsar avers he was still suspicious of the Germans. However, he told them he should not advance more than four miles that day, this for the sake of finding water. Let the Germans come to him at that point in good numbers (the proviso, in "good numbers" seems significant—was Cæsar's perfidious purpose already in his mind?) and he would talk with them. Meanwhile Cæsar sent orders to his vanguard not to fight unless attacked.

Now occurs an incident which it is very difficult to understand. Cæsar says that as soon as the enemy got sight of the Roman horse, five thousand strong, the German horse, only eight hundred strong, fell upon these and threw them into disorder. The Roman cavalry thereupon making a stand, the Germans leaped from their steeds, stabbed Cæsar's horses in the belly, and, overthrowing many of his soldiers, put the rest to flight. For the first time in his history, Cæsar tells the number of his fallen. There were seventy-five, among them an illustrious Aquitanian, sacred from having had a grandfather who was once styled "friend" by the Roman senate.

What follows in Cæsar's narrative is so grave in its illustrative bearing upon Cæsar's character, that we are going to satisfy the just curiosity of our readers by letting them see exactly how the writer states the business for himself. Here, then, are Cæsar's own words, in sufficiently strict translation:

After this battle, Cæsar resolved neither to give audience to their ambassadors nor admit them to terms of peace, seeing they had treacherously applied for a truce, and afterwards of their own accord broken it. He likewise considered that it would be downright madness to delay coming to an action until their army should be augmented and their cavalry join them; and the more so, because he was perfectly well acquainted with the levity of the Gauls, among whom they had already acquired a considerable reputation by this successful attack, and to whom it therefore behooved him by no means to allow time to enter into measures against him. Upon all these accounts he determined to come to an engagement with the enemy as soon as possible, and communicated his design to his quæstor and lieutenants. A very lucky accident fell out to bring about Cæsar's purpose, for the day after, in the morning, the Germans persisting in their treachery and dissimulation, came in great numbers to the camp: all their nobility and princes making part of their embassy. Their design was, as they pretended, to vindicate themselves in regard to what had happened the day before; because, contrary to engagements made and come under at their own request, they had fallen upon our men; but their real motive was to obtain if possible another insidious truce. Cæsar, overjoyed to have them thus in his power, ordered them to be secured and immediately drew his forces out of the camp. The cavalry, whom he supposed terrified with the late engagement, were commanded to follow in the rear.

Having drawn up his army in three lines and made a very expeditious march of eight miles, he appeared before the enemy's camp before they had the least apprehension of his design. All things conspiring to throw them into a sudden consternation, which was not a little increased by our unexpected appearance, and the absence of their own officers; and, hardly any time left them either to take counsel or fly to arms, they were utterly at a loss what course to take, whether to draw out their forces and oppose the enemy or content themselves with defending the camp or, in fine, to seek for safety in flight. As this fear was evident from the tumult and uproar we perceived among them, our soldiers, instigated by the remembrance of their treacherous behavior the day before, broke into the camp. Such as could first provide themselves with arms made a show of resistance and for some time maintained the fight amidst the baggage and carriages. But the women and children (for the Germans had brought all their families and effects with them over the Rhine) betook themselves to flight on all sides. Cæsar sent the cavalry in pursuit of them.

The Germans, hearing the noise behind them, and seeing their wives and children put to the sword, threw down their arms, abandoned their ensigns, and fled out of the camp. Being arrived at the confluence of the Rhine and the Meuse, and finding it impossible to continue their flight any farther; after a dreadful slaughter of those that pretended to make resistance, the rest threw themselves into the river; where, what with fear, weariness, and the force of the current, they almost all perished. Thus our army, without the loss of a man, and with very few wounded, returned to their camp, having put an end to this formidable war in which the number of the enemy amounted to four hundred and thirty thousand. Cæsar offered those whom he had detained in his camp liberty to depart; but they, dreading the resentment of the Gauls, whose lands they had laid waste, chose rather to remain with him, and obtained his consent for that purpose.

Cæsar had effectually dispelled the present danger. While the terror and horror of such an atrocity were still benumbing men's minds, he could safely display his skill and his daring in a feat well calculated to impress barbarian sensibilities with a useful idea of Roman power. He would do what no Roman had ever yet done, he would bridge the Rhine and cross it. It was to be barren demonstration, so far as anything beyond impression on the imagination was concerned. For he would recross almost immediately. "Avidity of fame," Plutarch attributes as Cæsar's motive, in this action of his. He wished to be the first Roman to put his head in the lion's mouth by invading Germany. He crossed and he recrossed the Rhine, and he had his reward.

Cæsar's bridge was fourteen hundred feet long, furnishing a solid roadway thirty or forty feet wide, all finished promptly enough to have the whole army got in safety across—at least with no casualty reported—within ten days from the time when the first blow of a Roman ax startled those distant forests. Just where it was situated, is a matter of much dispute—some say at Cologne and some say at Bonn.

Cæsar now turns his attention to another enterprise, that of invading Great Britain. In due time a flotilla is ready, and a few hours' sail brings Cæsar to the British coast. The cliffs are alive with islanders, prepared to receive their visitor with warlike welcome.

The Britons are alert, and they dash along the coast, with horsemen and with chariots of war, to meet the invasion where it threatened. The Romans have a sad time of it getting ashore. Cæsar notes it that his soldiers seemed not to take their chance of floundering through the shoal water to land, with anything like their wonted appetite for fighting on dry ground. There occurred a little incident which Cæsar, with a for him quite unusual condescension to dramatic representation, relates in what grammarians call (*oratio recta*) direct discourse. Our readers must have this rare specimen of Cæsar in the lively mood, without change—except the necessary change of literal translation from Latin into English :

While our men were hesitating chiefly on account of the depth of the sea, he who carried the eagle of the tenth legion, after supplicating the gods, that the matter might turn out favorably to the legion, exclaimed, " Leap, fellow-soldiers, unless you wish to betray your eagle to the enemy. I, for my part, will perform my duty to the commonwealth and my general." When he had said this with a loud voice, he leaped from the ship and proceeded to bear the eagle toward the enemy. Then our men, exhorting one another that so great a disgrace should not be incurred, all leaped from the ship. When those in the nearest vessels saw them, they speedily followed and approached the enemy.

We hardly need follow with further detail the incidents of this British adventure of Cæsar. The historian tries to give the affair something like historic dignity. The truth, however, is that Cæsar's first visit to Great Britain was by no means a very glorious thing. Cæsar in fact did well that he got off from Great Britain at all. But he had a thanksgiving of twenty days decreed to him for the success of the campaign as a whole.

The fifth book is mainly a record of disaster to Cæsar's arms, disaster retrieved, but barely retrieved, from being irreparable disaster. There is an episode to begin with—the episode of a second and last expedition, on Cæsar's part, to Great Britain. Without much more effort, that is permitted to appear in his story, than the mere word of command from his mouth, Cæsar gets together a fleet of some eight hundred sail all told—there are reckoned into this total a number of private bottoms, probably ventures in merchant speculation—and with this numerically formidable armada he reaches the coast of Great Britain.

Having landed and encamped, he encounters once more a former enemy of his—a British storm. His ships are badly shattered. But what can withstand Cæsar? He speaks a word, and his ships are tugged and lugged with main strength on shore, and there fortified within the same lines as his camp. This operation took about ten days and nights, for the men worked continuously—in relays, let us trust—all the twenty-four hours through.

Of attack and repulse, of retreat and pursuit, of slaughter and capture, of embassy and reply, of surrender proposed and hostages demanded, of all the vicissitudes of this wanton and gratuitous war, the upshot is that Cæsar gets off at last in safety, and, as he represents it, even in a certain barren and ambiguous triumph. The account closes with a passage worth our quoting. Cæsar covers the emptiness of his military performance in Britain with a rhetorical flourish about his own good fortune. This is a topic on which he never tires of enlarging. It is not mere curiosity on his own part that prompts the treatment of this topic, nor is it a good-natured wish to gratify the curiosity of his readers. It is a motive of thrift. Prosperity prospers. Cæsar wants everybody to understand that Cæsar is prosperous. Here, then, is the passage in which Cæsar thinks it comportable with his dignity to dismiss the story of his adventures in Britain :

And it so happened, that out of so large a number of ships, in so many voyages, neither in this nor in the previous year was any ship missing which conveyed soldiers; but very few out of those which were sent back to him from the continent empty, as the soldiers of the former convoy had been disembarked, and out of those (sixty in number) which Labienus had taken care to have built, reached their destination; almost all the rest were driven back, and when Cæsar had waited for them for some time in vain, lest he should be deterred from a voyage by the season of the year, inasmuch as the equinox was at hand, he of necessity stowed his soldiers the more closely, and, a very great calm coming on, after he had weighed anchor at the beginning of the second watch, he reached land at break of day and brought in all the ships in safety.

Returned to Gaul, Cæsar found that the harvests there, on account of droughts, were poor. He felt compelled, accordingly, to depart from his prudent previous practice, and for that winter distribute his legions. This seemed to offer to the natives their chance. There was a general movement commenced to fall on all the Roman camps simultaneously, and overpower them one by one. This movement had already prospered to the extent of the nearly complete destruction of one whole legion, when Quintus Cicero, the great Cicero's brother, a lieutenant of Cæsar's, was attacked in his camp.

The annihilated Nervii, of whom Cæsar told us in the second book of his Commentaries, re-appeared unaccountably here, and, it would seem, for an annihilated nation, in very considerable force. Here is what Cæsar tells us of them and of their work. How much, think you, did eagerness for revenge stimulate these brave, fierce fellows in their incredible toils?

The Nervians . . . surrounded the camp with a line, whose rampart was eleven feet high, and ditch fifteen feet deep. They had learned something of this in former wars with Cæsar, and the prisoners they had made gave them further instructions. But being unprovided with the tools necessary in this kind of service, they were obliged to cut the turf with their swords, dig up the earth with their hands, and carry it in their cloaks. And hence it will be easy to form some judgment of their number; for in less than three hours they completed a line of fifteen miles in circuit. The following days were employed in raising towers, proportioned to the height of our rampart, and in preparing scythes, and wooden galleries, in which they were again assisted by the prisoners.

In near sequel to this comes an episode so very romantic, and so far outside of the limits within which Cæsar usually confines his narration, that our readers will like to have seen it in the translated text of the original:

In this legion were two centurions of distinguished valor, T. Pul'fi-o and L. Va-re'nus, who stood fair for being raised to the first rank of their order. These were perpetually disputing with one another the pre-eminence in courage and at every year's promotion contended with great eagerness for precedence. In the heat of the attack before the ramparts, Pulfio addressing Varenus, "What hinders you now [says he] or what more glorious opportunity would you desire of signalizing your bravery? This, this is the day for determining the controversy between us." At these words he sallied out of the camp and rushed amid the thickest of the Gauls. Nor did Varenus decline the challenge; but thinking his honor at stake, followed at some distance. Pulfio darted his javelin at the enemy, and transfixed a Gaul that was coming forward to engage him; who, falling dead of the wound, the multitude advanced to cover him with their shields, and all poured their darts upon Pulfio, giving him no time to retire. A javelin pierced his shield and stuck fast in his belt. This accident, entangling his right hand, prevented him from drawing his sword, and gave the enemy time to surround him. Varenus, his rival, flew to his assistance, and endeavored to rescue him. Immediately the multitude, quitting Pulfio, as fancying the dart had dispatched him, all turned upon Varenus. He met them with his sword drawn, charged them hand to hand, and having laid one dead at his feet, drove back the rest; but, pursuing with too much eagerness, stepped into a hole, and fell down. Pulfio, in his turn, hastened to extricate him; and both together, after having slain a multitude of the Gauls, and acquired infinite applause, retired unhurt within the intrenchments. Thus fortune gave such a turn to the dispute that each owed his life to his adversary; nor was it possible to decide to which of them the prize of valor was due.

The situation, meantime, became daily more critical for distressed Cicero. But he was relieved at last by the coming of Cæsar. It was an occasion in some features like Havelock's famous relief of Lucknow. The final result was decisive victory for the Romans.

The chief peril was now past, but the winter kept bringing fresh anxieties to Cæsar, who had this time to forego his accustomed annual visit to Italy.

The fifth book closes without mention made of any thanksgiving decreed at Rome for Cæsar's successes, and Cæsar has no concluding paragraph in self-complacent celebration of his own good fortune.

Cæsar resolved to show the Gauls how Romans behaved themselves in the presence of reverses to their arms. This is set forth in the sixth book of the Gallic Commentaries, which is accordingly a stimulating chapter of the narrative. He made a new levy of troops; the cohorts lost under Titurius he replaced with a double number of soldiers, and he borrowed a legion from his fellow-triumvir, Pompey. Thus strengthened in force, Cæsar further strengthened himself with speed; for he began his new campaign before the winter was over. Observing that in the customary annual congress of Gaul, summoned by him, the Sen'o-nes failed to appear, Cæsar, with prompt audacity, at once transfers the place of meeting to their neighborhood. He goes to Paris (Lu-te'tia Par-is-i-o'rum). How modern and how real this name makes the history seem. From Paris, with those forced marches of his which so often accomplished so much for his cause, he brings his legions into the country of the Senones. Acco, the head of the revolt, calls on the Senones to muster into their towns. But the sudden apparition of the Romans overawes them, and they send in their surrender. Cæsar accepts their submission—for the sake of his friends, the Æduans, to whom he hands over for safe keeping the hundred hostages exacted. It will turn out to have been a confidence ill placed. In the end, even the trusted Æduans will rise against Cæsar.

Cæsar never, perhaps, in any other instance, evinced so much personal feeling to ripple the habitual viscid flux of his glacial cold-bloodedness, as in the instance of Am-bi'o-rix, that subtle deceiver and destroyer of Titurius with his legion. With noticeable energy of expression, Cæsar remarks that, the Senones disposed of, he " applied himself entirely, both in mind and in soul, to the war with the Trev'i-ri and Ambiorix." It might be said that to make an end of Ambiorix the campaign is chiefly directed. It seems not so much victory as revenge that Cæsar seeks. He fairly thirsts for Ambiorix's blood. Cæsar will die thirsting, for Ambiorix's blood he is destined never to taste. But it was a hot and eager hunt, with many a slip 'twixt cup and lip for the hunter, and many a hairbreadth escape for the hunted. Cæsar's good fortune was at fault again.

Cæsar hunted with as much of patience and of prudence as of zeal. He first went at the Me-na'pi-i and the Treviri, and disposed of them.

But now Ambiorix might find refuge among the Germans. Cæsar must bridge the Rhine again and provide against that. The Suevi have, he learns on getting over, retired to the farther boundary of their possessions, there to await the on-coming of the Romans. With this space between himself and his foe, Cæsar pauses to amuse his readers with a circumstantial account of the Germans and the Gauls, described in mutual contrast with each other. Almost everybody likes to read travelers' stories; and when the traveler is Caius Julius Cæsar and the scene of the travels is ancient France and Germany, the story is likely to be worth reading. Still, the inexorable laws of space forbid our including it here.

From his geographical digression, Cæsar gets back to say that he resolved not to follow the Suevi into their forests. Not, however, entirely to free the Germans from uncertain apprehension as to what he may yet do, he leaves a large part of his bridge standing. He now himself in person sets forth in chase of Ambiorix.

But Cæsar's phlegm was too much quickened. He could not wait. He sent on the cavalry in advance, "all the cavalry," to surprise Ambiorix, if possible. The cavalry are not to build campfires. The enemy would see them. They must take their rations cold, perhaps raw ; bare grain, very likely, which they must champ like their steeds. The cavalry surpass themselves in speed. They surprise and capture "many in the field"—many, but not Ambiorix. Cæsar has to moralize about "fortune." The cavalry came fairly upon Ambiorix. They got everything that belonged to him, his horses, his chariots, his weapons, but him not. A few followers of his made a momentary stand against the Roman onset. They meantime mounted Ambiorix, and he escaped.

But Ambiorix's people had a lamentable lot. They were dispersed in every direction, each man looking out for himself. Ambiorix's colleague, King Cat-i-vol'cus, infirm and old, called down every curse on Ambiorix and poisoned himself. Cæsar's purpose was fell. He wished to root out that "stock of wicked men." In order not to risk precious Roman soldiers in the forest, he called in the neighboring tribes to the hunt, making Ambiorix's nation, the Eb'u-ro'nes, a free and common prey to all. It was better economy, Cæsar thought, to throw away Gallic lives than Roman, in so dangerous a chase. But at some rate, "the stock and the name of the state" must "for such a crime be abolished." Again Cæsar feels called upon to speak of the powerful influence exercised in war by fortune. His promising plan for the extermination of the Eburones comes near costing him a lieutenant and a legion.

For, from even beyond the Rhine, who should hear of this fine free hunt in progress, and come forward for their share of the booty, but the Si-cam'bri? These freebooters, the Sicambri, however, have it whispered to them that there is a richer chance. What need prevent their surprising and taking Quintus Cicero with his command? The prize would be immense. Cicero, by order from Cæsar, is keeping his soldiers very close within the intrenchments. At length, however, a party of the recovered sick and wounded, with a large retinue of slaves and beasts of burden, make a sally for foraging. At this very moment, up come the Germans and throw the camp into panic confusion. This is the selfsame spot on which Titurius and his legion were destroyed. Not till Cæsar arrives do they recover from their fright. It affected Cæsar sadly to reflect how what he had plotted well for the injury of Ambiorix had thus turned out actually to the advantage of that detestable man.

However, the hunt was resumed. Thorough work Cæsar made of it. His plan was nothing less than to remove every cover that could hide the fugitive. Far and wide the horsemen rode to burn every human dwelling in the land of the Eburones. The soldiers, many of them, kindled with the hope of acquiring the highest favor with Cæsar, almost killed themselves, he tells us, with their exertions to catch Ambiorix. They again and again just missed him, but he finally never was caught. Cæsar had to content himself, as best he could, without his Ambiorix.

He closes his sixth book with mention of several matters despatched by him before his setting out for Italy. Among these was the execution of Acco, the head of the late confederate revolt. Our readers will perhaps be interested to know how this was accomplished. Well, to use Cæsar's own soft phrase, Acco was put to death "in accordance with the custom of the fathers." This meant, if we may trust the explanation supplied by Suetonius in his "Life of Nero," that, stripped naked, the victim was fastened by the neck in a forked stake, and then scourged till he died. With much justness of sentiment, Cæsar hints in passing that this sentence of his on Acco was "rather sharp." We can only guess what would have happened to Ambiorix had he been captured. Perhaps, indeed, Acco suffered a little vicariously, to satisfy the exasperated feelings of Cæsar disappointed of his prey in the person of hateful Ambiorix, hunted by him so long in vain.

The seventh book is of tragic interest. One man looms large in it, as the doomed Hector of a contest in which no one can stand before the prowess of mighty Achilles. Ver-cin-get'o-rix is this hero's name. He becomes the head of a last, the greatest, confederate revolt of Gaul against Rome. In this character he experiences various and violent vicissitudes of fortune, appearing always high-hearted and noble whether in prosperity or in adversity. The end was inevitable, for he contended with Cæsar and with Rome. Vercingetorix is fatally defeated and is captured. It is one of the many deep and indelible stains on the glory of Cæsar that, while he as conqueror was enjoying his triumph at Rome, his gallant captive, Vercingetorix, at the selfsame moment suffered death in his Roman dungeon.

The eighth and last book was written by Cæsar's lieutenant, Hirtius. Hirtius relates that Cæsar, "convinced that his lenity was known to all men," and so not fearing the charge of "cruelty," once "cut off the hands of those who had borne arms against him. Their lives he spared, that the punishment of their rebellion might be the more conspicuous."

If we are hastily inclined to charge such atrocity in warfare exclusively to a pagan spirit abolished with the entrance and spread of Christianity, let us remember Cortes, nay, even Columbus, and be rebuked and ashamed.

In one of his triumphs, Cæsar made an immense artificial lake, on the surface of which he exhibited a sea fight—not a sham fight, but a real fight—in which thousands of

Egyptians and thousands of Tyrians, respectively, killed each other for the delight of the populace. There were murmurs at this feature of Cæsar's displays—not, however, because it was cruel, but because it was wasteful. No wonder De Quincey called the Roman Empire founded by Cæsar a magnificently masked essential barbarism. Cæsar himself, De Quincey nevertheless pronounces—and with this sentence let us dismiss the present subject—"unquestionably, for comprehensive talents, the Lucifer, the protagonist, of all antiquity."

CHAPTER V.

CICERO.

CICERO is beyond comparison the most modern of the ancients. We scarcely seem to be breathing the atmosphere of antiquity when we are dealing with Cicero. Especially in reading his letters, we unconsciously forget that the writer of these living lines died near nineteen hundred years ago. Cicero was a most human-hearted man, possessing breadth enough of temperament and of sympathy to ally him with all races and all ages of his kind. In Arpinum in Italy, the birthplace of one of Rome's greatest generals, Rome's greatest orator was born. Caius Marius and Marcus Tullius Cicero were fellow-townsmen by birth. Cicero was not of patrician blood; but his father was a gentleman in circumstances that enabled him to give his son the best advantages for education. These of course were to be found in Rome, and to Rome accordingly young Cicero was sent. Here, at sixteen years of age, the future orator began his studies in law.

As a good Roman, with his fortune to make, Cicero must needs have some experience in army life. This, with subsequent tours of foreign travel, took him away from the metropolis of the world, which however in due time drew him back into its all-devouring vortex. Cicero rapidly made himself conspicuous at Rome. Round after round, he climbed the ladder of political promotion, until he became quæstor in Sicily. The quæstorship was an office that had to do with revenue and finance. Cicero distinguished himself as quæstor by his ability and by his probity. The Sicilians were delighted with this upright, accomplished, and genial official from Rome. Their praises almost turned the young fellow's head. Cicero afterwards rallied himself in public with admirable humor for the weakness of vanity indulged by him on occasion of the displays that were made in his honor by the grateful and effusive Sicilians. The allusion to this experience of his over-susceptible youth was artfully introduced by the orator to enliven a certain speech that he was making. "I thought in my heart," Cicero said, "that the people at Rome must be talking of nothing but my quæstorship." He was duly discharged of this pleasing illusion—he proceeds to tell us how.   Cicero conceived the following strain of allusion to himself—which may be taken as a good specimen of the Ciceronian pleasantry, and Cicero was rated a very lively man :

The people of Sicily had devised for me unprecedented honors. So I left the island in a state of great elation, thinking that the Roman people would at once offer me everything without my seeking. But when I was leaving my province and on my road home, I happened to land at Pu-te'o-li just at the time when a good many of our most fashionable people are accustomed to resort to that neighborhood. I very nearly collapsed, gentlemen, when a man asked me what day I had left Rome and whether there was any news stirring? When I made answer that I was returning from my province—"Oh! yes, to be sure," said he; "Africa, I believe?" "No," said I to him, considerably annoyed and disgusted; "from Sicily." Then somebody else, with an air of a man who knew all about it, said to him—"What! don't you know that he was quæstor at *Syracuse?* " [It was at Li-ly-bæ'um— quite a different district.] No need to make a long story of it; I swallowed my indignation and made as though I, like the rest, had come there for the waters.

Cicero's "improvement" of the lesson was highly characteristic, both of the Roman and of Cicero. He says he learned from it how important it was for his own profit that he should keep himself constantly familiar before the eyes of his countrymen at Rome and that he should sedulously practice every art of popularity. The following are the orator's own words :

But I am not sure, gentlemen, whether that scene did not do me more good than if everybody then and there had publicly congratulated me. For after I had thus found out that the people of Rome have somewhat deaf ears, but very keen and sharp eyes, I left off cogitating what people would hear about me ; I took care that thenceforth they should see me before them every day: I lived in their sight, I stuck close to the Forum ; the porter at my gate refused no man admittance—my very sleep was never allowed to be a plea against an audience.

How thoroughly a politician in spirit Cicero was, and how willingly he confessed that fact to the people of Rome—whom he flattered in the very act of so confessing it—is well shown in the following sentences from the same speech :

This is the inalienable privilege of a free people, and especially of this the chief people of the world, the lord and conqueror of all nations, to be able by their votes to give or to take away what they please to or from any one. And it is our duty,—ours, I say, who are driven about by the winds and waves of this people, to bear the whims of the people with moderation, to strive to win over their affections when alienated from us, to retain them when we have won them, to tranquilize them when in a state of agitation. If we do not think honors of any great consequence, we are not bound to be subservient to the people; if we do strive for them, then we must be unwearied in soliciting them.

The Roman people enforced a good deal of meekness in their candidates for office. Successful politicians had to learn the distasteful art of stooping to conquer.

The first really great display of oratory from Cicero, was his impeachment of Verres. Verres had been prætor in Sicily, and had there signalized his administration of office with more than normal Roman cruelty. Cicero brought him to trial. From this moment Cicero was the foremost orator of Rome. Everything now lay possible before him. He was soon consul. His merit and his fortune together made his consulship the most illustrious in the annals of Rome. That year was the year of the conspiracy of Catiline. This great political crime, Cicero had the good luck and the sagacity mingled, to detect, the courage, with the eloquence, to denounce, and the practical address completely to foil. His conduct gave him the proud title of Father of his Country. No one ever relished success more frankly than did Cicero. He never wearied of sounding out the praises of his own consulship. Cicero in fact was deeply encased with panoply of self-complacency. This armor served him well for defense against many an inward wound; but Cicero's vanity and an insincerity in him that was close of kin to vanity have proved indelible blemishes on the fair face of his fame.

Out of the heart itself of the success achieved by him in the matter of Catiline, sprang one of the greatest of the calamities that marked Cicero's checkered, and at last tragical career. A bill was introduced into the senate empowering Pompey, now returned in triumph from the war against Mithridates, to "restore the violated constitution." This ominous language had Cicero for its aim. Cicero had put Roman citizens to death without regular trial. Julius Cæsar was demagogue enough to support the bill. The bill failed in the senate, but Cicero did not escape. A personal enemy of his got the people of Rome to pass sentence of banishment upon him.

But a great compensation awaited the disconsolate exile. After a year and a half, Cicero was brought back to Rome like a conqueror. No military triumph decreed him could have done him half the honor or have yielded him half the generous joy that now overflowingly filled his cup in the magnificent popular ovation spontaneously prolonged to the returning patriot through an imperial progress on his part of twenty-four days from Brundusium to Rome. Cicero's heart swelled with unbounded elation. The height of the joy was as had been the depth of the sorrow. Let Cicero himself describe his triumph for us:

Who does not know what my return home was like? How
the people of Brundusium held out to me, as I might say, the right
hand of welcome on behalf of all my native land? From thence
to Rome my progress was like a march of all Italy. There was no
district, no town, corporation, or colony, from which a public
deputation was not sent to congratulate me. Why need I speak of
my arrival at each place? how the people crowded the streets
in the towns; how they flocked in from the country—fathers of
families with wives and children? How can I describe those days,
when all kept holiday, as though it were some high festival of the
immortal gods, in joy for my safe return? That single day was to
me like immortality; when I returned to my own city, when I saw
the senate and the population of all ranks come forth to greet me,
when Rome herself looked as though she had wrenched herself
from her foundations to rush to embrace her preserver. For she
received me in such sort, that not only all sexes, ages, and callings,
men and women of every rank and degree, but even the very
walls, the houses, the temples, seemed to share the universal joy.

Returning to Rome from a governorship in Cilicia, with the
mild glory of just and successful administration surrounding
him, he found the issue ready to be joined in deadly duel for
empire between Cæsar and Pompey. He cast in his own lot
with Pompey. But he did not wholly trust Pompey. Indeed
he despaired of the republic—whichever might win, Pompey
or Cæsar. Cæsar won. But the term was brief of Cæsar's
enjoyment of that supreme power which, as Pliny tells us the
conqueror himself used to say, it had cost a million and a half
of human lives, in Gaul alone, to win. Cicero was not one
of those who conspired against Cæsar, but he rejoiced at the
great man's bloody death—openly, almost savagely, rejoiced.
He thought that the republic—that dream, that ideal, of his
love—was about to be restored. But he thought wrong and he
paid the price of his mistake with his blood.

The period during which, after Cæsar's death, Cicero, with
his tongue, waged war against Antony, was the most truly
glorious of his life. Rufus Choate has celebrated it, with pomp
of numerous prose, beating in a rhythm answering to the
rhythm of Cicero himself, in a splendid discourse on the

"Eloquence of Revolutionary Periods." Cicero was a true hero now. His face, his form, his gait, are transfigured, like those of O-dys′seus at the gift of Pallas Ath-e′ne. One is pathetically comforted and glad, to behold the orator, the statesman, the philosopher, the man—whom, before this, one could not wholly admire—divested at length of the weakness of vanity and of fear, marching forward erect and elate, like a demigod out of Homer, and as with a kind of menacing and triumphing welcome to his doom. His doom met him with equal advancing steps. The story is familiar, but it bears to be told again and again.

The triumvirate had triumphed over the republicans, and therefore over Cicero. They made out a list for death, and Antony included Cicero's name. It was the usurper's revenge for Cicero's philippics against him. Cicero was at his Tusculan villa when he heard that he was proscribed. He sought to escape from the country. But life was no longer dear to him, and, after some irresolution, he decided to die by his own act. He would first rest a while, and then go hence. While he was resting, Antony's emissaries came. Cicero's servants hastened with their master borne on a litter toward the sea. But the soldiers were too quick for them. The servants affectionately and bravely addressed themselves for fight with their pursuers. But Cicero forbade them. He stretched forth his head and neck from the litter, and summoned the soldiers to take what they wanted. They wanted his head and his hands. These they bore with speed to Antony in the forum. Antony feasted his famished grudge with the sight and had them fixed for general view on the rostra from which, in better times, Cicero so often had spoken. The tears that Rome shed were wept perhaps as much for herself, as for her Tully.

Tully's praises were silent during the time of Augustus—for to praise Cicero would have been to blame the emperor—but they broke out again soon after, and they have since filled the world.

Cicero's writings form what has been finely called a library of reason and eloquence. They comprise orations, letters, and essays in what is conventionally called philosophy. Let us first deal with the orations.

Of Cicero as an orator it may summarily be said that he was, first of all, and always, as clear as a sunbeam—this, both as to his general order in the speech and as to the structure of the particular sentence—full in matter, copious, while pure, in diction, harmonious in rhythm, in temper by preference urbane, though capable of the utmost truculence, unsurpassed in skill of self-adjustment to the demands of his occasion. Readers who, in the companion volume to this, that on Greek literature, study the eloquence of Demosthenes, may see the Roman's style in a still stronger light by comparing and contrasting it with the style of the Greek. The English Burke, we believe, consciously modeled his own oratory on the oratory of Cicero.

To show Cicero first on that more gracious side of his oratory with which the greater part of our citation from him will be in bold, even violent, contrast, we present a very brief extract from his celebrated oration on Marcus Marcellus. Marcellus had fought against Cæsar in the civil war, and for that reason now kept himself in exile. His cousin one day in full senate prostrated himself before Cæsar to implore the dictator's pardon for his kinsman. The whole body of the senators did likewise. Cæsar yielded and pardoned the exile. Hereupon Cicero responded in a speech which is preserved for us in written form. We give only a single paragraph in specimen :

O Caius Cæsar, those military glories of yours will be celebrated not only in our own literature and language, but in those of almost all nations; nor is there any age which will ever be silent about your praises. But still, deeds of that sort, somehow or other, even when they are read, appear to be overwhelmed with the cries of the soldiers and the sound of the trumpets. But when we hear or read of anything which has been done with clemency, with humanity, with justice, with moderation, and with wisdom, especially in a time of anger, which is very adverse to prudence, and in the hour of victory, which is naturally insolent and haughty, with what ardor are we then inflamed (even if the actions are not such as have really been performed, but are only fabulous) so as often to love those whom we have never seen! But as for you, whom we behold present among us, whose mind and feelings and countenance we at this moment see to be such, that you wish to preserve everything which the fortune of war has left to the republic, O with what praises must we extol you? with what zeal must we follow you? with what affection must we devote ourselves to you? The very walls, I declare, the very walls of this senate-house appear to me eager to return you thanks: because, in a short time, you will have restored their ancient authority to this venerable abode of themselves and of their ancestors.

Now no one can read intelligently the foregoing representative extract, inadequate through brevity as it is, from this senatorial speech of Cicero, without perceiving that, both in the lines and between the lines of the speech, there unmistakably betrays itself the spirit of the patriot consenting to speak, nay, generously rejoicing to speak, in the words of the personal encomiast. The orator hoped well concerning the republic. Cicero's letters, written about the date of this speech, make it probable that the trust was not yet extinct in his breast that Cæsar was going to restore the ancient freedom and constitution. Cæsar should be helped on to any such goal of his thought by every incitement of appreciation shown him beforehand. The praise, then, was less mere adulation, than pregnant wisdom of oratory and statesmanship.

Before—but not many years before—Cæsar went to Gaul, there was a wide-spread dangerous political movement on foot at Rome, desperate enough in its aim and in its measures, as also in the character of the men concerned in it, to be justly branded a conspiracy. Of this conspiracy, the leading spirit was Lucius Catilina, commonly now among us called Catiline. Catiline was a member of the senate, and many of his fellow-conspirators belonged to the same body. He was bankrupt in fortune and in name—by general agreement an abandoned man. But he was as able as he was unscrupulous.

Cicero had proposed a new law against bribery. Catiline felt himself aimed at and plotted against Cicero's life. Cicero in open senate charged on him this design, and the consuls to meet the emergency were by decree invested with dictatorial powers. Catiline's hopes of election and his plot to assassinate Cicero were thwarted together.

Desperate now, he rushed into courses the most extreme. A general rising was to be instigated throughout Italy. Rome was to be fired in numerous places at once, the senate were all to be put to death, likewise the personal and political enemies of the conspirators. Pompey's sons, however, were to be kept alive as hostages to secure the proper behavior of Pompey who, in command of an army in the East, held the really effective power in the state.

Of all this stupendous iniquity, plotted in darkness, Cicero was fortunate enough and skillful enough to learn from one of the conspirators gained over through the arts of that conspirator's mistress. Cicero managed the affair with perfect adroitness. Things proceeded until he summoned a meeting of the senate in the temple of Jupiter at the foot of the Palatine Hill (some say on the Capitoline Hill), a place of assembling resorted to only under circumstances of the most threatening danger. Catiline was brazen enough to attend himself this session of the senate. His entrance created a sensation, and that sensation Cicero heightened by breaking into the following strain of personal invective, taken from what is known as the first oration against Catiline. There are four such orations in all. Of these the first and last were delivered in the senate, the second and third in the forum to the popular assembly of citizens. The style, or rather the course of treatment adopted, differs according to the character of the audience addressed and according to the object sought to be accomplished by the orator. Here, then, is a condensation of the

FIRST ORATION AGAINST CATILINE.

When, O Catiline, do you mean to cease abusing our patience? How long is that madness of yours still to mock us? When is there to be an end of that unbridled audacity of yours, swaggering about as it does now? Do not the night guards placed on the Palatine Hill—do not the watches posted throughout the city—does not the alarm of the people, and the union of all good men—does not the precaution taken of assembling the senate in this most defensible place—do not the looks and countenances of this venerable body here present, have any effect upon you? Do you not feel that your plans are detected? Do you not see that your conspiracy is already arrested and rendered powerless by the knowledge which every one here possesses of it? What is there that you did last night, what the night before—where is it that you were—who was there that you summoned to meet you—what design was there which was adopted by you, with which you think that any one of us is unacquainted?

Shame on the age and on its principles! The senate is aware of these things; the consul sees them; and yet this man lives. Lives! ay, he comes even into the senate. He takes a part in the public deliberations; he is watching and marking down and checking off for slaughter every individual among us. And we, gallant men that we are, think that we are doing our duty to the republic if we keep out of the way of his frenzied attacks.

You ought, O Catiline, long ago to have been led to execution by command of the consul. That destruction which you have been long plotting against us ought to have already fallen on your own head.

What? Did not that most illustrious man, Publius Scipio, the Pontifex Maximus, in his capacity of a private citizen, put to death Tiberius Gracchus, though but slightly undermining the constitution? And shall we, who are the consuls, tolerate Catiline, openly desirous to destroy the whole world with fire and slaughter? For I pass over older instances, such as how Caius Servilius A-ha'la with his own hand slew Spurius Mælius when plotting a revolution in the state. There was—there was once such virtue in this republic, that brave men would repress mischievous citizens with severer chastisement than the most bitter enemy. For we have a resolution of the senate, a formidable and authoritative decree against you, O Catiline; the wisdom of the republic is not at fault, nor the dignity of this senatorial body. We, we alone—I say it openly—we, the consuls, are wanting in our duty.

The senate once passed a decree that Lucius O-pim'i-us, the consul, should take care that the republic suffered no injury. Not one night elapsed. There was put to death, on some mere suspicion of disaffection, Caius Gracchus, a man whose family had borne the most unblemished reputation for many generations. There was slain Marcus Fulvius, a man of consular rank, and all his children. By a like decree of the senate the safety of the republic was intrusted to Caius Marius and Lucius Valerius, the consuls. Did not the vengeance of the republic, did not execution overtake Lucius Sat'ur-ni'nus, a tribune of the people, and Caius Servilius, the prætor, without the delay of one single day? But we, for these twenty days, have been allowing the edge of the senate's authority to grow blunt, as it were. For we are in possession of a similar decree of the senate, but we keep it locked up in its parchment—buried, I may say, in the sheath; and according to this decree you ought, O Catiline, be put to death this instant. You live—and you live, not to lay aside, but to persist in your audacity.

I wish, O conscript fathers, to be merciful; I wish not to appear negligent amid such danger to the state; but I do now accuse myself of remissness and culpable inactivity. A camp is pitched in Italy, at the entrance of Etruria, in hostility to the republic; the number of the enemy increases every day; and yet the general of that camp, the leader of those enemies, we see within the walls— ay, and even in the senate—planning every day some internal injury to the republic. If, O Catiline, I should now order you to be arrested, to be put to death, I should, I suppose, have to fear lest all good men should say that I had acted tardily, rather than that any one should affirm that I acted cruelly. But yet this, which ought to have been done long since, I have good reason for not doing as yet; I will put you to death, then, when there shall be not one person possible to be found so wicked, so abandoned, so like yourself, as not to allow that it has been rightly done. As long as one person exists who can dare to defend you, you shall live; but you shall live as you do now, surrounded by my many and trusty guards, so that you shall not be able to stir one finger against the republic; many eyes and ears shall still observe and watch you, as they have hitherto done, though you shall not perceive them.

.   .   .   .

O ye immortal gods, where on earth are we? in what city are we living? what constitution is ours? There are here—here in our body, O conscript fathers, in this the most holy and dignified assembly of the whole world, men who meditate my death and the death of all of us, and the destruction of this city and of the whole world. I, the consul, see them; I ask them their opinion about the republic, and I do not yet attack, even by words, those who ought to be put to death by the sword.

· · · · · · · ·

But now, what is that life of yours that you are leading? For I will speak to you not so as to seem influenced by the hatred I ought to feel, but by pity, nothing of which is due to you. You came a little while ago into the senate: in so numerous an assembly, who of so many friends and connections of yours saluted you? If this in the memory of man never happened to any one else, are you waiting for insults by word of mouth, when you are overwhelmed by the most irresistible condemnation of silence? Is it nothing that at your arrival all those seats were vacated? that all the men of consular rank, who had often been marked out by you for slaughter, the very moment you sat down, left that part of the benches bare and vacant? With what feelings do you think you ought to bear this? On my honor, if my slaves feared me as all your fellow-citizens fear you, I should think I must leave my house. Do not you think you should leave the city? If I saw that I was even undeservedly so suspected and hated by my fellow-citizens, I would rather flee from their sight than be gazed at by the hostile eyes of every one. And do you who, from the consciousness of your wickedness, know that the hatred of all men is just and has been long due to you, hesitate to avoid the sight and presence of those men whose minds and senses you offend? If your parents feared and hated you, and if you could by no means pacify them, you would, I think, depart somewhere out of their sight. Now, your country, which is the common parent of all of us, hates and fears you, and has no other opinion of you, than that you are meditating parricide in her case; and will you neither feel awe of her authority, nor deference for her judgment, nor fear of her power?

And she, O Catiline, thus pleads with you, and after a manner silently speaks to you: There has now for many years been no crime committed but by you; no atrocity has taken place without you; you alone unpunished and unquestioned have murdered the citizens, have harassed and plundered the allies; you alone have had power not only to neglect all laws and investigations, but to overthrow and break through them. Your former actions, though they ought not to have been borne, yet I did bear as well as I could; but now that I should be wholly occupied with fear of you alone, that at every sound I should dread Catiline, that no design should seem possible to be entertained against me which does not proceed from your wickedness, this is no longer endurable. Depart, then, and deliver me from this fear; that, if it be a just one, I may not be destroyed; if an imaginary one, that at least I may at last cease to fear.

.   .   .   .

I will let you see what these men [Catiline's fellow-senators] think of you. Be gone from the city, O Catiline, deliver the republic from fear; depart into banishment, if that is the word you are waiting for. What now, O Catiline? Do you not perceive, do you not see the silence of these men? they permit it, they say nothing; why wait you for the authority of their words, when you see their wishes in their silence?

But had I said the same to this excellent young man, Publius Sextius, or to that brave man, Marcus Marcellus, before this time the senate would deservedly have laid violent hands on me, consul though I be, in this very temple. But as to you, Catiline, while they are quiet they approve, while they permit me to speak they vote, while they are silent they are loud and eloquent.

.   .   .   .

O conscript fathers, let the worthless begone—let them separate themselves from the good—let them collect in one place—let them, as I have often said before, be separated from us by a wall; let them cease to plot against the consul in his own house—to surround the tribunal of the city prætor—to besiege the senate-house with words—to prepare brands and torches to burn the city; let it, in short, be written on the brow of every citizen, what are his sentiments about the republic. I promise you this, O conscript fathers, that there shall be so much diligence in us the consuls, so much authority in you, so much virtue in the Roman knights, so much unanimity in all good men, that you shall see everything made plain and manifest by the departure of Catiline—everything checked and punished.

With these omens, O Catiline, begone to your impious and nefarious war, to the great safety of the republic, to your own misfortune and injury, and to the destruction of those who have joined themselves to you in every wickedness and atrocity. Then do you, O Jupiter, who were consecrated by Romulus with the same auspices as this city, whom we rightly call the stay of this city and empire, repel this man and his companions from your altars and from the other temples—from the houses and walls of the city—from the lives and fortunes of all the citizens; and overwhelm all the enemies of good men, the foes of the republic, the robbers of Italy, men bound together by a treaty and infamous alliance of crimes, dead and alive, with eternal punishments.

The effect of a speech so very unconventionally frank, on the person against whom it was aimed, seems not to have been immediately and overwhelmingly discomposing. Catiline begged that the senate would not be hasty in giving credit to the wild accusations of Cicero. The senate responded with cries of "Traitor!" and "Parricide!" This enraged Catiline, and he declared that the flame which his enemies were kindling around him he would quench in the general ruin. He flung fiercely out of the temple.

Cicero had now a task of justifying himself before the people of Rome. For Catiline's friends got it reported that Catiline had gone into voluntary exile to Marseilles, driven forth by the violence of the consul. To meet the popular odium sought thus to be excited against himself, and in general to satisfy public opinion in Rome that what had been done had been wisely done, Cicero harangued the people in the forum. We give some extracts from this address, usually called the

SECOND ORATION AGAINST CATILINE.

At length, O Romans, we have dismissed from the city, or driven out, or, when he was departing of his own accord, we have pursued with words, Lucius Catiline, mad with audacity, breathing wickedness, impiously planning mischief to his country, threatening fire and sword to you and to this city. He is gone, he has departed, he has disappeared, he has rushed out. No injury will now be prepared against these walls within the walls themselves by that monster and prodigy of wickedness. . . . Now he lies prostrate, O Romans, and feels himself stricken down and abject and often casts back his eyes toward this city, which he mourns over as snatched from his jaws, but which seems to me to rejoice at having vomited forth such a pest and cast it out of doors.

But if there be any one of that disposition which all men should have, who yet blames me greatly for the very thing in which my speech exults and triumphs—namely, that I did not arrest so capital mortal an enemy rather than let him go—that is not my fault, O citizens, but the fault of the times. Lucius Catiline ought to have been visited with the severest punishment and to have been put to death long since; and both the customs of our ancestors and the rigor of my office and the republic, demanded this of me; but how many, think you, were there who did not believe what I reported?

how many who out of stupidity did not think so? how many who even defended him? how many who, out of their own depravity, favored him? If, in truth, I had thought that, if he were removed, all danger would be removed from you, I would long since have cut off Lucius Catiline, had it been at the risk, not only of my popularity, but even of my life.

.   .   .   .

There is no nation for us to fear—no king who can make war on the Roman people. All foreign affairs are tranquilized, both by land and sea, by the valor of one man [Pompey]. Domestic war alone remains. The only plots against us are within our own walls—the danger is within—the enemy is within. We must war with luxury, with madness, with wickedness. For this war, O citizens, I offer myself as the general. I take on myself the enmity of profligate men. What can be cured, I will cure, by whatever means it may be possible. What must be cut away, I will not suffer to spread to the ruin of the republic. Let them depart or let them stay quiet; or if they remain in the city and in the same disposition as at present, let them expect what they deserve.

.   .   .   .

I will tell you, O Romans, of what classes of men those forces are made up, and then, if I can, I will apply to each the medicine of my advice and persuasion.

There is one class of them, who, with enormous debts, have still greater possessions, and who can by no means be detached from their affection to them. . . . But I think these men are the least of all to be dreaded, because they can either be persuaded to abandon their opinions or, if they cling to them, they seem to me more likely to form wishes against the republic than to bear arms against it.

There is another class of them, who, although they are harassed by debt, yet are expecting supreme power; they wish to become masters. . . . If these had already got that which they with the greatest madness wish for, do they think that in the ashes of the city and blood of the citizens, which in their wicked and infamous hearts they desire, they will become consuls and dictators and even kings? Do they not see that they are wishing for that which, if they were to obtain it, must be given up to some fugitive slave or to some gladiator?

There is a third class, already touched by age, but still vigorous from constant exercise. . . . These are colonists, who, from becoming possessed of unexpected and sudden wealth, boast themselves extravagantly and insolently; these men, while they build like rich men, while they delight in farms, in litters, in vast families of slaves, in luxurious banquets, have incurred such great debts, that, if they would be saved, they must raise Sylla from the dead. . . . Let them cease to be mad, and to think of proscriptions and dictatorships; for such a horror of these times is ingrained into the city, that not even men, but it seems to me that even the very cattle, would refuse to bear them again.

There is a fourth class, various, promiscuous, and turbulent; . . . not so much active soldiers as lazy insolvents. . . . As to these, I do not understand why, if they cannot live with honor, they should wish to die shamefully; or why they think they shall perish with less pain in a crowd, than if they perish by themselves.

There is a fifth class, of parricides, assassins; in short, of all infamous characters, whom I do not wish to recall from Catiline, and indeed they cannot be separated from him. Let them perish in their wicked war, since they are so numerous that a prison cannot contain them.

There is a last class, last not only in number but in the sort of men and in their way of life; the especial body-guard of Catiline, of his levying; ay, the friends of his embraces and of his bosom; whom you see with carefully-combed hair, glossy, beardless, or with well-trimmed beards; with tunics with sleeves, or reaching to the ankles; clothed with veils, not with robes, all the industry of whose life, all the labor of whose watchfulness, is expended in suppers lasting till daybreak.

.   .   .   .

On the one side are fighting modesty, on the other, wantonness; on the one, chastity, on the other, uncleanness; on the one, honesty, on the other, fraud; on the one, piety, on the other, wickedness; on the one, consistency, on the other, insanity; on the one, honor, on the other, baseness; on the one, continence, on the other, lust; in short, equity, temperance, fortitude, prudence, all the virtues, contend against iniquity with luxury, against indolence, against rashness, against all the vices; lastly, abundance contends against destitution, good plans against baffled designs, wisdom against madness, well-founded hope against universal despair. In a contest and war of this sort, even if the zeal of men were to fail, will not the immortal gods compel such numerous and excessive vices to be defeated by these most eminent virtues?

.   .   .   .

Now once more I wish those who have remained in the city, and who, contrary to the safety of the city and of all of you, have been left in the city by Catiline, although they are enemies, yet because they were born citizens, to be warned again and again by me. . . . If any one stirs in the city, and if I detect not only any action, but any attempt or design against the country, he shall feel that there are in this city vigilant consuls, eminent magistrates, a brave senate, arms, and prisons, which our ancestors appointed as the avengers of nefarious and convicted crimes.

. . . An internal civil war the most cruel and terrible in the memory of man, shall be put an end to by me alone in the robe of peace acting as general and commander-in-chief. . . . And this I promise you, O Romans, relying neither on my own · prudence, nor on human counsels, but on many and manifest intimations of the will of the immortal gods; under whose guidance I first entertained this hope and this opinion; who are now defending their temples and the houses of the city, not afar off, as they were used to, from a foreign and distant enemy, but here on the spot, by their own divinity and present help. And you, O Romans, ought to pray to and implore them to defend from the nefarious wickedness of abandoned citizens, now that all the forces of all enemies are defeated by land and sea, this city which they have ordained to be the most beautiful and flourishing of all cities.

Look back and observe the sagacity with which the orator, instead of assuming the attitude of self-defense, begins by boldly making a merit of his conduct.

The third oration is interesting. It has even something of the interest of plot described, as well as of eloquence. It is addressed to the people, and it details, in masterly narration, the incidents of the discovery of full documentary evidence against the conspirators. The Al-lob′ro-ges had at the moment an embassy in Rome, with whom the conspirators had tampered. But Cicero received from these Gallic envoys a hint of the approaches made to them. He bade them go on and obtain full knowledge of the plans of the conspirators. This they did. At Cicero's suggestion they demanded credentials in black and white which they might carry home to their nation. Such were supplied, and then, as they were withdrawing homeward, they were arrested and brought back with their papers in possession. The evidence was so unquestionable that the conspirators could not gainsay it, and one of them made a clean breast of the whole crime.   Such in brief is what Cicero in this admirable popular speech recites to his hearers.

The subject of the fourth speech delivered in the senate is the disposal to be made of the conspirators now in custody. Cicero spoke in favor of the capital sentence.   His weight and eloquence prevailed.   The conspirators were strangled by torchlight in their underground dungeon.   The suppression of this conspiracy was an occasion of triumph to Cicero.   No civilian's glory had ever been so great at Rome.   He was saluted *Pater Patriæ*, "Father of his Fatherland."

From this fourth speech we extract briefly to show, according to Cicero's statement of them, the tenor of Cæsar's remarks.   The advice of Silanus, consul elect, to put the conspirators to death, is contrasted with that of Julius Cæsar, thus:

The other [Cæsar] feels that death was not appointed by the immortal gods for the sake of punishment, but that it is either a necessity of nature or a rest from toils and miseries; therefore wise men have never met it unwillingly, brave men have often encountered it even voluntarily.   But imprisonment, and that too perpetual, was certainly invented for the extraordinary punishment of nefarious wickedness: therefore he proposes that they should be distributed among the municipal towns.   This proposition seems to have in it injustice if you command it, difficulty if you request it; however, let it be so decreed if you like.

For I will undertake and, as I hope, I shall find one who will not think it suitable to his dignity to refuse what you decide on for the sake of the universal safety.   He imposes, besides, a severe punishment on the burgesses of the municipal town if any of the prisoners escape; he surrounds them with the most terrible guard, and with everything worthy of the wickedness of abandoned men.   And he proposes to establish a decree that no one shall be able to alleviate the punishment of those whom he is condemning, by a vote of either the senate or the people.   He takes away even hope, which alone can comfort men in their miseries; besides this, he votes that their goods should be confiscated; he leaves life alone to these infamous men, and, if he had taken that away, he would have relieved them by one pang of many tortures of mind and body and of all the punishment of their crimes.   Therefore, that there might be some dread in life to the wicked, men of old have believed that there were some punishments of that sort appointed for the wicked in the shades below; because in truth they perceived that if this were taken away death itself would not be terrible.

Now, O conscript fathers, I see what is my interest. If you follow the opinion of Caius Cæsar (since he has adopted this path in the republic, which is accounted the popular one) perhaps as he is the author and promoter of this opinion, the popular violence will be less to be dreaded by me. If you adopt the other opinion, I know not but I am likely to have more trouble. Still, let the advantage of the republic outweigh the consideration of my danger. For we have from Caius Cæsar, as his own dignity and as the illustrious character of his ancestors demanded, a vote as a hostage of his lasting good will to the republic. It has been clearly seen how great is the difference between the lenity of demagogues, and a disposition really attached to the interests of the people.

This most gentle and merciful man does not hesitate to commit Publius Lentulus to eternal darkness and imprisonment, and he establishes a law to all posterity that no one shall be able to boast of alleviating his punishment or hereafter to appear a friend of the people to the destruction of the Roman people. He adds, also, the confiscation of their goods, so that want also and beggary may be added to all the torments of mind and body. Wherefore, if you decide on this, you give me a companion in my address dear and acceptable to the Roman people.

The comity proper between senators is carefully observed in Cicero's answer to Cæsar. Nay, you feel that Cicero is conscious of dealing now with a man whose popular influence is at least to be respected, perhaps to be feared. How much self-control, combined with how much fine courage, was displayed by Cicero, if, within himself, he indeed knew, what Mommsen supposes to be certainly true, that Cæsar was all the time, by secret encouragement, in complicity with the conspirators! In that case, however, you cannot acquit Cicero of being crafty at some expense of candor. We can seldom be quite sure, in a great game of statesmanship or diplomacy, what motives behind the mask of decent appearance really work in the breasts of those engaged in it.

The range of Cicero's eloquence is so wide, that adequately

to represent it would require a whole volume as large as this. There is, however, one other cycle of Cicero's speeches too important in itself, and too important for illustration of the orator's genius and character, not to be spoken of here, and exemplified in at least a few extracts.

We refer to the fourteen orations that go by the name of the philippics—a style of designation imitated and appropriated from the famous harangues of Demosthenes against Philip of Macedon. Cicero's philippics were directed against Mark Antony. They were delivered, part of them to the senate, and part of them before the people, within the period following Julius Cæsar's death during which it remained doubtful what course of public policy would be pursued by young Octavian (Cæsar Augustus), named in Cæsar's will as his political heir. Cicero still hoped that the destined future emperor might be induced to restore the republic.

Antony meantime, who, as having been Cæsar's colleague in nominal consulship, had succeeded to the place of chief actual power in the state, was manifestly taking measures to confirm himself in a kind of imperial usurpation. He had been in negotiation and collusion with the assassins—Liberators, it was the fashion to call them—but he was evidently beginning to revive Cæsarism by such contrivances of administration as, for that purpose, he dared adventure upon. He convened the senate to confer some additional divine honors on the dead dictator. That day's session, Cicero, though specially requested by Antony to do so, did not attend. He was against the measure proposed. Antony, provoked, talked threateningly in the senate about pulling down the recusant ex-consul's house about his ears.

The next day, Cicero went to the senate and, Antony in his turn being absent, delivered a speech in dignified, moderate, but quite firm, opposition to Antony. Provoked again, Antony replied in a violent personal invective. To this,

Cicero prudently abstained from replying in the senate ; but he wrote out a speech in response, which, having previously sent it in private to some of his friends, he finally published as the second philippic. This second philippic, conceived and composed as if addressed in immediate reply to Antony before the senate, constitutes what is generally esteemed the master-piece of Cicero's eloquence.

The contrast in tone, in style, in matter, which this philippic, in common with the rest of the series, presents to the other orations of Cicero, not excepting even the vehement onslaughts upon Catiline, is more than merely strong, it is violent. You could hardly believe it possible for the author of the courtly orations for the poet Archias, for the Manilian Law, for Marcus Marcellus, to produce discourse so indignant, so impetuous, so direct, so hard-hitting, nay, so savage, as the orations against Antony. The flowing robes are flung off, and the orator speaks like an athlete, rather like a warrior, stripped to hew his antagonist to the ground.

Antony was, undoubtedly, one of the most shamelessly profligate of men. Otherwise such accusations as Cicero brought must have reacted with his audience against the bringer.

We must content ourselves with brief citations. Here is the opening of the speech [we condense by omissions] :

To what destiny of mine, O conscript fathers, shall I say that it is owing, that none for the last twenty years has been an enemy to the republic without at the same time declaring war against me? Nor is there any necessity for naming any particular person ; you yourselves recollect instances in proof of my statement. They have all hitherto suffered severer punishments than I could have wished for them; but I marvel that you, O Antonius, do not fear the end of those men whose conduct you are imitating. And in others I was less surprised at this. None of these men of former times was a voluntary enemy to me ; all of them were attacked by me for the sake of the republic. But you, who have never been injured by me, not even by a word, in order to appear more audacious than Catiline, more frantic than Clodius, have of your own accord attacked me with abuse.

.   *   *   *   *   *   *   *

Did he think that it was easiest to disparage me in the senate? a body which has borne its testimony in favor of many most illustrious citizens that they governed the republic well, but in favor of me alone, of all men, that I preserved it. Or did he wish to contend with me in a rivalry of eloquence? This, indeed, is an act of generosity! for what could be a more fertile or richer subject for me than to have to speak in defense of myself, and against Antonius?   ·

*   *   *   *   *   *   *   *

In that complaint [Cicero's first philippic], mournful indeed and miserable, but still unavoidable for a man of that rank in which the senate and people of Rome have placed me, what did I say that was insulting? that was otherwise than moderate? that was otherwise than friendly? and what instance was it not of moderation to complain of the conduct of Marcus Antonius, and yet to abstain from any abusive expressions? especially when you had scattered abroad all relics of the republic; when everything was on sale at your house by the most infamous traffic; when you confessed that those laws which had never been promulgated had been passed with reference to you and by you; when you, being augur, had abolished the auspices, being consul, had taken away the power of interposing the veto; when you were escorted in the most shameful manner by armed guards; when, worn out with drunkenness and debauchery, you were every day performing all sorts of obscenities in that chaste house of yours. But I, as if I had to contend against Marcus Crassus, with whom I have had many severe struggles, and not with a most worthless gladiator, while complaining in dignified language of the state of the republic, did not say one word which could be called personal. Therefore, to-day I will make him understand with what great kindness he was then treated by me.

*   *   *   *   *   *   *   *

Since, O conscript fathers, I have many things which I may say both in my own defense and against Marcus Antonius, one thing I ask you, that you will listen to me with kindness while I am speaking for myself; the other I will insure myself, namely, that you shall listen to me with attention while speaking against him. At the same time also, I beg this of you: that if you have been acquainted with my moderation and modesty throughout my whole life, and especially as a speaker, you will not, when to-day I answer this man in the spirit in which he has

attacked me, think that I have forgotten my usual character.
I will not treat him as a consul, for he did not treat me as a man of
consular rank; and although he in no respect deserves to be
considered a consul, whether we regard his way of life or his
principle of governing the republic or the manner in which he was
elected, I am beyond all dispute a man of consular rank.

. . . .

On one occasion [addressed directly as to Antony] you attempted
even to be witty. O ye good gods, how little did that attempt
suit you! And yet you are a little to be blamed for your failure
in that instance, too. For you might have got some wit from your
wife, who was an actress. "Arms to the gown must yield."
[*Cedant arma togæ*—"let military yield to civil power." This is a
bit of verse from Cicero himself; Antony had evidently been rally-
ing his antagonist on it; Cicero meant it in praise of his own
exploits.] Well, have they not yielded? But afterward the gown
yielded to your arms. Let us inquire, then, whether it was better
for the arms of wicked men to yield to the freedom of the Roman people or that our liberty should yield to your arms. Nor
will I make any further reply to you about the verses. I will only
say briefly that you do not understand them, nor any other
literature whatever.

The free and frequent change, on Cicero's part, from addressing the senate to addressing Antony, indicates the highly
dramatic play of delivery in which the orator must have been
accustomed to indulge. Antony, it seems, inculpated Cicero
as in complicity with the assassins of Cæsar. Cicero points
out the inconsistency of Antony's praising, as Antony did, the
conspirators, and, at the same time, blaming Cicero. Cicero,
however, shows, as to himself, that though he approved
the deed when the deed had been done, he could have had
no part in the doing of the deed, since, were it otherwise,
his name must have been associated with it in the popular
fame of so illustrious an exploit. Evidently, at that point
of time, it was the prevailing opinion at Rome that Cæsar's
murder was a praiseworthy act of liberation for the state.
Cicero goes over Antony's life and finds abundant matter
of invective:

Let us speak of his meaner descriptions of worthlessness. You, with those jaws of yours, and those sides of yours, and that strength of body suited to a gladiator, drank such quantities of wine at the marriage of Hippia, that you were forced to vomit the next day in the sight of the Roman people.   O action disgraceful not merely to see, but even to hear of!   If this had happened to you at supper amid those vast drinking-cups of yours who would not have thought it scandalous ?   But in an assembly of the Roman people, a man holding a public office, a master of the horse, to whom it would have been disgraceful even to belch, vomiting filled his own bosom and the whole tribunal with fragments of what he had been eating reeking with wine.

.   .   .   .

Cicero comes to an incident in Antony's career the mention of which, as the author's lively imagination prompts him, writing in his closet, to suppose, makes Antony start:

He does not dissemble, O conscript fathers: it is plain that he is agitated; he perspires; he turns pale.   Let him do what he pleases, provided he is not sick, and does not behave as he did in the Minucian colonnade. . . .   Your colleague [Julius Cæsar] was sitting in the rostra, clothed in a purple robe, on a golden chair, wearing a crown.   You mount the steps; you approach his chair (if you were a priest of Pan, you ought to have recollected that you were consul too); you display a diadem.   There is a groan over the whole forum.   Where did the diadem come from ?   For you had not picked it up when lying on the ground, but you had brought it from home with you, a premeditated and deliberately planned wickedness.   You placed the diadem on his head amid the groans of the people; he rejected it amid great applause.   You then alone, O wicked man, were found, both to advise the assumption of kingly power, and to wish to have him for your master who was your colleague; and also to try what the Roman people might be able to bear and to endure.   Moreover, you even sought to move his pity; you threw yourself at his feet as a suppliant; begging for what? to be a slave? You might beg it for yourself, when you had lived in such a way from the time that you were a boy that you could bear everything and would find no difficulty in being a slave; but certainly you had no commission from the Roman people to try for such a thing for them.

O how splendid was that eloquence of yours, when you harangued the people stark naked!   What could be more foul than this? more shameful than this? more deserving of every sort of punishment?   Are you waiting for me to prick you more?   This that I am saying must tear you and bring blood enough, if you have any feeling at all.   I am afraid that I may be detracting from the glory of some most eminent men. Still my indignation shall find a voice. What can be more scandalous than for that man to live who placed a diadem on a man's head, when every one confesses that that man was deservedly slain who rejected it? And, moreover, he caused it to be recorded in the annals, under the head of Lupercalia, "That Marcus Antonius, the consul, by command of the people, had offered the kingdom to Caius Cæsar, perpetual dictator; and that Cæsar had refused to accept it."

  •   •   •   •   •   •

Cicero again alludes to the killing of Cæsar :

The name of peace is sweet; the thing itself is most salutary. But between peace and slavery there is a wide difference. Peace is liberty in tranquillity: slavery is the worst of all evils—to be repelled, if need be, not only by war, but even by death. But if those deliverers of ours have taken themselves away out of our sight, still they have left behind the example of their conduct. They have done what no one else had done. Brutus pursued Tarquinius with war, who was a king when it was lawful for a king to exist in Rome. Spurius Cassius, Spurius Mœlius, and Marcus Manlius were all slain because they were suspected of aiming at regal power. These are the first men who have ever ventured to attack, sword in hand, a man not aiming at regal power, but actually reigning. And their action is not only of itself a glorious and godlike exploit, but it is also one put forth for our imitation; especially since by it they have acquired such glory as appears hardly to be bounded by heaven itself. For although in the very consciousness of a glorious action there is a certain reward, still I do not consider immortality of glory a thing to be despised by one who is himself mortal.

  •   •   •   •   •   •   •

Contrasting Antony with Julius Cæsar, Cicero says :

In that man were combined genius, method, memory, literature, prudence, deliberation, and industry. He had performed exploits in war which, though calamitous for the republic, were nevertheless mighty deeds. Having for many years aimed at being a king, he had with great labor and much personal danger accomplished what he intended. He had conciliated the ignorant multitude by presents, by monuments, by largesses of food, and by banquets; he had bound his own party to him by rewards, his adversaries by the appearances of clemency. Why need I say much on such a subject? He had already brought a free city, partly by fear, partly by patience, into a habit of slavery.

With him I can, indeed, compare you as to your desire to reign ; but in all other respects you are in no degree to be compared to him. But from the many evils which by him have been burned into the republic there is still this good, that the Roman people has now learned how much to believe every one, to whom to trust itself, and against whom to guard. Do you never think on these things? And do you not understand that it is enough for brave men to have learned how noble a thing it is as to the act, how grateful it is as to the benefit done, how glorious as to the fame acquired, to slay a tyrant? When men could not bear him, do you think they will bear you? Believe me, the time will come when men will race with one another to do this deed and when no one will wait for the tardy arrival of an opportunity.

Consider, I beg you, Marcus Antonius, do some time or other consider the republic: think of the family of which you are born, not of the men with whom you are living. Be reconciled to the republic. However, do you decide on your conduct. As to mine, I myself will declare what that shall be. I defended the republic as a young man; I will not abandon it now when I am old. I scorned the sword of Catiline; I will not quail before yours. No, I will rather cheerfully expose my own person, if the liberty of the city can be restored by my death.

May the indignation of the Roman people at last bring forth what it has been so long laboring with. In truth, if twenty years ago in this very temple I asserted that death could not come prematurely upon a man of consular rank, with how much more truth must I now say the same of an old man? To me, indeed, O conscript fathers, death is now even desirable, after all the honors which I have gained and the deeds which I have done. I only pray for these two things: One, that dying I may leave the Roman people free. No greater boon than this can be granted me by the immortal gods. The other, that every one may meet with a fate suitable to his deserts and conduct toward the republic.

Thus the second philippic of Cicero ends.

Our own great jurist and orator, Rufus Choate, speaking on the general subject of "The Eloquence of Revolutionary Periods," enters, at one point, without notice upon a magnificent version, his own, no doubt, of a representative passage of Cicero's patriot oratory, as follows:

Lay hold on this opportunity of our salvation, conscript fathers— by the immortal gods I conjure you! — and remember that you are the foremost men here, in the council-chamber of the whole earth.

Give one sign to the Roman people that even as now they pledge their valor, so you pledge your wisdom to the crisis of the state. But what need that I exhort you? Is there one so insensate as not to understand that if we sleep over an occasion such as this, it is ours to bow our necks to a tyranny not proud and cruel only, but ignominious—but sinful? Do ye not know this Antony? Do ye not know his companions? Do ye not know his whole house— insolent,—impure,—gamesters,—drunkards? To be slaves to such as he, to such as these, were it not the fullest measure of misery, conjoined with the fullest measure of disgrace? If it be so—may the gods avert the omen—that the supreme hour of the republic has come, let us, the rulers of the world, rather fall with honor, than serve with infamy! Born to glory and to liberty, let us hold these bright distinctions fast or let us greatly die! Be it, Romans, our first resolve to strike down the tyrant and the tyranny. Be it our second to endure all things for the honor and liberty of our country. To submit to infamy for the love of life can never come within the contemplation of a Roman soul! For you, the people of Rome—you, whom the gods have appointed to rule the world—for you to own a master is impious.

You are in the last crisis of nations. To be free or to be slaves— that is the question of the hour. By every obligation of man or states it behooves you in this extremity to conquer—as your devotion to the gods and your concord among yourselves encourage you to hope—or to bear all things but slavery. Other nations may bend to servitude; the birthright and the distinction of the people · of Rome is liberty.

Our previous extracts were from the best translations accessible, but the rendering which Choate thus gives of a passage of Cicero may serve to show what a different power there is in Cicero's eloquence according as he is translated or not by a man with the sense in him, and the capacity, of style. With Mr. Choate's fine bit of translation, let us consider our presentation of Cicero as orator closed.

Now for Cicero's letters. And first an extract from one written to his friend Atticus about a visit of omnipotent Cæsar to Cicero's house. It needs to be explained that there was apparently a tacit playful understanding between Cicero and his half-Greek friend Atticus, that they should freely interlard the text of their correspondence with phrases borrowed from Greek. Mr. Jeans, our translator, has, with excellent judgment, sought to reproduce the effect for us, by putting the Greek used by Cicero into an equivalent of French. Those readers of ours who know French will readily excuse it if, for the benefit of those readers of ours who do not, we hint in English the meaning of the few foreign phrases that here occur:

Oh, what a formidable guest to have had! and yet *je n'en suis pas fâché* [I am not sorry], he was in such a very agreeable mood. But after his arrival at Philippus's house, on the evening of the second day of the Saturnalia, the whole establishment was so crowded with soldiers that even the room where Cæsar himself was to dine could hardly be kept clear from them; it is a fact that there were two thousand men! Of course I was nervous about what might be the case with me next day, and so Cassius Barba came to my assistance; he gave me some men on guard. The camp was pitched out of doors; my villa was made secure. On the third day of the Saturnalia he stayed at Philippus's till near one, and admitted nobody (accounts with Balbus, I suppose); then took a walk on the beach. After two to the bath: then he heard about Ma-mur'ra; he made no objection. He was then rubbed down with oil, and dinner began. It was his intention *se faire vomir* [to take a vomit], and consequently he ate and drank *sans peur* [freely], and with much satisfaction. And certainly everything was very good, and well served; nay more, I may say that

> " Though the cook was good,
> 'Twas Attic salt that flavored best the food."

There were three dining rooms besides, where there was a very hospitable reception for the gentlemen of his *suite;* while the inferior class of freedmen and slaves had abundance at any rate; for as to the better class, they had a more refined table. In short, I think I acquitted myself like a man. The guest, however, was not the sort of person to whom you would say, "'I shall be most delighted if you will come here again on your way back "; once is enough. As to our conversation, it was mostly like that of two *savants* [men of letters]; nothing was said *au grand serieux* [in a very serious vein]. Well, I will only say that he was greatly pleased and seemed to enjoy himself. He told me that he should be one day at Puteoli, and the next near Baiæ. Here you have the story of his visit—or shall I say "billeting"?—which, I told you, was a thing one would shrink from, but did not give much trouble. I am for Tusculum next after a short stay here.

When he was passing Dolabella's house, but nowhere else, the whole guard was paraded in arms on either side of him as he rode; I have it from Nicias.

The allusion about Mamurra is obscure. Generally it is taken to mean certain scathing epigrams on Cæsar and Mamurra, from the pen of the poet Catullus. "He never changed countenance," is Middleton's rendering, in place of Mr. Jeans's "he made no objection."

The taking of a vomit before and after meals was a not uncommon Roman habit of the times. It was not only an epicure's expedient for better enjoying, and enjoying more safely, the pleasures of the table, but it was a current medical prescription for improving the health. Cæsar's purposed post-prandial vomit (ante-prandial, Middleton makes it) was not therefore an exceptional bit of epicurism. Rather, it is to be regarded as good guestship on his part. Cæsar thus intimated to Cicero that he expected a good dinner, and was intending to do his host's fare full dictatorial justice.

The quotation in verse is from Lucilius. Cicero has it again in his De Finibus. "Or shall I say 'billeting'?" is Cicero's way of implying to Atticus that Cæsar's visit, having been accepted rather than invited, might be looked upon as in the nature of a military quartering of himself by Cæsar on his host's hospitality. We may venture however to guess, both from Cicero's characteristic genial good nature and from his shrewd eye to the main chance, that Cæsar was not suffered to feel any lack of seeming-spontaneous cordiality, in that day's entertainment.

A letter of Sulpicius, included in Mr. Jeans's selection from the correspondence of Cicero, is one of consolation to his illustrious friend on the death of his daughter Tullia. This is a famous literary antique. It admirably shows what was the best that ancient paganism could offer in the way of

comfort to souls bereaved.   Here is a specimen extract from
the letter of Sulpicius:

A reflection which was such as to afford me no light consolation I
cannot but mention to you, in the hope that it may be allowed
to contribute equally toward mitigating your grief. As I was
returning from Asia, when sailing from Æ-gi'na in the direction of
Meg'a-ra, I began to look around me at the various places by
which I was surrounded.   Behind me was Ægina, in front, Megara;
on the right, the Piræus, on the left, Corinth: all of these towns,
that in former days were so magnificent, are now lying prostrate
and in ruins before one's eyes.   "Alas!" I began to reflect to myself, "we poor feeble mortals, who can claim but a short life in
comparison, complain as though a wrong was done us if one of our
number dies in the course of nature or has fallen on the field
of battle; and here in one spot are lying stretched out before
me the corpses of so many cities! Servius, why do you not control
yourself, and remember that that is man's life into which you have
been born?" Believe me, I found myself in no small degree
strengthened by these reflections.   Let me advise you, if you agree
with me, to put the same prospect before your eyes too. How
lately at one and the same time have many of our most illustrious
men fallen! how grave an encroachment has been made on the
rights of the sovereign people of Rome! every country in the
world has been convulsed: if the frail life of a helpless woman has
gone too, who being born to our common lot must have died
in a few short years, even if the time had not come for her now,
are you thus utterly stricken down?

Cicero replied as follows to the tender of sympathy and consolation from Sulpicius:

I join with you, my dear Sulpicius, in wishing that you had been
in Rome when this most severe calamity befell me.   I am sensible
of the advantage I should have received from your presence, and I
had almost said your equal participation of my grief, by having
found myself somewhat more composed after I had read your
letter.   It furnished me, indeed, with arguments extremely proper
to soothe the anguish of affliction and evidently flowed from a
heart that sympathized with the sorrows it endeavored to assuage.
But although I could not enjoy the benefit of your own good offices
in person, I had the advantage, however, of your son's, who gave
me proof, by every tender assistance that could be contributed
upon so melancholy an occasion, how much he imagined that
he was acting agreeably to your sentiments when he thus dis-

covered the affection of his own. More pleasing instances of his friendship I have frequently received, but never any that were more obliging. As to those for which I am indebted to yourself, it is not only the force of your reasonings and the very considerable share you take in my afflictions, that have contributed to compose my mind; it is the deference, likewise, which I always pay to the authority of your sentiments. For, knowing, as I perfectly do, the superior wisdom with which you are enlightened, I should be ashamed not to support my distresses in the manner you think I ought; I will acknowledge, nevertheless, that they sometimes almost entirely overcome me; and I am scarce able to resist the force of my grief when I reflect, that I am destitute of those consolations which attended others, whose examples I propose to my imitation. Thus Quintus Maximus lost a son of consular rank and distinguished by many brave and illustrious actions; Lucius Paulus was deprived of two sons in the space of a single week; and your relation Gallus, together with Marcus Cato, had both of them the unhappiness to survive their respective sons, who were endowed with the highest abilities and virtues. Yet these unfortunate parents lived in times when the honors they derived from the republic might, in some measure, alleviate the weight of their domestic misfortunes. But as for myself, after having been stripped of those dignities you mention, and which I had acquired by the most laborious exertion of my abilities, I had one only consolation remaining—and of that I am now bereaved! I could no longer divert the disquietude of my thoughts, by employing myself in the causes of my friends or the business of the state; for I could no longer, with any satisfaction, appear either in the forum or the senate. In short, I justly considered myself as cut off from the benefit of all those alleviating occupations in which fortune and industry had qualified me to engage. But I considered, too, that this was a deprivation which I suffered in common with yourself and some others; and, whilst I was endeavoring to reconcile my mind to a patient endurance of those ills, there was one to whose tender offices I could have recourse, and in the sweetness of whose conversation I could discharge all the cares and anxiety of my heart. But this last fatal stab to my peace has torn open those wounds which seemed in some measure to have been tolerably healed: for I can now no longer lose my private sorrows in the prosperity of the commonwealth, as I was wont to dispel the uneasiness I suffered upon the public account, in the happiness I received at home. Accordingly, I have equally banished myself from my house and from the public,—as finding no relief in either from the calamities I lament in both. It is this, therefore, that

heightens my desire of seeing you here; as nothing can afford me
a more effectual consolation than the renewal of our friendly intercourse; a happiness which I hope, and am informed indeed, that I
shall shortly enjoy. Among the many reasons I have for impatiently wishing your arrival, one is, that we may previously
concert together our scheme of conduct in the present conjunc-
ture—which, however, must now be entirely accommodated to
another's will. This person [Cæsar], it is true, is a man of great
abilities and generosity, and one, if I mistake not, who is by
no means my enemy—as I am sure he is extremely your friend.
Nevertheless, it requires much consideration, I do not say in what
manner we shall act with respect to public affairs, but by what
methods we may best obtain his permission to retire from them.
Farewell.

We go from Cicero the letter-writer to Cicero the philosopher.

In his quality of philosopher, Cicero wrote on morals. "De
Officiis" ["Concerning Duties"] is the title of his great
treatise on this subject. A comparative estimate of Cicero's
De Officiis and of his philosophical writings in general, presented by Luther, will be read with interest. Out of this
great man's teeming "table talk" so-called, happily in
such large measure preserved to us, we take the following
extract:

"Cicero is greatly superior to Aristotle in philosophy and in
teaching. The Officia of Cicero are greatly superior to the Ethica
of Aristotle; and although Cicero was involved in the cares of
government and had much on his shoulders, he greatly excels
Aristotle, who was a lazy ass, and cared for nothing but money and
possessions, and comfortable, easy days. Cicero handled the
greatest and best questions in his philosophy, such as: Is there a
God? What is God? Does he give heed to the actions of men?
Is the soul immortal? etc. Aristotle is a good and skillful dialec-
tician, who has observed the right and orderly method in teaching,
but the kernel of matters he has not touched. Let those who wish
to see a true philosophy read Cicero. Cicero was a wise and indus-
trious man, and he suffered much and accomplished much. I
hope that our Lord God will be generous to him and the like of
him. Of this we are not entitled to speak with certainty.
Although the revealed word must abide: 'He who believeth, and
is baptized, shall be saved.' (Mark xvi., 16), yet it is possible that

God may dispense with it in the case of the heathen. There will be a new heaven and a new earth, much larger than the present; and he can give to every one according to his good pleasure.'

Cicero was an eminently practical man, a man of affairs, a man of real life. The practical interest accordingly with him always dominated the speculative. The De Officiis is by no means conceived as an exhaustive philosophical treatise on the subject of ethics. It is rather a manual of maxims, reasoned and elucidated maxims, adapted to guide the conduct of a young man seeking to be a good citizen in the Roman state and a candidate there for political preferment.

The work is divided into three books. The first book treats the right, the second, the expedient, the third, the relation between the right and the expedient. The main interest of the De Officiis centers in the third book, the book in which the author treats of apparent conflicts between the expedient and the right. Let us go to that book; but let us, while going, cull here and there an interesting thing on the way.

"The first demand of justice," says Cicero, "is that no one do harm to another, *unless provoked by injury*." We italicize the exceptive clause—the clause will occur a second time toward the end of the treatise—as constituting a point of contrast between the De Officiis and the New Testament.

Julius Cæsar (dead at the date of this composition) is more than once made by Cicero to do duty as an example by way of warning. Generosity, as well as justice, is, according to Cicero, a demand of morality. But the lavish munificence of Cæsar was not to be accounted generosity. Cæsar had taken wrongfully what he bestowed magnificently; and "nothing," insists Cicero, "is generous that is not at the same time just."

Cicero himself was rich, but hardly rich with such a spirit as to be condemned by his own sentiment, expressed in the following words:

Nothing shows so narrow and small a mind as the love of riches; nothing is more honorable and magnificent than to despise money, if you have it not—if you have it, to expend it for purposes of beneficence and generosity.

When, however, Cicero immediately went on, "The greed of fame also must be shunned," perhaps he was, whether he knew it or not, fairly hit by a boomerang return upon himself of his own weapon.

"One person," Cicero teaches, "ought, while another person, under the same circumstances, ought not, to commit suicide." Elsewhere in his writings, he makes suicide wrong.

Is not this that follows almost like the apostle Paul giving instruction to the Corinthian Christians about the use of the various supernatural "gifts"?

It is better to speak fluently, if wisely, than to think, no matter with what acuteness of comprehension, if the power of expression be wanting; for thought begins and ends in itself, while fluent speech extends its benefit to those with whom we are united in fellowship.

Cicero, as from the foregoing might be inferred, insists strongly on "altruism"—in the form of making self-indulgence in study and culture severely subordinate to activities that may tend to the good of one's fellow-creatures.

That is a wholesome inculcation, in which Cicero, discussing the expedient, teaches his son that, even for his own sake, he ought to seek to be loved. He draws warning example again, anonymously this time, from Cæsar, and Ennius is quoted (not for the first time in this treatise):

But of all things nothing tends so much to the guarding and keeping of resources as to be the object of affection; nor is anything more foreign to that end than to be the object of fear. Ennius says most fittingly:

"Hate follows fear; and plotted ruin, hate."

It has been lately demonstrated, if it was before unknown, that

no resources can resist the hatred of a numerous body. It is
not merely the destruction of this tyrant . . . that shows how
far the hatred of men may prove fatal; but similar deaths of other
tyrants, hardly one of whom has escaped a like fate, teach this
lesson.

Cicero constantly enlivens and enlightens his ethical page
with instance drawn by the writer from great resources of
knowledge in possession. Here is an example of this
method of his. He is pointing out how on the whole it is
for you yourself more profitable to exercise kindness toward
really good men than toward men simply well placed in
life :

I think a kindness better invested with good men than with men
of fortune. In fine, we should endeavor to meet the claims of
those of every class; but if it come to a competition between rival
claimants for our service, Themistocles may be well quoted as
an authority, who, when asked whether he would marry his
daughter to a good poor man, or to a rich man of less respectable character, replied, " I, indeed, prefer the man who lacks
money to the money that lacks a man."

Cicero holds good sound doctrine on financial questions.
Repudiation of debt, under whatever form proposed, and with
whatever pretext, excites his abhorrence. He has his thrust
at Julius Cæsar again :

Nothing holds the state more firmly together than good faith,
which cannot possibly exist unless the payment of debts is obliga-
tory. . . . He, indeed, of late conqueror, but at that time
conquered [that is, when Catiline's conspiracy was suppressed—
Cicero assumes Cæsar, deeply in debt at the moment, to
have taken part in the plot], carried out what he had then
planned after he had ceased to have any personal interest in it. So
great was his appetite for evil-doing, that the very doing of evil
gave him delight, even when there was no special reason for it.
From this kind of generosity, then—the giving to some what is
taken from others—those who mean to be guardians of the state
will refrain, and will especially bestow their efforts, that through
the equity of the laws and of their administration every man
may have his own property made secure, and that neither the
poorer may be defrauded on account of their lowly condition,

nor any odium may stand in the way of the rich in holding or recovering what belongs to them.

The third book, as has been said, is occupied with the relation of the right to the expedient. Cicero, with repetition and with emphasis, insists that there is never any conflict between these two—that always what is right is expedient, and that never is anything expedient which is not right. But he draws many distinctions and admits many qualifications. A thing generally wrong may, under certain circumstances, be right. He instances Brutus's act in stabbing Cæsar, as an illustration in point:

What greater crime can there be than to kill not only a man, but an intimate friend? Has one, then, involved himself in guilt by killing a tyrant, however intimate with him? This is not the opinion of the Roman people, who of all deeds worthy of renown regard this as the most noble. Has expediency, then, got the advantage over the right? Nay, but expediency has followed in the direction of the right.

It is the Stoic philosophy that Cicero mainly follows in the De Officiis, but, as disciple also of Plato, he claims much latitude of view and discussion. Here is a noble passage that will recall Paul's ethics, and even Paul's rhetoric:

For a man to take anything wrongfully from another, and to increase his own means of comfort by his fellow-man's discomfort, is more contrary to nature than death, than poverty, than pain, than anything else that can happen to one's body or his external condition. In the first place, it destroys human intercourse and society; for if we are so disposed that every one for his own gain is ready to rob or outrage another, that fellowship of the human race which is in the closest accordance with nature must of necessity be broken in sunder. As if each member of the body were so affected as to suppose itself capable of getting strength by appropriating the strength of the adjacent member, the whole body must needs be enfeebled and destroyed, so if each of us seizes for himself the goods of others, and takes what he can from every one for his own emolument, the society and intercourse of men must necessarily be subverted.

To the same purport again :

This, then, above all, ought to be regarded by every one as an established principle, that the interest of each individual and that of the entire body of citizens are identical, which interest if any one appropriate to himself alone, he does it to the sundering of all human intercourse. . . . Those, too, who say that account is to be taken of citizens, but not of foreigners, destroy the common sodality of the human race, which abrogated, beneficence, liberality, kindness, justice, are removed from their very foundations.

The following fine anecdote illustrates Cicero's open-minded hospitality toward what he found good in other nations than the Roman:

The-mis'to-cles, after the victory in the Persian war, said in a popular assembly, that he had a plan conducive to the public good, but that it was not desirable that it should be generally known. He asked that the people should name some one with whom he might confer. Aristi'des was named. Themistocles said to him that the fleet of the Lacedæmonians, which was drawn ashore at Gy-the'um, could be burned clandestinely, and if that were done, the power of the Lacedæmonians would be inevitably broken. Aristides, having heard this, returned to the assembly amidst the anxious expectation of all, and said that the measure proposed by Themistocles was very advantageous, but utterly devoid of right. Thereupon the Athenians concluded that what was not right was not expedient, and they repudiated the entire plan which they had not heard, on the authority of Aristides.

Several cases narrated or supposed by Cicero, and then considered by him on the one side and on the other—cases of apparent conflict between the right and the expedient—give rise to discussion at his hands which strikingly shows to what height of moral standard the conscience of man, unassisted by Divine revelation, could attain. The now so much vaunted ethics of Buddhism suffer cruelly in contrast with Cicero's De Officiis.

With one brief sentence more from this remarkable volume, we end our extracts from the De Officiis of Cicero. The sentence is one which sums up, in a single blended expression, at once the strange loftiness and the strange limitation of Cicero's moral ideal;

If one would only develop the idea of a good man wrapped up in his own mind, he would then at once tell himself that he is a good man who benefits all that he can, and does harm to no one unless provoked by injury.

"Unless provoked by injury"! The wings seemed strong enough to raise their possessor quite clear of the ground ; but, alas, there was a hopeless clog tied fast to the feet. How easily that untaught young Judæan to be born a generation later, will say :

"Love your enemies, bless them that curse you, do good to them that hate you, and pray for them which despitefully use you and persecute you."

The De Senectute (Concerning Old Age) of Cicero is an essay such almost as Addison, for example, might have issued in parts continued through several numbers of his Spectator. It is a charming meditation on a theme that Cicero's time of life when he wrote it inclined him and fitted him to make the subject of discourse. It was probably written not far from the date of the composition of the De Officiis. The literary form is that of a dialogue after the manner of Plato, in which Cato the Elder—an idealized and glorified man, as Cicero finely misrepresents the sturdy but boorish old censor of actual history—is the chief speaker. It is the gracious personality of the writer himself, rather than the repellent, not to say repulsive, personality of the historic character represented, which diffuses that indescribable charm over the exquisite pages of the De Senectute. Cicero balances the good and the ill of old age, with a serene and suave philosophy, which, while you read, makes you feel as if it would be a thing delightful to grow old. We take a single passage, only too brief, from the concluding part of the dialogue. This passage will be found to disclose something of the spirit in which the transmitted influence of Socrates and Plato enabled Cicero, at least in his better, his more transfigured, moments, to contemplate the prospect of death. It forms a bland and beautiful contrast to the hideous squalor of the old man depicted in Juvenal's satirical portrait. Cato is speaking to his younger companions in conversation—sons they of illustrious sires. He alludes to a son of his own, deceased,—" my Cato," he calls him,—with pathetic reminiscence reminding one of Burke's uttered sorrow over his similar bereavement, and of Webster's over his. What we give brings the dialogue to its end :

I am transported with desire to see your fathers whom I revered and loved; nor yet do I long to meet those only whom I have known, but also those of whom I have heard and read, and about whom I myself have written. Therefore one could not easily turn me back on my lifeway, nor would I willingly, like Pelias, be plunged in the rejuvenating caldron. Indeed, were any god to grant that from my present age I might go back to boyhood or become a crying child in the cradle, I should steadfastly refuse; nor would I be willing, as from a finished race, to be summoned back from the goal to the starting point. For what advantage is there in life? Or rather, what is there of arduous toil that is wanting to it? But grant all that you may in its favor, it still certainly has its excess or its fit measure of duration. I am not, indeed, inclined to speak ill of life, as many and even wise men have often done, nor am I sorry to have lived; for I have so lived that I do not think that I was born to no purpose. Yet I depart from life, as from an inn, not as from a home; for nature has given us here a lodging for a sojourn, not a place of habitation. O glorious day, when I shall go to that divine company and assembly of souls, and when I shall depart from this crowd and tumult! I shall go, not only to the men of whom I have already spoken, but also to my Cato, than whom no better man was ever born, nor one who surpassed him in filial piety, whose funeral pile I lighted,— the office which he should have performed for me,—but whose soul, not leaving me, but looking back upon me, has certainly gone into those regions whither he saw that I should come to him. This my calamity I seemed to bear bravely. Not that I endured it with an untroubled mind; but I was consoled by the thought that there would be between us no long parting of the way and divided life. For these reasons, Scipio, as you have said that you and Lælius have observed with wonder, old age sits lightly upon me. Not only is it not burdensome; it is even pleasant. But if I err in believing that the souls of men are immortal, I am glad thus to err, nor am I willing that this error in which I delight shall be wrested from me so long as I live; while if in death, as some paltry philosophers think, I shall have no consciousness, the dead philosophers cannot ridicule this delusion of mine. But if we are not going to be immortal, it is yet desirable for man to cease living in his due time; for nature has its measure, as of all other things, so of life. Old age is the closing act of life, as of a drama, and we ought in this to avoid utter weariness, especially if the act has been prolonged beyond its due length. I had these things to say about old age, which I earnestly hope that you may reach, so that you can verify by experience what you have heard from me.

We feel like performing an act of expiation. In preceding pages, we gave hard measure in judgment of the Roman character. We cannot revoke our sentence; for our sentence, we think, was mainly just. But we should like to strengthen our recommendation to mercy. Cicero, both by what he himself was, and by noble things that he here and there reports of his countrymen, inclines us, willingly persuaded, to relent from our extreme severity. They were a great race, not unworthy of their fame,—those ancient Romans; and Alpine flowers of moral beauty bloomed amid the Alpine snow and ice of their austere pride, their matter-of-fact selfishness.

As for Tully, his glory is secure. His own writings are his imperishable monument. Spoken against he may be, but he will continue to be read; and as long as he is read, he will enjoy his triumph. For no one can read Cicero, and not feel, in the face of whatever faults discovered, irresistibly propitiated toward him.

If, in an historic view of Rome, one might call Cæsar the sun of Roman history, with not less truth certainly might one call Cicero the sun of Roman literature.

CHAPTER VI.

NEXT to the Iliad of Homer, and hardly second to that, the Æneid of Virgil is the most famous of poems. The two poems, like the two poets, are joined forever in an inseparable comparison, contrast, and fellowship of fame. It would, however, be right that Homer's Odyssey, not less than his Iliad, should be associated in thought with the Æneid of Virgil. For the Æneid partakes quite as much of the character of the Odyssey as it does of the character of the Iliad. It is, in fact, a composite reproduction of both those poems, Virgil's poetic invention consisting rather in a cunning of composition and harmony to blend the Iliad and the Odyssey into one new whole, an authentic creation of the Roman poet's proper genius—Virgil's invention, we say, consisting rather in this, than in power to produce really original material of his own.

The literary history of the Æneid is remarkable. There has, in fact, happened no parenthesis of neglect in the long sentence of study and approval which posterity has pronounced on the genius and fame of this fortunate poet. For it is Virgil's good fortune, not less than it is his merit, that he is so safely and universally famous. Or possibly his fame belongs in part to the man as distinct from the poet. For Virgil had what has been called the genius to be loved.

This simple fact about his character, that he was lovable, together with the complementary fact about his life, that he was loved, is the most important thing that we know of Virgil the man. Publius Virgilius Maro was born (70 B. C.) a country boy in the hamlet of Andes (Northern Italy), near Mantua—whence "the Mantuan" has become a designation for him. He grew to early manhood in the rustic region of his birth. His little farm was not little enough to escape confiscation when the discharged legionaries of Octavius (Augustus) were to be furnished with settlements of land to keep them quiet and contented. Virgil had already won some friend at court who now proved influential enough to get back again for him, from the grace of Augustus, his confiscated patrimony.

There is a pretty story told of Virgil's composing a couplet of verses in praise of the emperor, and posting them secretly and anonymously on the palace gate. Augustus, having had the good taste to be pleased with the lines, made an effort to discover the author. Virgil's modesty kept him in the background, until some unscrupulous fellow thought it safe to claim the verses for his own. The impostor was handsomely rewarded. Virgil at this was so much vexed that he took measures to redress himself. With all his modesty and all his genius, Virgil seems not to have wanted a certain thrifty knack for making his way in the world. His present contrivance, however, was the contrivance of a poet, as well as of a man of sense. Under the original distich he wrote an additional verse, running

I made these lines, another took the praise,

together with the first words of a verse to follow—which same first words were written four times, in form and order as if beginning four successive verses purposely left unfinished. Here was a puzzle and a mystery. Augustus condescended to require that the lines should be completed. Several attempts to complete them ignominiously failed. Virgil at last revealed himself as the author, and finished the lines. They read as follows :

> Thus you not for yourselves build nests, O birds ;
> Thus you not for yourselves bear fleeces, flocks ;
> Thus you not for yourselves make honey, bees ;
> Thus you not for yourselves draw plows, O oxen.

The neat symmetrical look of the verses is necessarily lost in an English rendering. It is needless to say that the fortune of the poet was made.

Virgil was, it is believed, a man of exceptionally pure life, for a Roman of his time. His poetry agrees with this estimate of his morals. Toward the close of his life, he lived chiefly at Naples, Par-then'o-pe, as it used to be called. He ended his peaceful and prosperous life in his fifty-first year, a very well-to-do man. He was buried, according to Roman custom, by the wayside. They still point out the spot to the tourist. It lies on the road leading to Puteoli, out from Naples.

Virgil's works consist of three classes of poems. The order of production must be exactly inverted to give the order of comparative importance. That is, Virgil's poetic achievement formed a regular climax to its close. He was still, after finishing the Æneid, younger than Milton was when he began his Paradise Lost. Finishing, we say ; but, according to the poet's own standard, the Æneid never was finished. It is even reported that one of his parting directions was to have the manuscript of the poem burned. Augustus intervened to prevent the act of destruction.

We had better let our own order of treatment follow Virgil's order of production. First, then, of Virgil's pastoral poems.

These are called sometimes bucolics (Greek for "pastorals," which latter term is Latin), and sometimes eclogues (Greek for "select pieces"). There are in all ten eclogues of Virgil now extant. They vary somewhat in length, averaging about eighty lines each. They are written in the same meter as that of the Æneid, dactylic hexameter. The idea of such poems is derived from a Greek original. Theocritus in particular was Virgil's master in this species of composition. The pupil, however, puts into some of his eclogues what he found no hint of anywhere in his master. This is pre-eminently the case with the "Pollio," so-called, which is short enough to be presented in full. The "Pollio" happens to be the piece least truly pastoral in its quality of all Virgil's pastoral poems. However—nay, for that very reason—it is at the same time the most highly characteristic, not, to be sure, of the eclogues as bucolics, but of the eclogues as purely conventional productions of an artificial age, and of a true poet rendered artificial by the influences surrounding him.

The "Pollio" has for ostensible subject the birth of a marvelous boy, variously supposed to be son of Antony, son of Pollio, son of Augustus—even, by retrospective license on the poet's part, to be Augustus himself. The terms of allusion to this offspring, and of description of a blessed state of things to accompany and follow his birth, are, at points, singularly coincident with prophecies of Holy Writ concerning Jesus. The date of the poem is startlingly near that of the nativity of our Saviour. One can easily conceive in reading it that we have here an articulate utterance of the unconscious desire of all nations for a Redeemer. In it, the Sibyl is spoken of by Virgil as having foretold this happy age. Fragments still exist alleged to be authentic parts of the Sibylline oracles. But we cannot be sure. Those oracles, whatever they originally were, have been tampered with, for reasons of state and of church, until nothing of them remains that is unquestionably genuine. That old Latin hymn, so familiar to us all, the Dies Iræ, has a line,

Teste David cum Sibylla,

—"David, along with the Sibyl, bearing witness"—which keeps the idea of a Sibylline prophecy concerning Jesus fresh in modern recollection. Cuma was the Sibyl's dwelling-place.

Here, then, is Virgil's "Pollio." We use the prose translation of Professor Conington, of whose fruitful labors on Virgil we shall hereafter speak. The Muses of Sicily, you will observe, are invoked. Virgil thus acknowledges or rather proclaims, that he derives his pastoral verse from Theocritus, a Sicilian Greek, of Syracuse:

POLLIO.

Muses of Sicily, let us strike a somewhat louder chord. It is not for all that plantations have charms, or groundling tamarisks. If we are to sing of the woodland, let the woodland rise to a consul's dignity.

The last era of the song of Cuma has come at length: the grand file of the ages is being born anew; at length the virgin is returning to the reign of Saturn; at length a new generation is descending from heaven on high. Do but thou smile thy pure smile on the birth of the boy who shall at last bring the race of iron to an end, and bid the golden race spring up all the world over—thou Lucina—thine own Apollo is at length on his throne. In thy consulship it is—in thine, Pollio—that this glorious time shall come on, and the mighty months begin their march. Under thy conduct, any remaining trace of our national guilt shall become void, and release the world from the thraldom of perpetual fear. He shall have the life of the gods conferred on him, and shall see gods and heroes mixing together, and shall himself be seen of them, and with his father's virtues shall govern a world at peace.

For thee, sweet boy, the earth, of her own unforced will, shall pour forth a child's first presents—gadding ivy and foxglove everywhere, and Egyptian bean blending with the bright smiling acanthus. Of themselves, the goats shall carry home udders distended with milk; nor shall the herds fear huge lions in the way. Of itself, thy grassy cradle shall pour out flowers to caress thee. Death to the serpent, and to the treacherous plant of poisoned juice. Assyrian spices shall spring up by the wayside.

But soon as thou shalt be of an age to read at length of the glories of heroes and thy father's deeds, and to acquaint thyself with the nature of manly work, the yellow of the waving corn shall steal gradually over the plain, and from briers, that know naught of culture, grapes shall hang in purple clusters, and the stubborn heart of oak shall exude dews of honey. Still, under all this show, some few traces shall remain of the sin and guile of old—such as may prompt men to defy the ocean goddess with their ships, to build towns with walls around them, to cleave furrows in the soil of earth. A second Tiphys shall there be in those days—a second Argo to convey the flower of chivalry; a second war of heroes, too, shall there be, and a second time shall Achilles be sent in his greatness to Troy.

Afterward, when ripe years have at length made thee man, even the peaceful sailor shall leave the sea, nor shall the good ship of pine exchange merchandise—all lands shall produce all things, the ground shall not feel the harrow, nor the vineyard the pruning-hook; the sturdy plowman, too, shall at length set his bullocks free from the yoke; nor shall wool be taught to counterfeit varied hues, but of himself, as he feeds in the meadows, the ram shall transform his fleece, now into a lovely purple dye, now into saffron-yellow—of its own will, scarlet shall clothe the lambs as they graze. Ages like these, flow on!—so cried to their spindles the Fates, uttering in concert the fixed will of destiny.

Assume thine august dignities—the time is at length at hand—thou best-loved offspring of the gods, august scion of Jove! Look upon the world as it totters beneath the mass of its overhanging dome—earth and the expanse of sea and the deep of heaven—look how all are rejoicing in the age that is to be! O may my life's last days last long enough, and breath be granted me enough to tell of thy deeds! I will be o'er-matched in song by none—not by Or'pheus of Thrace, nor by Linus though that were backed by his mother, and this by his father—Orpheus by Cal-li'o-pe, Linus by Apollo in his beauty. Were Pan himself, with Arcady looking on, to enter the lists with me, Pan himself, with Arcady looking on, should own himself vanquished.

Begin, sweet child, with a smile, to take notice of thy mother. . .

Pope's "Messiah, a Sacred Eclogue, in imitation of Virgil's Pollio," would prove interesting read in comparison with its famous Latin original.

In the Georgics, we have a poem on farming. The title itself, Georgics, means farming, from *ge* (Greek for "earth," appearing in geography, geology, geometry) and *ergo* (an old Greek root, meaning "work"). The object of the poem was to encourage agricultural pursuits. Augustus desired that the empire should be peace, and he wanted to see every sword turned into a sickle—that is, every sword but his own. It is doubtful if Virgil's Georgics ever made many men farmers, or made many farmers better farmers than they were before. The theory and practice of farming exhibited are hardly up to the mark of the present scientific times. Quite probably, too, the farmers of Virgil's own day might have criticised the poet's suggestions at points. However, there is much good sense in the poem, mingled with much superstition. The tenor of didactics is pleasantly interrupted by occasional episode.

The Georgics are divided into four books. (The verse is dactylic hexameter.) The first book treats of raising what English people call corn, and we Americans call grain, or, in commercial dialect, cereal crops. The second book has the culture of fruits, especially of the grape, for its subject. The third book deals with the breeding and treatment of farm animals. The fourth book is given up to the topic of the management of bees. An aggressive religious earnestness appears throughout, animating the author, as it were out of time.

Virgil, in his Georgics, as in all his other poetry, follows Greek originals. Hesiod—in antiquity and in traditionary character, to be associated with Homer—has a poem, not very poetical, entitled "Works and Days," in which, after giving a legendary account of the history of the earth, he proceeds to furnish farmers with practical suggestions about their husbandry. Virgil draws from Hesiod. To other Greek authors Virgil owes an obligation, the extent of which it is no longer possible to estimate.

We give the opening lines, containing, first, what might be called the argument and dedication, and, secondly, the invocation. We use Dryden's version—iambic pentameters, or heroics, varied from uniformity by triplets, frequently replacing couplets, of lines, and by Alexandrines occurring at irregular intervals, whether sometimes through defect of ear in the rhymer, or always in the exercise of conscious art on his part, it might be a doubtful matter to determine. The brevity and simplicity of the argument, as also of the dedication, are admirable in the original. The length and multiplicity, to say nothing of the adulatory blasphemy, of the invocation, are to be admired, if admired at all, rather for the ingenuity which they afford opportunity to display, than for any merit of a higher sort exhibited. The idea of the poet seems to have been to muster into his prayer as many of the national divinities as could in any way be associated with farming, and then to cap his climax with a sweetmeat of compliment to Augustus as large and as rich as the imperial stomach could be supposed equal to digesting. Whether the genius of the flatterer succeeded in sating the appetite of the flattered, our readers may be left to guess each one for himself. Here are the lines:

> What makes a plenteous harvest, when to turn
> The fruitful soil, and when to sow the corn;
> The care of sheep, of oxen, and of kine;
> And how to raise on elms the teeming vine;
> The birth and genius of the frugal bee,
> I sing, Mæcenas, and I sing to thee.
> Ye deities! who fields and plains protect,
> Who rule the seasons, and the year direct,
> Bacchus and fostering Ceres, powers divine,
> Who gave us corn for mast, for water, wine—
> Ye Fauns, propitious to the rural swains,
> Ye Nymphs that haunt the mountains and the plains,
> Join in my work, and to my numbers bring
> Your needful succor; for your gifts I sing.
> And thou, whose trident struck the teeming earth,
> And made a passage for the courser's birth;
> And thou, for whom the Cean shore sustains
> The milky herds, that graze the flowery plains;
> And thou the shepherds' tutelary god,
> Leave, for a while, O Pan, thy loved abode;
> And, if Arcadian fleeces be thy care,
> From fields and mountains to my song repair,
> Inventor, Pallas, of the fattening oil,
> Thou founder of the plow and plowman's toil;

And thou, whose hands the shroud-like cypress rear,
Come, all ye gods and goddesses, that wear
The rural honors, and increase the year ;
You who supply the ground with seeds of grain ;
And you, who swell those seeds with kindly rain ;
And chiefly thou, whose undetermined state
Is yet the business of the gods' debate,
Whether in after times, to be declared,
The patron of the world, and Rome's peculiar guard,
Or o'er the fruits and seasons to preside,
And the round circuit of the year to guide—
Powerful of blessings, which thou strew'st around,
And with thy goddess mother's myrtle crowned,
Or, wilt thou, Cæsar, choose the watery reign
To smooth the surges, and correct the main ?
Then mariners, in storms, to thee shall pray ;
E'en utmost Thule shall thy power obey ;
And Neptune shall resign the fasces of the sea.
The watery virgins for thy bed shall strive,
And Tethys all her waves in dowry give.
Or wilt thou bless our summers with thy rays,
And, seated near the Balance, poise the days,
Where in the void of heaven a space is free,
Betwixt the Scorpion and the Maid, for thee ?
The Scorpion, ready to receive thy laws,
Yields half his region, and contracts his claws.
Whatever part of heaven thou shalt obtain
(For let not hell presume of such a reign ;
Nor let so dire a thirst of empire move
Thy mind, to leave thy kindred gods above :
Though Greece admires Elysium's blest retreat,
Though Proserpine affects her silent seat,
And, importuned by Ceres to remove,
Prefers the fields below to those above),
Be thou propitious, Cæsar ! guide my course,
And to my bold endeavors add thy force ;
Pity the poet's and the plowman's cares ;
Interest thy greatness in our mean affairs,
And use thyself betimes to hear and grant our prayers.

We go on a few verses :

While yet the spring is young, while earth unbinds
Her frozen bosom to the western winds ;
While mountain snows dissolve against the sun,
And streams, yet new, from precipices run ;

> E'en in this early dawning of the year,
> Produce the plow, and yoke the sturdy steer,
> And goad him till he groans beneath his toil,
> Till the bright share is buried in the soil.

We make now a bold bound forward and light upon the end of Virgil's Georgics. The last book, our readers will remember, is devoted to the subject of bees. A climax is sought and found by the poet in a queer bit of thaumaturgy. He tells how bees, having once been quite lost to the world, were renewed in their stock by a process which he describes at great length in one of the most elaborate episodes of the poem. Proteus figures in the episode—Proteus, a humorous old sea-god who has it for his specialty to be a cheat of the first water. He can slip from form to form in the very hands of those who hold him. But bind him, caught asleep, and you have him at advantage. Unless he manages still to deceive you as to his own true identity and so to make his escape from your hand, you can compel him to tell you anything whatever, past, present, or future, you may desire to know. The upshot is that the bee-seeker is directed to slay four fine bulls and four fair heifers and have their carcasses exposed. The wonderful sequel is thus told by the poet (Professor Conington's prose translation once more) :

After, when the ninth morn-goddess had ushered in the dawn, he sends to Orpheus a funeral sacrifice, and visits the grove again. And now a portent, sudden and marvelous to tell, meets their view; through the whole length of the kine's dissolving flesh bees are seen, buzzing in the belly and boiling out through the bursten ribs, and huge clouds lengthen and sway, till at last they pour altogether to the tree's top, and let down a cluster from the bending boughs.

The conclusion of the poem follows immediately :

Such was the song I was making; a song of the husbandry of fields and cattle, and of trees ; while Cæsar, the great, is flashing war's thunderbolt over the depths of Euphrates, and dispensing among willing nations a conqueror's law, and setting his foot on the road to the sky. In those days I was being nursed in Parthenope's delicious lap, embowered in the pursuits of inglorious peace—I, Virgil, who once dallied with the shepherd's muse, and with a young man's boldness, sang of thee, Tityrus, under the spreading beechen shade.

The poetry of the Georgics is of a texture more finished than is that of the poetry of the Æneid. Thomson's Seasons may be read as in some respects a parallel for Virgil's Georgics.

We come to the Æneid. This great epic has attracted many translators. We here shall have no doubt, no hesitation, in choosing from among the number. Mr. Conington, the late Professor John Conington, of Oxford, England, is unquestionably our man. Other translators than he have their merits; but for exhaustive learned preparation, scholarlike accuracy, divining insight, conscientious fidelity, sure good sense, resourceful command of language, unflagging spirit, Mr. Conington is easily the best of all Virgil's English metrical translators.

A serious abatement has to be made. Mr. Conington has chosen for his verse a measure, not only such that the proper stately Virgilian movement is lost in the English form which the poem assumes, but such that this movement suffers change to a gait entirely different, indeed violently contrasted. Virgil's line is like the Juno he describes in one of his own memorably fine, almost untranslatable, expressions; it moves with measured tread as queen. Mr. Conington's translation gives us a line that always hastens, and that sometimes runs with breathless speed. The high, queenly, sweeping, dactylic gait that Virgil taught his verse is transformed by Mr. Conington into a quick, springing, eager, forward, iambic bound. Perhaps, too, in a poem so long, the versification is felt at last to be a little monotonous. Mr. Conington adopts the octosyllabic wayward irregular meter, made so popular in the handling of Sir Walter Scott. You read the Æneid as if you were reading another Lady of the Lake.   The flowing robes of the dactylic hexameter are cinctured and retrenched into the neat, trim, smart frock of a Scottish lassie.

The setting forth of the subject of the poem is excellent literary art, in Virgil's text. Mr. Conington translates as follows :

> Arms and the man I sing, who first,
> By Fate of Ilian realm amerced,
> To fair Italia onward bore,
> And landed on Lavinium's shore :—
> Long tossing earth and ocean o'er,
> By violence of heaven, to sate
> Fell Juno's unforgetting hate :
> Much labored, too, in battle-field,
> Striving his city's walls to build,
>   And give his gods a home :
> Thence come the hardy Latin brood,
> The ancient sires of Alba's blood,
>   And lofty-rampired Rome.

Dryden's rendering is this :

> Arms, and the man I sing, who, forced by Fate,
> And haughty Juno's unrelenting hate,
> Expelled and exiled, left the Trojan shore.
> Long labors, both by sea and land, he bore,
> And in the doubtful war, before he won
> The Latian realm, and built the destined town ;
> His banished gods restored to rites divine,
> And settled sure succession in his line,
> From whence the race of Alban fathers come
> And the long glories of majestic Rome.

The Æneid is of set deliberate purpose a national epic in the strictest sense. Such the Iliad, Hellenic as that poem is throughout, is not. The Iliad happened, as it were, to be Greek. That is, it is Greek because Homer was Greek, not because the poet planned to produce a Greek poem. Virgil expressly designed to produce a poem that should be Roman and national. The Æneid is accordingly, in its plan, a larger poem than the Iliad. The wrath of Achilles suffices to Homer for theme. Virgil's theme must be nothing less than the founding of Rome.   The Iliad, personal by intention, is only by accident national.   The Æneid, national by intention, is only by accident personal.   Virgil is second and secondary to Homer.   But nobody can deny that the conception of Virgil's poem, as a whole, though it may lack the attribute of spontaneity, may be cold-bloodedly intentional and conventional, is at least nobler in breadth and magnitude, perhaps also in height and aspiration, than is the conception of the Iliad. . The Iliad grew to be what it was.   The Æneid was made such as we have it by a first great act of invention on the part of the poet.   Virgil's poem was, from the first, what, with few intervals, it has always remained, a school-book.   Its national character eminently fitted it to be, as it was, a school-book to Roman boys.

A short summary of the action of the Æneid may help the reader follow intelligently the sequence of events.   Virgil really does, what Homer is often said to do, but does not, plunge into the midst of things with his story.

In the first book, Æneas, the hero of the poem, the seventh summer after the fall of Troy, lands with his companions on the Carthaginian coast.   Here, Ulysses-like, he relates to Carthaginian Queen Dido the story of his previous adventures and wanderings.   This narration occupies two more books of the poem.   The fourth book contains the episode of the mutual passion between Dido and Æneas, ending tragically for Dido in his faithless desertion of her and in her death by cruel suicide.   The fifth book describes the games celebrated by the Trojans on the hospitable shores of Sicily in honor of Æneas's dead father, Anchises (An-ki'ses).   In the sixth book, Æneas, arrived in Italy, makes his descent into the lower world.   The rest of the poem relates the fortunes of Æneas in obtaining a settlement for the Trojans in Italy. There is war.   Against the invaders, a great Italian champion appears, who serves the same purpose of foil to Æneas as long before did Hector to Achilles. The end, of course, is victory for Æneas.

We now return to let Virgil himself, speaking by the voice of English interpreter Conington, take us forward the first stage of his poem. There is, in the whole Æneid, no more finished versification, no more skillful narrative, no greater wealth of quotable and quoted phrases, than are found in the first book of the poem. We begin with a citation long enough to include a fine example of Virgil's sublimity, appearing in the description of a storm and shipwreck. Æneas, with his companions, refugees from ruined Troy, is escaping by sea when this tempest arises.

We need not tell our readers that the machinery with which the raising and calming of the tempest are brought about, was already in Virgil's time nearly as much an exploded superstition at Rome as is the case in our own day. There is in the introduction, on Virgil's part, of this absurd supernaturalism a certain lack of genuineness apparent, which in Homer we nowhere discover. The tempest-raising part of Æolus in this action is a transfer from Homer. Æolus has just responded favorably to an appeal from Juno for his intervention against the hated Trojans. His intervention is prompt. It was, literally, a word and a blow;

> He said, and with his spear struck wide
> The portals in the mountain side:
> At once, like soldiers in a band,
> Forth rush the winds, and scour the land:
> Then lighting heavily on the main,
> East, South, and West with storms in train,
> Heave from its depth the watery floor,
> And roll great billows to the shore.
> Then come the clamor and the shriek,
> The sailors shout, the main-ropes creak:
> All in a moment sun and skies
> Are blotted from the Trojan's eyes:
> Black night is brooding o'er the deep,
> Sharp thunder peals, live lightnings leap:

The stoutest warrior holds his breath,
And looks as on the face of death.
At once Æneas thrilled with dread ;
Forth from his breast, with hands outspread,
  These groaning words he drew :
" O happy, thrice and yet again,
Who died at Troy like valiant men,
  E'en in their parents' view !
O Diomed, first of Greeks in fray,
Why pressed I not the plain that day,
  Yielding my life to you,
Where stretched beneath a Phrygian sky
Fierce Hector, tall Sarpedon lie :
Where Simois tumbles 'neath his wave
Shields, helms, and bodies of the brave ? "

Now, howling from the north, the gale,
While thus he moans him, strikes his sail :
The swelling surges climb the sky ;
The shattered oars in splinters fly ;
The prow turns round, and to the tide
Lays broad and bare the vessel's side ;
On comes a billow mountain-steep,
Bears down, and tumbles in a heap.
These stagger on the billow's crest,
Those to the yawning depth deprest
See land appearing 'mid the waves,
While surf with sand in turmoil raves.
Three ships the South has caught and thrown
On scarce hid rocks, as altars known,
Ridging the main, a reef of stone.
Three more fierce Eurus from the deep,
A sight to make the gazer weep,
Drives on the shoals, and banks them round
With sand, as with a rampire-mound.
One, which erewhile from Lycia's shore
Orontes and his people bore,
E'en in Æneas's anguished sight
A sea down crashing from the height
Strikes full astern : the pilot, torn
From off the helm, is headlong borne :
Three turns the foundered vessel gave,
Then sank beneath the engulfing wave.
There in the vast abyss are seen
The swimmers, few and far between,

> And warrior's arms and shattered wood,
> And Trojan treasures strew the flood.
> And now Ilioneus, and now
> 　　Aletes old and gray,
> Abas and brave Achates bow,
> 　　Beneath the tempest's sway;
> Fast drinking in through timbers loose
> At every pore the fatal ooze,
> 　　Their sturdy barks give way.

Neptune at this point

> His calm broad brow o'er ocean rears.

He speaks with highly pacific effect thus described :

> As when sedition oft has stirred
> In some great town the vulgar herd,
> And brands and stones already fly—
> For Rage has weapons always nigh—
> Then should some man of worth appear
> Whose stainless virtue all revere,
> They hush, they list: his clear voice rules
> Their rebel wills, their anger cools:
> So ocean ceased at once to rave,
> When, calmly looking o'er the wave,
> Girt with a range of azure sky,
> The father bids his chariot fly.

The foregoing simile is a celebrated one. The allusion in it is, with great probability, held to be to an incident in Cicero's oratorical career. Roscius Otho had been greeted in a theater with a tumultuary storm of hisses. The disturbance grew to a riot. Cicero was summoned. He got the people into a temple near by, and there, with infinite skill, rebuked and rallied them out of their ill-temper. It was a striking triumph of oratory seconded by character.

The "tempest-tossed Æneadæ" (Trojans) struggle ashore, and there make themselves as comfortable as they can. Æneas gets a shot (with bow and arrow) at some deer that come within sight and range. He kills just a deer apiece for his seven ships, and, with this good fortune to support him, he harangues his comrades :

> Comrades and friends! for ours is strength
>   Has brooked the test of woes;
> O worse-scarred hearts! these wounds at length
>   The gods will heal, like those.
> You that have seen grim Scylla rave,
>   And heard her monsters yell,
> You that have looked upon the cave
>   Where savage Cyclops dwell,
> Come, cheer your souls, your fears forget;
> *This suffering will yield us yet*
>   *A pleasant tale to tell.*
> Through chance, through peril lies our way
> To Latium, where the fates display
> A mansion of abiding stay:
> There Troy her fallen realm shall raise:
> Bear up, and live for happier days.

The couplet italicized translates

> Et hæc olim meminisse juvabit

(literally: Even these things hereafter to remember will afford delight), a sentiment often quoted by modern authors in Virgil's own happy expression.

The next day Æneas had an adventure that was worth while. He met his goddess-mother, Venus, not confessed in her true divine identity, but wearing a disguise of virgin loveliness, which Virgil beautifully describes as follows:

> In mien and gear a Spartan maid,
> Or like Harpalyce arrayed,
> Who tires fleet coursers in the chase,
> And heads the swiftest streams of Thrace.
> Slung from her shoulders hangs a bow;
> Loose to the wind her tresses flow;
> Bare was her knee; her mantle's fold
> The gathering of a knot controlled.

The colloquy which ensued we have no room to give at large. The goddess informs Æneas where he is, and how, under present circumstances, he ought to manage matters. The bewitching creature uses one simile, to convey her encouragement to her son, that is divine enough to be reported to our readers:

> Mark those twelve swans, that hold their way
> In seemly jubilant array,
> Whom late, down swooping from on high,
> Jove's eagle scattered through the sky;
> Now see them o'er the land extend
> Or hover, ready to descend:
> They, rallying, sport on noisy wing,
> And circle round the heaven, and sing:
> E'en so your ships, your martial train,
> Have gained the port, or stand to gain.
> Then pause not further, but proceed
> Still following where the road shall lead.

The immediate sequel was tantalizing in the extreme. Venus revealed herself as Venus and—instantly vanished:

> She turned, and flashed upon their view
> Her stately neck's purpureal hue;
> Ambrosial tresses round her head
> A more than earthly fragrance shed:
> Her falling robe her footprints swept,
> And showed the goddess as she stept.
>
> .   .   .   .   .
>
> She through the sky to Paphos moves,
> And seeks the temple of her loves.

The two Trojans, Æneas and his faithful companion, Achates, shrouded by Venus in a cloud, invisibly visit the scene of the labors in progress for the founding of Carthage. The description is very fine in Virgil, and it loses nothing of spirit in the finished version of Mr. Conington. A simile occurs in it, one of Virgil's best, which our readers must not lose. The various busy labor of the Carthaginian builders is the subject:

> So bees, when springtime is begun
> Ply their warm labor in the sun,
> What time along the flowery mead
> Their nation's infant hope they lead;   —
> Or with clear honey charge each cell,
> And make the hive with sweetness swell,
> The workers of their loads relieve,
> Or chase the drones, that gorge and thieve:
> With toil the busy scene ferments,
> And fragrance breathes from thymy scents.

Æneas—Achates is now neglected by the poet—looks about him at his leisure. At length he was interrupted by the approach of Queen Dido, whom the poet ushers in to us with a stately simile.

Dido seats herself and gives out laws—when, behold, some of those Trojans who were shipwrecked make their appearance. Invisible Æneas and Achates are overjoyed, but they wait and listen while one of their Trojan friends delivers himself of an extremely well-conceived appeal, for favorable consideration, to the queen and her subjects. The speaker makes flowing promises of the most honorable conduct on the part of his companions, and on that of the Trojans in general, by way of return for the hospitality they crave.

The Carthaginian queen responds with the utmost grace of majesty. She says she will send to seek their great Æneas. Æneas himself, with his friend Achates, amid the clouds can scarcely keep from crying out. The cloud seems to feel by sympathy the effects of his impulse to speak. It parts

And purges brightening into day.

And now an Homeric miracle. The goddess-mother of Æneas does for her son what readers of the Odyssey will remember Pallas Athene more than once did for her favorite warrior and sage, Ulysses—she glorifies Æneas into godlike grace and beauty. The transfiguration is beautifully portrayed by Virgil, and Mr. Conington as translator is not wanting to the occasion :

Æneas stood, to sight confest,
A very god in face and chest:
For Venus round her darling's head
A length of clustering locks had spread,
Crowned him with youth's purpureal light,
And made his eyes gleam glad and bright:
Such loveliness the hands of art
To ivory's native hues impart:
So 'mid the gold around it placed
Shines silver pale or marble chaste.

Radiant Æneas makes to Dido a very gallant speech, full of chivalrous engagement. You would have taken him for the soul of honor. But honor, as we Christians understand the idea, was by no means Æneas's forte. Æneas's specialty was "piety"—piety in the sense of reverence for the gods and for parents, and of regard for duties owed to country. Virgil's attribution of piety to Æneas did not in the least imply that he, pious soul, might not all the same be a very poor reliance in relations other than the ones above specified. This, Dido, to her undoing, was presently to learn. Unconsciously, or indeed perhaps consciously, Virgil incorporated the very spirit of the ideal Roman character in his hero Æneas. To this "pious" man nothing could be wrong that would tend to further his fortunes. But we anticipate.

Dido lavishes refreshment on the Trojan crews, and sets her palace in order for the entertainment of their goddess-born and godlike leader, Æneas. He meantime, "loth to lose the father in the king," sends to have brought to him his son, the lovely lad variously named I-u′lus, I-lus, As-ca′ni-us.

This quest of the father's gives Venus a chance, not to be lost. She plans a deceit. Her boy Cupid shall go personate Ascanius and, nestling, at the feast to be, in the bosom of Dido, shall infix ineradicably there a sweet sting of love for Æneas. The true Ascanius, her grandson, the goddess transports elsewhere and

soft amaracus receives
And gently curtains him with leaves.

The plot prospers. Cupid enters sympathetically into the humor of his part. As Mr. Conington featly and daintily translates,

Young Love obeyed, his plumage stripped,
And, laughing, like Iulus tripped.

Unconscious Dido at the feast caresses her doom. The roguish Cupid having first

> satisfied the fond desire
> Of that his counterfeited sire,
> Turns him to Dido. Heart and eye
> She clings, she cleaves, she makes him lie
> Lapped in her breast, nor knows, lost fair,
> How dire a god sits heavy there.
> But he, too studious to fulfill
> His Acidalian mother's will,
> Begins to cancel trace by trace
> The imprint of Sychæus' face,
> And bids a living passion steal
> On senses long unused to feel.

Dido is lost. She commits herself in boundless pledge to the Trojans. In a pause made, she solemnly appeals to Olympus. With her invocation of the Olympians, a full pledge in golden wine was poured out. Then the part performed by Demodocus at Homer's Phæacian banquet to Ulysses is repeated at this Didonian feast given in honor of Æneas. I-o′pas is the name of Virgil's bard. This name has never become so famous in subsequent song and story as has the name Demodocus. Nevertheless, the performance did not lack matter, as will show the following brilliant programme, itself poetry and song of potent spell to the imagination. How charmingly Mr. Conington has rendered it ! Virgil had a marked tendency toward philosophical poetry. Lucretius drew him strongly. Observe how he here makes Iopas go, as it were philosophically, not less than poetically, into the secret of things :

> He sings the wanderings of the moon,
> The sun eclipsed in deadly swoon,
> Whence human kind and cattle came,
> And whence the rain-spout and the flame,
> Arcturus and the two bright Bears,
> And Hyads weeping showery tears,
> Why winter suns so swiftly go,
> And why the weary nights move slow.

Discourse succeeds to feast and song. Dido asks Æneas to tell the company all about his own various fortune—with which request ends book first of the Æneid.

The second book, with the third, is made up of Æneas's autobiographical story.

He sets out with the incident of the celebrated Wooden Horse. Of this incident, only alluded to in our treatment of Homer, we proceed to give Virgil's account in full, or nearly enough in full for the full satisfaction of our readers:

> The Danaan chiefs, with cunning given
> By Pallas, mountain-high to heaven
> A giant horse uprear,
> And with compacted beams of pine
> The texture of its ribs entwine:
> A vow for their return they feign,
> So runs the tale, and spreads amain.
> There in the monster's cavernous side
> Huge frames of chosen chiefs they hide,
> And steel-clad soldiery finds room
> Within that death-producing womb.

This huge image of a horse the Greeks leave on shore, and withdraw in their ships from the Trojans' sight. The delighted Trojans swarm out of the gates to survey the deserted camp of the Greeks. One of them proposes that they draw the colossal horse within the walls of the city. As to the expediency of this there are conflicting views, and La-oc'o-on— note the name, there is a sequel awaiting associated with this priest of Neptune—runs down to discountenance the project. His speech is full of prophet's wisdom and fire.

The disposition to be made of the horse hangs in doubt, when a Greek captive is brought in who plays a very deep part. Si'non is the man's name. On the desperate chance of getting himself believed in a most improbable tale, this man has risked his life by thus throwing himself into the power of the Trojans. He pretends to have escaped from dreadful death at the hands of his own countrymen, having been, as he says, destined by them to perish, a human sacrifice, for their safe return from Troy. The upshot is that Sinon gets himself believed. His fetters are stricken off and, at Priam's kindly challenge, he has his desired chance to cheat the Trojans to the full, under sanction of protestations volunteered by him with gratuitous eloquence of perjury. Tell us honestly, Sinon, Priam says, what does the horse mean?

Sinon's satisfaction to the old king's curiosity is ingeniously fabricated. He says that Pallas turned against the Greeks, aggrieved by profanation done to her image at the hands of ruthless Ulysses and Ty-di'des. These chieftains had plucked the sacred statue—Palladium, it was called—from its seat in the temple in Troy, and stained it with blood. The Greek prophet Calchas [Kal'kas], so Sinon glibly relates, assures his countrymen that they must return home and there renew the omens, or they will never take Troy. Meantime they fashion the colossal horse in Pallas's honor,

> An image for an image given
> To pacify offended Heaven.

Calchas, Sinon with skillful surplusage of lying, says, bade the Greeks rear the horse so high that the Trojans could not get it through their city gates, lest, taken within, it should make Troy impregnable, and endanger Greece.

To second and support the lithe lying of Sinon, a ghastly omen fell. Now comes in the story of Laocoön, which is too famous and too characteristic of Virgil not to be given to our readers without retrenchment, as Virgil tells it:

> Laocoön, named as Neptune's priest,
> Was offering up the victim beast,
> When lo! from Tenedos—I quail,
> E'en now, at tolling of the tale—
> Two monstrous serpents stem the tide,
> And shoreward through the stillness glide.
> Amid the waves they rear their breasts,
> And toss on high their sanguine crests;
> The hind part coils along the deep,
> And undulates with sinuous sweep.
> The lashed spray echoes: now they reach
> The inland belted by the beach,

> And rolling bloodshot eyes of fire,
> Dart their forked tongue and hiss for ire.
> We fly distraught; unswerving they
> Toward Laocoön hold their way;
> First round his two young sons they wreathe,
> And grind their limbs with savage teeth:
> Then, as with arms he comes to aid,
> The wretched father they invade
> And twine in giant folds; twice round
> His stalwart waist their spires are wound,
> Twice round his neck, while over all
> Their heads and crests tower high and tall.
> He strains his strength their knots to tear,
> While gore and slime his fillets smear,
> And to the unregardful skies
> Sends up his agonizing cries:
> A wounded bull such moaning makes,
> When from his neck the axe he shakes,
> Ill-aimed, and from the altar breaks.
> The twin destroyers take their flight
> To Pallas' temple on the height;
> There by the goddess' feet concealed
> They lie and nestle 'neath her shield.

No wonder that the Trojans now, seeing an apparent punishment so dire befall Laocoön, are shocked into unqualified credit of Sinon's tale. With resistless enthusiasm, they rush to drag the fateful horse within the walls. Virgil's description of this madness and this action is instinct with fire.

The sequel of the contrivance of the Wooden Horse is thus told:

> And now from Tenedos set free
> The Greeks are sailing on the sea,
> Bound for the shore where erst they lay,
> Beneath the still moon's friendly ray:
> When in a moment leaps to sight
> On the king's ship the signal light,
> And Sinon, screened by partial fate,
> Unlocks the pine-wood prison's gate.
> The horse its charge to aid restores
> And forth the armed invasion pours.
> Thessander, Sthenelus, the first,
> Slide down the rope; Ulysses curst,

> Thoas and Acamas are there,
> And great Pelides' youthful heir,
> Machaon, Menelaus, last
> Epeus, who the plot forecast.
> They seize the city, buried deep
> In floods of revelry and sleep,
> Cut down the warders of the gates,
> And introduce their conscious mates.

Among the touching incidents of the last night of Troy with which the teeming invention of Virgil crowds his swift-revolving kaleidoscopic narrative, there is, perhaps, no other so pathetic as that of aged Priam's girding on the armor of his youth, to sally out and do battle with the foe. Hecuba, his wife, espies him in his panoply, and exclaims with vain deprecation at the noble madness of the old man.

The end of Priam comes by the hand of Pyrrhus, son of Achilles. Priam had just seen his own son Po-li'tes slain at his very feet by Pyrrhus, and with aged ire had upbraided the slayer as degenerate offspring of an illustrious sire. He had even hurled against Pyrrhus an impotent weapon. Now a few lines of Virgil according to Conington:

> Then Pyrrhus: "Take the news below,
> And to my sire Achilles go:
> Tell him of his degenerate seed,
> And that and this my bloody deed.
> Now die": and to the altar stone
>   Along the marble floor
> He dragged the father sliddering on
>   E'en in his child's own gore;
> His left hand in his hair he wreathed,
>   While with the right he plied
> His flashing sword, and hilt-deep sheathed
>   Within the old man's side.
> So Priam's fortunes closed at last:
> So passed he, seeing as he passed
> His Troy in flames, his royal tower
> Laid low in dust by hostile power.
> Who once o'er land and peoples proud
> Sat, while before him Asia bowed:

> Now on the shore behold him dead,
> A nameless trunk, a trunkless head.

The last line of Conington affords an admirable instance of this accomplished translator's quality as rhetorician rather than poet. What consummate rhetoric is

> A nameless trunk, a trunkless head!

The sense is exactly Virgil's, the rhetoric exactly Conington's. That repetition, in transposed order, of the word trunk—it is brilliant, but it is rhetoric rather than poetry.

Æneas, trying to save his father, has trouble with the spirited old man, who refuses to be saved. Whereupon Æneas is as spirited as he, and, unrestrained by his wife Cre-u′sa's entreaty, is on the point of rushing forth again into the street brim with its battle and flame, when, behold a prodigy!   A lovely lambent flame lights on the head of little Iulus, as his mother is eloquently presenting him in argument to his father. The parents try to quench it, but prophetic grandfather Anchises is enraptured at the sight. He prays for confirmation of the omen. A clap of thunder on the left, and a sliding meteor above the palace roof! Anchises chants—but we should profane a holy phrase with such an application—we were about to say his "Nunc dimittis"—Anchises, in short, now consents to flee with Æneas. The pious son arranges a place of meeting for Creusa, outside the city, and starts, bearing his father on his shoulders and leading his boy by the hand—an immortal picture of filial fidelity.

Creusa got parted from her company and met a fate unknown. Æneas did what a faithful husband was bound to do ; he returned to the city in search of his wife. Her specter met him and bade him farewell. She was not to be his companion. He tried to embrace her, but he embraced emptiness. Æneas was wifeless.

The second book ends with Æneas's return to his father and

son, where he had left them in order to seek his wife. He there found a number of Trojans ready to join their fate with his.

The third book is crowded with matter; but we must pass it altogether.

The fourth book is devoted to the sad tale of Dido and her fatal passion for her guest. The episode is interesting, but it has not the interest of a story of love, such as Christianity, with its gospel of woman's equality with man, has taught us moderns to understand love between the sexes. Of that love, pagan antiquity knew nothing. The relation between Dido and Æneas was not one of true love, but one of passion, in which the passion was chiefly on the hapless woman's side. We moderns cannot enter into the sympathy of it. Dido you pity indeed, but hardly respect. You feel more satisfaction in heartily execrating Æneas with his everlastingly applauded piety. You wish he were a little less pious and a little more honorable.

There are celebrated passages of fine poetry in this book which we must lay before our readers; but poor Dido's moon-struck maunderings to her confidant sister Anna, together with her love-sick wheedling of Æneas kind, and her crazy objurgation of Æneas treacherous—this detail may well be spared. Virgil does it all with great skill, displaying in it great knowledge of the human heart. But the story rather revolts the modern taste. Let us pass it. The sum of it is that Dido is helplessly enamored of Æneas, that Æneas be-trays and deserts her, and that then Dido takes refuge in suicide, having first provided to perish in a funeral pyre that shall flame high enough to be a baleful sign to Æneas off at sea. Thus is a quasi-historic reason found or feigned by Virgil for the immortal enmity that subsisted between Cartha-ginian and Roman blood. It should be said that the rascal Olympian divinities come in to be, as usual, mutually an-tagonist artificers of fraud.

After Dido's fall, she seeks at once to cover her disgrace :

> She calls it marriage now; such name
> She chooses to conceal her shame.

What follows is perhaps as famous a passage as any in ancient poetry.   It is a magnificent description of fame, report, or rumor personified—gossip, we might familiarly call the creature :

> Now through the towns of Libya's sons
>   Her progress Fame begins,
> Fame than whom never plague that runs
>   Its way more swiftly wins;
> Her very motion lends her power ;
> She flies and waxes every hour.
> At first she shrinks, and cowers for dread :
>   Ere long she soars on high :
> Upon the ground she plants her tread,
>   Her forehead in the sky.
> Wroth with Olympus, parent Earth
>   Brought forth the monster to the light,
> Last daughter of the giant birth,
>   With feet and rapid wings for flight.
> Huge, terrible, gigantic Fame !
> For every plume that clothes her frame
> An eye beneath the feather peeps,
> A tongue rings loud, an ear upleaps.
> Hurtling 'twixt earth and heaven she flies
> By night, nor bows to sleep her eyes ;
> Perched on a roof or tower by day
> She fills great cities with dismay ;
> How oft soe'er the truth she tell,
> She loves a falsehood all too well.

Here is another fine passage.   It is descriptive of night—the calm night on which, while wakeful Dido communed with herself about ways of yet regaining her lover, that lover, himself first roused by Mercury, messenger of Jove, roused in turn his men, and faithlessly, though piously, set sail for Italy.   The contrast of the universal quiet, in a few strokes so strongly depicted, with Dido's unrest, is very effective :

'Tis night: earth's tired ones taste the balm,
The precious balm of sleep,
And in the forest there is calm,
  And on the savage deep:
The stars are in their middle flight:
  The fields are hushed: each bird or beast
That dwells beside the silver lake
Or haunts the tangles of the brake
  In placid slumber lies, released
From trouble by the touch of night;
All but the hapless queen.

The fifth book is largely occupied with an elaborate account
of games celebrated on a friendly shore by the Trojans under
the imperio-paternal eye of Æneas, in honor of the anniversary
of his father Anchises's death.   They have a galley race, a foot
race, a boxing match, a trial of archery, and, to crown all,
a gallant competition of horsemanship in mimic tournament,
on the part of the boys.

The sixth book is a long and splendid tract of poetry.   The
matter of it is Æneas's descent into Hades.   This descent is
accomplished with much antecedent as well as accompanying
circumstance and ceremony.   Resort is had to the residence
of the Sibyl at Cumæ (Cuma).   This famous mythical person-
age is a well-known subject in the modern painter's art.   She
is thus introduced by Virgil:

Within the mountain's hollow side
A cavern stretches high and wide;
A hundred entries thither lead;
A hundred voices thence proceed,
Each uttering forth the Sibyl's rede.
The sacred threshold now they trod:
" Pray for an answer! pray! the god,"
  She cries, "the god is nigh!"
And as before the doors in view
She stands, her visage pales its hue,
Her locks dishevelled fly,
Her breath comes thick, her wild heart glows,
Dilating as the madness grows,
Her form looks larger to the eye,

> Unearthly peals her deep-toned cry,
> As breathing nearer and more near
> The god comes rushing on his seer.
> "So slack," cried she, "at work divine?
> Pray, Trojan, pray! not else the shrine
>   Its spellbound silence breaks."

Thus adjured, Æneas falls to praying with pious pagan zeal. The result is marked and immediate. The maiden seer is as drunk as a pantheist with god, that is, with Apollo:

> The seer, impatient of control,
>   Raves in the cavern vast,
> And madly struggles from her soul
>   The incumbent power to cast:
> He, mighty Master, plies the more
> Her foaming mouth, all chafed and sore,
> Tames her wild heart with plastic hand,
> And makes her docile to command.
> Now, all untouched, the hundred gates
> Fly open, and proclaim the fates.

The fates are troubled, ending in conquest, for Æneas. The prophet-maid has a dreadful convulsion all the time, which Æneas waits to see a little composed before he boastfully prefers his request to be admitted to the lower world. The Sibyl told him, in words that have become as famous as any in poetry,

> Facilis descensus Averni, etc.,

which Mr. Conington translates:

> The journey down to the abyss
>   Is prosperous and light:
> The palace-gates of gloomy Dis
>   Stand open day and night:
> But upward to retrace the way
> And pass into the light of day
> There comes the stress of labor; this
>   May task a hero's might.

She uses powerfully deterrent language, but bids Æneas, if he still will try the journey, go into the woods and look till he finds a certain mystic golden bough which may serve as passport to the regions of the dead. With much ado, this branch is found. Then sacrifice is offered and, with a warning cry, "Back, ye unhallowed," to all besides, she invites Æneas to follow her and plunges into the cave.

Here Virgil puts up a prayer in his own behalf for permission to go on and tell what he has resolved on telling :

> Eternal Powers, whose sway controls
> The empire of departed souls,.
> Ye too, throughout whose wide domain
> Black Night and grisly Silence reign,
> Hoar Chaos, awful Phlegethon,
> What ear has heard let tongue make known :
> Vouchsafe your sanction, nor forbid
> To utter things in darkness hid.

Permitted or not, Virgil proceeds with his disclosure. Of Æneas and his guide, he says :

> Along the illimitable shade
> Darkling and lone their way they made,
> Through the vast kingdom of the dead,
> An empty void, though tenanted :
> So travelers in a forest move
> With but the uncertain moon above,
> Beneath her niggard light,
> When Jupiter has hid from view
> The heaven, and Nature's every hue
> Is lost in blinding night.

The shapes that haunt, as porters and portresses, about the entrance of Hades are a grim group :

> At Orcus' portals hold their lair
> Wild Sorrow and avenging Care;
> And pale Diseases cluster there,
> And pleasureless Decay,
> Foul Penury, and Fears that kill,
> And Hunger, counselor of ill,
> A ghastly presence they :
> Suffering and Death the threshold keep
> And with them Death's blood-brother, Sleep :
> Ill Joys with their seducing spells
> And deadly War are at the door ;
> The Furies couch in iron cells

> And Discord maddens and rebels;
> Her snake-locks hiss, her wreaths drip gore.

The description of the journey proceeds:

> The threshold passed, the road leads on
> To Tartarus and to Acheron.
> At distance rolls the infernal flood,
> Seething and swollen with turbid mud,
> And into dark Cocytus pours
> The burden of its oozy stores.
> Grim, squalid, foul, with aspect dire,
> His eyeballs each a globe of fire,
> The watery passage Charon keeps,
> Sole warden of those murky deeps:
> A sordid mantle round him thrown
> Girds breast and shoulder like a zone.
> He plies the pole with dexterous ease,
> Or sets the sail to catch the breeze,
> Ferrying the legions of the dead
> In bark of dusky iron-red,
> Now marked with age; but heavenly powers
> Have fresher, greener eld than ours.
> Towards the ferry and the shore
> The multitudinous phantoms pour;
> Matrons, and men, and heroes dead,
> And boys and maidens yet unwed,
> And youths who funeral fires have fed
> Before their parents' eye:
> Dense as the leaves that from the treen
> Float down when autumn first is keen,
> Or as the birds that thickly massed
> Fly landward from the ocean vast,
> Driven over sea by wintry blast
> To seek a sunnier sky.
> Each in pathetic suppliance stands,
> So may he first be ferried o'er,
> And stretches out his helpless hands
> In yearning for the farther shore.
> The ferryman, austere and stern,
> Takes these and those in varying turn,
> While other some he scatters wide,
> And chases from the river side.
> Æneas, startled at the scene,
> Cries, "Tell me, priestess, what may mean
> This concourse to the shore?

What cause can shade from shade divide
That these should leave the river side,
   Those sweep the dull waves o'er?"
The ancient seer made brief reply:
"Anchises' seed, of those on high
   The undisputed heir,
Cocytus' pool, and Styx you see,
The stream by whose dread majesty
   No god will falsely swear.
A helpless and unburied crew
Is this that swarms before your view:
The boatman, Charon: whom the wave
Is carrying, these have found their grave.
For never man may travel o'er
That dark and dreadful flood before
   His bones are in the urn.
E'en till a hundred years are told
They wander shivering in the cold:
At length admitted they behold
   The stream for which they yearn."

There is now an encounter, on Æneas's part, with pilot Palinurus lost overboard on the voyage, disconsolate because his corpse lies unburied. The Sibyl promises the shade that the coast where he perished shall bear a name associated with his own—whereat his grief is comforted! What an irony, such comfort—irony probably not intended by Virgil, who was no cynic—on posthumous fame!

The two adventurers, Æneas and the Sibyl, come in due course to the banks of the Styx. Charon, the infernal ferryman, challenges Æneas, but the Sibyl speaks the hero's name and shows the golden branch. This satisfies Charon, and he lets Æneas step into his boat. The crazy bark sinks deep under living weight, but they all get safe across. It was to a gruesome place:

Lo! Cerberus with three-throated bark
   Makes all the region ring,
Stretched out along the cavern dark
   That fronts their entering.
The seer perceived his monstrous head

> All bristling o'er with snakes uproused,
> And toward him flings a sop of bread
>   With poppy-seed and honey drowsed.
> He with his triple jaws dispread
>   Snaps up the morsel as it falls,
> Relaxes his huge frame as dead,
>   And o'er the cave extended sprawls.
> The sentry thus in slumber drowned,
> Æneas takes the vacant ground,
> And quickly passes from the'side
> Of the irremeable tide.

("Ir-re′me-a-ble" (not to be repassed) is Virgil's own stately Latin polysyllable, *irremeabilis*, transferred almost without change into English. In making this impressive transfer Conington follows Dryden.)

> Hark! as they enter, shrieks arise,
>   And wailing great and sore,
> The souls of infants uttering cries
>   At ingress of the door,
> Whom, portionless of life's sweet bliss,
>   From mother's breast untimely torn,
> The black day hurried to the abyss
>   And plunged in darkness soon as born.
> Next those are placed whom Slander's breath
> By false arraignment did to death.
> Nor lacks e'en here the law's appeal,
> Nor sits no judge the lots to deal.
> Sage Minos shakes the impartial urn,
>   And calls a court of those below,
> The life of each intent to learn
>   And what the cause that wrought them woe.
> Next comes their portion in the gloom
> Who guiltless sent themselves to doom,
> And all for loathing of the day
> In madness threw their lives away:
> How gladly now in upper air
> Contempt and beggary would they bear,
>   And labor's sorest pain!
> Fate bars the way: around their keep
> The slow unlovely waters creep
>   And bind with ninefold chain.

Another class were there whom love had slain. Virgil, of

course, does not " slip the occasion "—indeed it was probably
an occasion expressly created by the poet—to bring about
a dramatic encounter between Æneas and Dido. The total
effect commends Virgil's art; for the reader is gratefully relieved in his feeling as to both the two personages concerned :

'Mid these among the branching treen
Sad Dido moved, the Tyrian queen,
Her death-wound ghastly yet and green.
Soon as Æneas caught the view
And through the mist her semblance knew,
Like one who spies or thinks he spies
Through flickering clouds the new moon rise,
The tear-drop from his eyelids broke,
And thus in tenderest tones he spoke:
" Ah Dido! rightly then I read
The news that told me you were dead,
   Slain by your own rash hand!
Myself the cause of your despair!
Now by the blessed stars I swear,
By heaven, by all that dead men keep
In reverence here 'mid darkness deep,
Against my will, ill-fated fair,
   I parted from your land.
The gods, at whose command to-day
Through these dim shades I take my way,
Thread the waste realm of sunless blight,
And penetrate abysmal night,
They drove me forth : nor could I know
My flight would work such cruel woe:
Stay, stay your step awhile, nor fly
So quickly from Æneas' eye.
Whom would you shun ? this brief space o'er,
Fate suffers us to meet no more."
Thus while the briny tears run down,
The hero strives to calm her frown,
   Still pleading 'gainst disdain:
She on the ground averted kept
Hard eyes that neither smiled nor wept,
Nor bated more of her stern mood
Than if a monument she stood
   Of firm Marpesian grain.
At length she tears her from the place

> And hies her, still with sullen face,
>   Into the embowering grove,
> Where her first lord, Sychæus, shares
> In tender interchange of cares
>   And gives her love for love;
> Æneas tracks her as she flies,
> With bleeding heart and tearful eyes.

As soon as Æneas could stanch his flowing heart and eyes, he with his guide advanced to the quarters of the warrior dead. Here Trojan ghosts recognized him :

> They cluster round their ancient friend ;
>   No single view contents their eye :
> They linger and his steps attend,
>   And ask him how he came, and why.

Upon the Grecian slain a quite different effect is produced by the sight of Æneas :

> Some huddle in promiscuous rout
>   As erst at Troy they sought the fleet ;
> Some feebly raise the battle-shout ;
> Their straining throats the thin tones flout
>   Unformed and incomplete.

The Sibyl checks a colloquy between Æneas and De-iph′o-bus with reminder that the time was passing. Deiphobus flees, and Æneas now beholds a gloomy prison house of pain. Virgil describes and, through the Sibyl, relates :

> Hark ! from within there issue groans
>   The cracking of the thong,
> The clank of iron o'er the stones
>   Dragged heavily along.
> Æneas halted, and drank in
> With startled ear the fiendish din :
> " What forms of crime are these? " he cries,
>   " What shapes of penal woe?
> What piteous wails assault the skies?
>   O maid! I fain would know."
> " Brave chief of Troy," returned the seer,
> " No soul from guilt's pollution clear
>   May yon foul threshold tread :
> But me when royal Hecate made
> Controller of the Avernian shade,

The realms of torture she displayed,
    And through their horrors led.
Stern monarch of these dark domains,
The Gnosian Rhadamanthus reigns:
He hears and judges each deceit,
    And makes the soul those crimes declare
Which, glorying in the empty cheat,
    It veiled from sight in upper air.
Swift on the guilty, scourge in hand,
    Leaps fell Tisiphone, and shakes
    Full in their face her loathly snakes,
And calls her sister band.
Then, not till then, the hinges grate,
And slowly opes the infernal gate.
See you who sits that gate to guard?
What presence there keeps watch and ward?
Within, the Hydra's direr shape
Sits with her fifty throats agape.
Then Tartarus with sheer descent
    Dips 'neath the ghost-world twice as deep
As towers above earth's continent
    The height of heaven's Olympian steep.
'Tis there the eldest born of earth,
The children of Titanic birth,
Hurled headlong by the lightning's blast,
Deep in the lowest gulf are cast.
Aloeus' sons there met my eyes,
Twin monsters of enormous size,
Who stormed the gate of heaven, and strove
From his high seat to pull down Jove.
Salmoneus too I saw in chains,
The victim of relentless pains,
While Jove's own flame he tries to mock
And emulate the thunder-shock.
By four fleet coursers chariot-borne
And scattering brands in impious scorn
    Through Elis' streets he rode,
All Greece assisting at the show,
And claimed of fellow-men below
    The honors of a god:
Fond fool! to think that thunderous crash
And heaven's inimitable flash
Man's puny craft could counterfeit
With rattling brass and horsehoof's beat.
Lo! from the sky the Almighty Sire

The levin-bolt's authentic fire
   'Mid thickest darkness sped
(No volley his of pine-wood smoke)
And with the inevitable stroke
   Dispatched him to the dead.
There too is Tityos the accurst,
By earth's all-fostering bosom nurst:
O'er acres nine from end to end
His vast unmeasured limbs extend:
A vulture on his liver preys:
The liver fails not nor decays;
Still o'er that flesh, which breeds new pangs,
With crooked beak the torturer hangs,
Explores its depth with bloody fangs,
   And searches for her food;
Still haunts the cavern of his breast,
Nor lets the filaments have rest,
   To endless pain renewed.
Why should I name the Lapith race,
Pirithous and Ixion base?
A frowning rock their heads o'ertops,
Which ever nods and almost drops:
Couches where golden pillars shine
Invite them freely to recline,
And banquets smile before their eyne
   With kingly splendor proud:
When lo! fell malice in her mien,
Beside them lies the Furies' queen:
From the rich fare she bars their hand,
Thrusts in their face her sulphurous brand,
   And thunders hoarse and loud.
Here those who wronged a brother's love,
   Assailed a sire's grey hair,
Or for a trustful client wove
   A treachery and a snare,
Who wont on hoarded wealth to brood,
In sullen selfish solitude,
Nor call their friends to share the good
   (The most in number they)
With those whom vengeance robbed of life
For guilty love of other's wife,
And those who drew the unnatural sword,
Or broke the bond 'twixt slave and lord,
   Await the reckoning day.
Ask not their doom, nor seek to know

What depth receives them there below.
Some roll huge rocks up rising ground,
Or hang, to whirling wheels fast bound:
There in the bottom of the pit
Sits Theseus, and will ever sit:
And Phlegyas warns the ghostly crowd,
Proclaiming through the shades aloud,
" Behold, and learn to practice right,
Nor do the blessed gods despite."
This to a tyrant master sold
His native land for cursed gold,
    Made laws for lucre and unmade:
That dared his daughter's bed to climb:
All, all essayed some monstrous crime,
    And perfected the crime essayed.
No—had I e'en a hundred tongues,
A hundred mouths, and iron lungs,
Those types of guilt I could not show,
Nor tell the forms of penal woe.

The Sibyl, ending thus, once more hastens Æneas, and they
go on to the dwelling place of the happy dead. At the entrance, Æneas deposits his golden bough. Virgil describes
Elysium and its inhabitants:

Green spaces, folded in with trees,
A paradise of pleasances.
Around the champaign mantles bright
The fullness of purpureal light;
Another sun and stars they know,
That shine like ours, but shine below.
There some disport their manly frames
In wrestling and palæstral games,
Strive on the grassy sward, or stand
Contending on the yellow sand:
Some ply the dance with eager feet
And chant responsive to its beat.
The priest of Thrace in loose attire
Makes music on his seven-stringed lyre;
The sweet notes 'neath his fingers trill,
Or tremble 'neath his ivory quill.
Here dwell the chiefs from Teucer sprung,
Brave heroes, born when earth was young,
Ilus, Assaracus, and he
Who gave his name to Dardany.

Marveling, Æneas sees from far
The ghostly arms, the shadowy car.
Their spears are planted in the mead :
Free o'er the plain their horses feed :
Whate'er the living found of charms
In chariot and refulgent arms,
Whate'er their care to tend and groom
Their glossy steeds, outlives the tomb.
Others along the sward he sees
Reclined, and feasting at their ease
    With chanted Pæans, blessed souls,
Amid a fragrant bay-tree grove,
Whence rising in the world above
Eridanus 'twixt bowing trees
    His breadth of water rolls.

Here sees he the illustrious dead
Who fighting for their country bled ;
Priests, who while earthly life remained
Preserved that life unsoiled, unstained ;
Blest bards, transparent souls and clear,
Whose song was worthy Phœbus' ear ;
Inventors, who by arts refined
The common life of human kind,
With all who grateful memory won
By services to others done :
A goodly brotherhood, bedight
With coronals of virgin white.
There as they stream along the plain
The Sibyl thus accosts the train,
Musæus o'er the rest, for he
Stands midmost in that company,
His stately head and shoulders tall
O'ertopping and admired of all :
"Say, happy souls, and thou, blest seer,
    In what retreat Anchises bides :
To look on him we journey here,
    Across the dread Avernian tides."
And answer to her quest in brief
Thus made the venerable chief :
" No several home has each assigned ;
We dwell where forest pathways wind,
Haunt velvet banks 'neath shady treen,
And meads with rivulets fresh and green ;
But climb with me this ridgy hill,

> Yon path shall take you where you will."
> He said, and led the way, and showed
> The fields of dazzling light:
> They gladly choose the downward road,
> And issue from the height.

They find Anchises busy at an employment which must have afforded that highly patriotic old gentleman much pleasure. He was surveying the yet unborn generations of his own destined progeny. For this Elysium seems to have been not only the home of the beatified dead, but a waiting-place, an ante-room, for those that were to live. Anchises descries Æneas and salutes him. The son striving to embrace the sire is cheated with an intangible phantom in his grasp. But a new sight diverts his mind:

> Deep woodlands, where the evening gale
> Goes whispering through the trees,
> And Lethe river, which flows by
> Those dwellings of tranquillity.
> Nations and tribes, in countless ranks,
> Were crowding to its verdant banks:
> As bees afield in summer clear
> Beset the flowerets far and near
> And round the fair white lilies pour:
> The deep hum sounds the champaign o'er.
> Æneas, startled at the scene,
> Asks wondering what the noise may mean,
> What river this, or what the throng
> That crowds so thick its banks along.

Anchises replying describes a kind of purgatory in which souls linger, to become pure through pain, until, after the lapse of a millennium, summoned they come to the banks of Lethe and thence drinking forget the past and are born anew into the world of men. Readers will hardly need to be told that Virgil has thus prepared his way for going over, in a novel and striking manner, the whole range of Roman history. It will be prophecy at excellent advantage, for it will be prophecy after the fact. There will be in it magnificent opportunity offered for compliment to the imperial house of Rome. Such compliment Virgil prepares, compliment more elaborate and more lofty than perhaps ever before or since in the annals of literature was laid by poet at the feet of his prince. Anchises leads his son Æneas with the Sibyl to a "specular mount,"

whence the eye
Might form and countenance descry,
As each one passed along.

Anchises then takes up the office of herald or usher, and announces the name and quality of the illustrious descendants who should prolong and decorate the Trojan line.   We quote:

"Now listen what the future fame
Shall follow the Dardanian name,
    What glorious spirits wait
Our progeny to furnish forth:
My tongue shall name each soul of worth,
    And show you of your fate.
See you yon gallant youth advance
Leaning upon a headless lance?
He next in upper air holds place,
First offspring of the Italian race
Commixed with ours, your latest child
By Alban name of Silvius styled,
Whom to your eye Lavinia fair
In silvan solitude shall bear,
King, sire of kings, by whom comes down
Through Trojan hands the Alban crown.
Nearest to him see Procas shine,
The glory of Dardania's line,
And Numitor and Capys too,
And one that draws his name from you,
Silvius Æneas, mighty he
Alike in arms and piety,
Should Fate's high pleasure e'er command
The Alban scepter to his land.
Look how they bloom in youth's fresh flower!
What promise theirs of martial power!
Mark you the civic wreath they wear,
The oaken garland in their hair?
These, these are they, whose hands shall crown

The mountain heights with many a town.
Shall Gabii and Nomentum rear,
There plant Collatia, Cora here,
And leave to after years their stamp
On Bola and on Inuus' camp:
Names that shall then be far renowned,
Now nameless spots of unknown ground.
There to his grandsire's fortune clings
 Young Romulus of Mars' true breed;
From Ilia's womb the warrior springs,
 Assaracus' authentic seed.
See on his helm the double crest,
The token by his sire impressed,
That marks him out betimes to share
The heritage of upper air.
Lo! by his fiat called to birth
 Imperial Rome shall rise,
Extend her reign to utmost earth,
 Her genius to the skies,
And with a wall of girdling stone
Embrace seven hills herself alone—
Blest in an offspring wise and strong:
So through great cities rides along
 The mighty Mother, crowned with towers,
Around her knees a numerous line,
A hundred grandsons, all divine,
 All tenants of Olympian bowers.

 "Turn hither now your ranging eye:
Behold a glorious family,
 Your sons and sons of Rome:
Lo! Cæsar there and all his seed,
Iulus' progeny, decreed
 To pass 'neath heaven's high dome.
This, this is he, so oft the theme
Of your prophetic fancy's dream,
 Augustus Cæsar, Jove's own strain;
Restorer of the age of gold
In lands where Saturn ruled of old:
O'er Ind and Garamant extreme
 Shall stretch his boundless reign.
Look to that land which lies afar
Beyond the path of sun or star,
Where Atlas on his shoulder rears
The burden of the incumbent spheres.

Egypt e'en now and Caspia hear
The muttered voice of many a seer,
And Nile's seven mouths, disturbed with fear,
    Their coming conqueror know:
Alcides in his savage chase
Ne'er traveled o'er so wide a space,
What though the brass-hoofed deer he killed,
And Erymanthus' forest stilled,
And Lerna's depth with terror thrilled
At twanging of his bow:
Nor stretched his conquering march so far,
Who drove his ivy-harnessed car
From Nysa's lofty height, and broke
The tiger's spirit 'neath his yoke.
And shrink we in this glorious hour
From bidding worth assert her power,
Or can our craven hearts recoil
From settling on Ausonian soil?

    " But who is he at distance seen
With priestly garb and olive green?
That reverend beard, that hoary hair
The royal sage of Rome declare,
Who first shall round the city draw
The limitary lines of law,
Called forth from Cures' petty town
To bear the burden of a crown.
Then he whose voice shall break the rest
That lulled to sleep a nation's breast,
And sound in languid ears the cry
Of Tullus and of victory.

        .   .   .   .

Say, shall I show you face to face
The monarchs of Tarquinian race,
And vengeful Brutus, proud to wring
The people's fasces from a king?
He first in consul's pomp shall lift
The axe and rods, the freeman's gift,
And call his own rebellious seed
For menaced liberty to bleed.
Unhappy father! howsoe'er
    The deed be judged by after days,
His country's love shall all o'erbear,
    And unextinguished thirst of praise.
There move the Decii, Drusus here,

Torquatus, too, with axe severe,
And great Camillus: mark him show
Rome's standards rescued from the foe!
But those who side by side you see
    In equal armor bright,
Now twined in bonds of amity
    While yet they dwell in night,
Alas! how terrible their strife,
If e'er they win their way to life,
    How fierce the shock of war,
This kinsman rushing to the fight
From castellated Alpine height,
That leading his embattled might
    From farthest morning star!
Nay, children, nay, your hate unlearn,
Nor 'gainst your country's vitals turn
    The valor of her sons:
And thou, do thou the first refrain;
Cast down thy weapons on the plain,
Thou, born of Jove's Olympian strain,
    In whom my lifeblood runs!

"One, victor in Corinthian war,
Up Capitol shall drive his car,
    Proud of Achæans slain:
And one Mycenæ shall o'erthrow,
The city of the Atridan foe,
And e'en Æacides destroy,
Achilles' long-descended boy,
In vengeance for his sires of Troy,
    And Pallas' plundered fane.
Who mighty Cato, Cossus, who
    Would keep your names concealed
The Gracchi, and the Scipios two,
    The levins of the field,
Serranus o'er his furrow bowed,
Or thee, Fabricius, poor yet proud?
Ye Fabii, must your actions done
The speed of panting praise outrun?
Our greatest thou, whose wise delay
Restores the fortune of the day.
Others, I ween, with happier grace
From bronze or stone shall call the face,
Plead doubtful causes, map the skies,
And tell when planets set or rise:

> But ye, my Romans, still control
>   The nations far and wide,
> Be this your genius—to impose
> The rule of peace on vanquished foes,
> Show pity to the humbled soul,
>   And crush the sons of pride."

Virgil, they say, read his sixth book aloud to Augustus. At the reading, Augustus's sister, Octavia, was present. This sister had then just lost a son, Marcellus, dead at twenty years of age. With exquisite art of adulation, perhaps too of sincerely sympathetic consolation, Virgil, as we are just about to show our readers, introduced at this point a noble and delicate tribute to young Marcellus. The story is that the mother fainted with emotion when she heard it. She rallied, to make the fortunate poet glad with a great gift of money. We proceed with the resumed prophetic strain of Anchises, allusive now to Marcellus :

> He ceased ; and ere their awe was o'er,
> Took up his prophecy once more:
> " Lo, great Marcellus ! see him tower
> With kingly spoils, in conquering power,
>   The warrior host above !
> He in a day of dire debate
> Shall stablish firm the reeling state,
> The Carthaginian bands o'erride,
> Break down the Gaul's insurgent pride,
> And the third trophy dedicate
>   To Rome's Feretrian Jove."
> Then spoke Æneas, who beheld
>   Beside the warrior pace
> A youth, full-armed, by none excelled
>   In beauty's manly grace,
> But on his brow was naught of mirth,
> And his fixed eyes were dropped on earth ;
> " Who, father, he, who thus attends
>   Upon that chief divine?
> His son, or other who descends
>   From his illustrious line?
> What whispers in the encircling crowd?
> The portance of his step, how proud ?

But gloomy night, as of the dead,
Flaps her sad pinions o'er his head."
The sire replies, while down his cheek
    The tear-drops roll apace:
" Ah son! compel me not to speak
    The sorrows of our race!
That youth the Fates but just display
To earth, nor let him longer stay:
With gifts like these for aye to hold,
Rome's heart had e'en been overbold.
Ah? what a groan from Mars's plain
    Shall o'er the city sound!
How wilt thou gaze on that long train,
Old Tiber, rolling to the main
    Beside his new-raised mound!
No youth of Ilium's seed inspires
With hope as fair his Latian sires:
Nor Rome shall dandle on her knee
A nursling so adored as he.
O piety! O ancient faith!
O hand untamed in battle scathe!
No foe had lived before his sword,
    Stemmed he on foot the war's red tide
Or with relentless rowel gored
    His foaming charger's side.
Dear child of pity! shouldst thou burst
The dungeon-bars of Fate accurst,
    Our own Marcellus thou!
Bring lilies here, in handfuls bring:
Their lustrous blooms I fain would fling:
Such honor to a grandson's shade
By grandsire hands may well be paid:
    Yet O! it 'vails not now!"

    Mid such discourse, at will they range
The mist-clad region, dim and strange.
So when the sire the son had led
Through all the ranks of happy dead,
And stirred his spirit into flame
At thought of centuries of fame,
With prophet power he next relates
The war that in the future waits,
Italia's fated realm describes,
Latinus' town, Laurentum's tribes,
And tells him how to face or fly

> Each cloud that darkens o'er his sky.—
> Sleep gives his name to portals twain:
>   One all of horn, they say,
> Through which authentic specters gain
>   Quick exit into day,
> And one which bright with ivory gleams,
> Whence Pluto sends delusive dreams.
> Conversing still the sire attends
>   The travelers on their road,
> And through the ivory portal sends
>   From forth the unseen abode.
> The chief betakes him to the fleet,
> Well pleased again his crew to meet:
> Then for Caieta's port sets sail,
>   Straight coasting by the strand:
> The anchors from the prow they hale,
>   The sterns are turned to land.

Let readers remark with what fine artistic self-restraint Virgil at the close dismisses the arduous subject of the sixth book. No effort at unnaturally sustaining the tension beyond its just end. The stream of his verse has writhed in long subterranean torture, but it issues placidly in light and peace, with calm unconscious resumption of the usual flow of the narrative. The basis of the whole episode is Homeric, but the majestic imperial sweep of execution is purely, inimitably, Virgilian.

What remains of the poem we may fairly dispatch, as necessarily we must, within very brief space. Æneas, thrifty soul, secures for himself a royal matrimonial alliance, which, however, involves him in war with a rival, Turnus by name. This Turnus is the foil to Æneas. The foil is almost too much for the hero. It is decidedly by a very narrow chance, if the reader's sympathies do not go over from cold-blooded Æneas to the side of Turnus foredoomed to be slain. After many oscillations of fortune in war, the narration of which is mixed and prolonged with many episodes and many dialogues, it is finally determined that Turnus and Æneas shall decide the strife by single combat. This combat, with its diversified incidents, fills up the measure of the twelfth and last book of the poem. It is the Iliad over again, but the Iliad fairly made into the Æneid, by a genius in Virgil as clearly his own as the genius of Homer was his. We quote the closing lines. Turnus is overthrown, after heroic struggle against a foregone and foreshown conclusion of the strife. He confesses defeat, resigns his betrothed to Æneas, but begs to be sent back, living or dead, to his father. Now Virgil (Turnus has previously slain Pallas, a Trojan friend of Æneas, and is now wearing as trophy the dead warrior's belt) :

> Rolling his eyes, Æneas stood,
> And checked his sword, athirst for blood.
> Now faltering more and more he felt
> The human heart within him melt,
> When round the shoulder wreathed in pride
> The belt of Pallas he espied,
> And sudden flashed upon his view
> Those golden studs so well he knew,
> Which Turnus from the stripling tore
>   When breathless on the field he lay,
> And on his breast in triumph wore,
>   Memorial of the bloody day.
> Soon as his eyes had gazed their fill
> On that sad monument of ill,
> Live fury kindling every vein,
> He cries with terrible disdain :
> "What! in my friend's dear spoils arrayed
>   To me for mercy sue?
> 'Tis Pallas, Pallas guides the blade :
> From your cursed blood his injured shade
>   Thus takes the atonement due."
> Thus as he spake, his sword he drave
>   With fierce and fiery blow
> Through the broad breast before him spread :
> The stalwart limbs grow cold and dead :
> One groan the indignant spirit gave,
>   Then sought the shades below.

We dismiss our task with Virgil by presenting to our readers the elaborate parallel that Pope, in the preface to his translation of the Iliad, draws between the Greek poet and the Roman:

"The beauty of his [Homer's] numbers is allowed by the critics to be copied but faintly by Virgil himself, though they are so just as to ascribe it to the nature of the Latin tongue. Indeed, the Greek has some advantages, both from the natural sound of its words, and the turn and cadence of its verse, which agree with the genius of no other language. Virgil was very sensible of this, and used the utmost diligence in working up a more intractable language to whatsoever graces it was capable of; and in particular never failed to bring the sound of his line to a beautiful agreement with its sense. [A celebrated instance of this occurs in the eighth.book, line 596:

Quadrupedante putrem sonitu quatit ungula campum,

to represent the measured numerous tread of galloping horses.] If the Grecian poet has not been so frequently celebrated on this account as the Roman, the only reason is that fewer critics have understood one language than the other. Dionysius of Halicarnassus has pointed out many of our author's beauties in this kind, in his treatise of the 'Composition of Words.' It suffices at present to observe of his numbers, that they flow with so much ease as to make one imagine Homer had no other care than to transcribe as fast as the Muses dictated; and at the same time with so much force and aspiring vigor that they awaken and raise us like the sound of a trumpet. They roll along as a plentiful river, always in motion, and always full; while we are borne away by a tide of verse, the most rapid and yet the most smooth imaginable.

"Thus, on whatever side we contemplate Homer, what principally strikes us is his invention. It is that which forms the character of each part of his work; and accordingly we find it to have made his fable more extensive and copious than any other, his manners more lively and strongly marked, his speeches more affecting and transported, his sentiments more warm and sublime, his images and descriptions more full and animated, his expression more raised and daring, and his numbers more rapid and various. I hope, in what has been said of Virgil, with regard to any of these heads, I have in no way derogated from his character. Nothing is more absurd and endless than the common method of comparing eminent writers by an opposition of particular passages in them, and forming a judgment from thence of their merit upon the whole. We ought to have a certain knowledge of the principal character and distinguishing excellence of each : it is in that we are to consider him, and in proportion to his degree in that we are to admire him. No author or man ever excelled all the world in more than one faculty : and as Homer has done this in invention, Virgil has in judgment ; not that we are to think Homer wanted judgment, because Virgil has it in a more eminent degree, or that Virgil wanted invention, because Homer possessed a larger share of it ; each of these great authors had more of both than perhaps any man besides, and are only said to have less in comparison with one another. Homer was the greater genius, Virgil the better artist. In one we most admire the man, in the other the work ; Homer hurries and transports us with a commanding impetuosity, Virgil leads us with an attractive majesty ; Homer scatters with a generous profusion, Virgil bestows with a careful magnificence ; Homer, like the Nile, pours out his riches with a boundless overflow ; Virgil, like a river in its banks, with a gentle and constant stream. When we behold their battles, methinks the two poets resemble the heroes they celebrate. Homer, boundless and irresistible as Achilles, bears all before him, and shines more and more as the tumult increases ; Virgil, calmly daring, like Æneas, appears undisturbed in the midst of the action, disposes all about him, and conquers with tranquillity. And when we look upon their machines, Homer seems like his own Jupiter in his terrors, shaking Olympus, scattering the lightnings, and firing the heavens; Virgil, like the same power in his benevolence, counseling with the gods, laying plans for empires, and regularly ordering his whole creation."

The shade of a writer worthy to have been thus elaborately paralleled by Pope with Homer might well lament that his great work in its original text should, in these latter times, have come to be studied so much more as a means of drill in language than as a consummate achievement in poetry.

But it is in the latter way, rather, that our readers have here had their opportunity to study the Æneid.

CHAPTER VII.

OF Livy the man little is known, except that he wrote one of the most delightful histories in the world. To him, more perhaps than to any other writer, is due the traditional fame of the Romans for traits of high character. Roman virtue is not wholly a figment of fancy ; for of virtue, in the antique sense of that word, the Romans, with the Spartans, certainly possessed a large share. But Livy is of all men the man who supplies the historic or mythologic material out of which the current lofty ideal of Roman character has been constructed. Cato, who lived before Livy, said that there were Roman stories as well worthy of immortal remembrance as any stories told of the Greeks—there wanted to Rome only the genius of some great writer to tell those stories properly. That occasion of reproach Livy took away.

Ti'tus Liv'i-us Pat-a-vi'nus we know was born at Pad'ua, in Italy. His last name was derived from the original Latin designation, Pa-ta'vi-um, for that city. He was the great prose poet of the reign of Augustus. Horace and Virgil were coevals of his. He was a boy of fifteen years when Cæsar fell at the base of Pompey's statue.

Besides being a historian, Livy was something of a philosopher. The things, however, that he wrote as philosopher survive only in the mention of Sen'e-ca. The two functions, that of philosopher and that of historian, he kept quite distinct. He did not write history philosophically.

Livy's history was a majestic work, covering the whole subject of the fortunes of Rome from the founding of the city down almost to the beginning of the Christian era. What an epic in prose was there! But of the hundred and fifty-two books in which the work was written, only thirty-five books remain. What we have is highly interesting; but what we have not, as well in quality as in quantity, would be a far more precious possession. We have lost we know not what; but we guess with certainty that Livy's account of the Italian War and his account of the Civil War between Marius and Sulla, which are among the many things missing, would have thrown on those great chapters of Roman story such a light as now is not to be collected from all other sources taken together.

Livy apparently published his work in installments. He must have been occupied not less than twenty years in the composition. This we gather from the fact that in the last parts of the history there are events recorded that did not take place until some twenty years subsequently to the issue of the first installment. The history has been divided up into sets of books, ten each in number, hence called "decades." The thirty-five books that remain give us the first decade, the third, and the fourth, entire, with half of the fifth. There are detached fragments from the rest.

The first decade deals with about five hundred years of history, from the founding of Rome to the subjugation by Rome of the Sam'nites. This portion of the work has little claim, and it makes little claim, to the character of history. It is confessedly mythical and legendary, rather than historical. But most entertaining narrative Livy makes of his material. "The brave days of old" live again, with power—a power communicated from vivific style—in his glowing pages.

One spirited legend out of Livy's treasury of such, and we will pass to something of his that is better entitled to credit.

The story of Cur'ti-us, as Livy tells it, well sums up the
Roman's ideal of civic wealth and civic virtue. The forum
yawned with a chasm in the midst. The gods said it would
close when the best that Rome owned was cast into the pit—
then, and not till then. She tried one precious thing after
another in vain. The bodeful chasm still stretched wide its
hungry jaws. Livy now :

Then young Marcus Curtius, a gallant soldier, chid them all for
doubting that there could be any better thing in Rome than good
weapons and a stout heart. He called for silence; and looking toward the temples of the immortal gods that crowned the forum,
and toward the capitol, he lifted his hands first to heaven, and then
stretching them downward, where the gulf yawned before him, in
supplication to the Powers below, he solemnly devoted himself to
death. Mounted on his horse, which he had clothed in the most
splendid trappings that could be found, he leaped, all armed, into
the chasm, while crowds of men and women showered in after
him precious gifts and fruits.

Of course, upon this costly act of self-sacrifice, there was
nothing left for the chasm to do, but close up and hold fast
what it had got. The fable is a splendid allegory of what
patriots do by thousands upon thousands whenever they offer
themselves up in battle to die for their country.

There is probably no part of extant Livy more vividly interesting, and interesting to a wider audience of modern minds,
than is the long and checkered story of that Punic War, so-
called, in which the figures of Han'ni-bal, of Fa'bi-us, and of
Scipio [Sip'i-o] loom large and splendid, in mutually effective
and ennobling contrast. It was more, far more—that long
strife—than a conflict of individual leaders, of rival nations,
of antagonistic races. It was also a war of contending political ideas, of opposing historical tendencies. It was now to be
decided what type of civilization, what spirit of civil polity,
should rule the future. The sympathies of readers will almost
certainly be enlisted on the side of Carthaginian Hannibal
doomed beforehand to final defeat. Such is the secret magic

of a great human personality. But we may console ourselves.
It was far better that Rome should conquer, as she did. In
this case, at any rate, it was the fitter that survived.

Carthage, when the long duel between Carthage and Rome
commenced, was apparently a full equal of her enemy in
promised extent and duration of empire. Rome, indeed, had
now become supreme mistress of Italy. But Carthage, besides her home possessions in Africa, had established important connections with many points on the Mediterranean
coast. She was a maritime power, as Rome was not. She
had strong foothold in Spain. Sar-din'i-a was hers and
Cor'si-ca and the Ba-le-ar'ic Isles. She was stretching
a cordon of colonies along the border of Sicily, with designs upon that great and rich island as a whole. This
might justly be deemed an indirect menace to Rome. Rome
had not long to wait for a desirable opportunity to take
up the gauntlet that Carthage threw down at her feet. The
two cities closed in a grapple that, having lasted twenty-
three years, left Rome in possession of Sicily. This struggle
is known in history as the First Punic War. (The Carthaginians were Phœnicians, and the Phœnicians were by the
Romans called Pœni, whence "Punic". as the name of the
war.)

The Second Punic War was a greater. The Carthaginian
hero of it was Hannibal. It is of this second war between
Carthage and Rome that we shall here let Livy treat. The
historian had a generous idea of the magnitude of the struggle. But his idea was not exaggerated. The fortune of the
world was decided by the event of this war. History
perhaps—or is this too much to suggest?—is Indo-European
instead of being Semitic, because Rome conquered and not
Carthage. Livy's language about this war will remind readers of what Thu-cyd'i-des, with so much less justness, said four
hundred years earlier about the Peloponnesian War. The two

historians' high estimate of the importance of the subjects they undertook to treat, might be accepted as a pledge on their part of devoting to the treatment the best exertions of which they were capable. The result in either case was a masterpiece of historical composition. What Livy, compared with Thucydides, lacks in breadth of comprehension and in depth of insight, he quite fully makes up in dash and brilliancy of narrative. Livy has the advantage of Thucydides in largeness of theme to handle, and in splendor of exploit to describe. The passage of Livy that we are about to present, namely, the narrative of the Second Punic War, stands as simply an important part of a much larger design, while the "Peloponnesian War" of Thucydides was conceived by its author as an historical monograph, complete in itself.

Here is the preface that Livy prefixes to his account of the Second Punic War. It marks the beginning of the third decade of his work; that is, the beginning of his twenty-first book:

I claim leave to preface a portion of my history by a remark which most historians make at the beginning of their whole work. I am about to describe the most memorable war ever waged, the war which the Carthaginians, under the leadership of Hannibal, waged against the people of Rome. Never have states or nations with mightier resources met in arms, and never had these two peoples themselves possessed such strength and endurance. The modes of warfare with which they encountered one another were not unfamiliar, but had been tested in the First Punic War. Again, so varying was the fortune of battle, so doubtful the struggle, that they who finally conquered were once the nearer to ruin. And they fought, too, with a hate well-nigh greater than their strength. Rome was indignant that the conquered should presume to attack the conqueror, Carthage that the vanquished had, she thought, been subjected to an arrogant and rapacious rule.

We must go on, and repeat the familiar story that immediately follows, of the oath taken by young Hannibal of enmity to Rome. Readers will like to learn that Livy is a source and

authority for this picturesque and grim legend of Carthaginian patriotism :

There is a story, too, of Hannibal when, at nine years of age, he
was boyishly coaxing his father Ham-il'car to take him with him
to Spain (Hamilcar had just finished the African war, and was
sacrificing before transporting his army to that country), how the
child was set by the altar, and there, with his hand upon the
victim, was made to swear that, so soon as he could, he would be
the enemy of the Roman people.

Livy gives us a spirited portrait in words of one of the
most remarkable military geniuses the world has ever beheld.
In drawing this portrait, he goes back a little in retrospect of
Hannibal's years of youthful service under Hasdrubal after
the untimely death of his own father, Hamilcar :

Hannibal was sent to Spain, and instantly on his arrival attracted
the admiration of the whole army. Young Hamilcar was restored
to them, thought the veterans, as they saw in him the same animated look and penetrating eye, the same expression, the same
features. Soon he made them feel that his father's memory was
but a trifling aid to him in winning their esteem. Never had man
a temper that adapted itself better to the widely diverse duties of
obedience and command, till it was hard to decide whether he was
more beloved by the general or the army. There was no one
whom Hasdrubal preferred to put in command, whenever courage
and persistency were specially needed, no officer under whom the
soldiers were more confident and more daring. Bold in the extreme in incurring peril, he was perfectly cool in its presence. No
toil could weary his body or conquer his spirit. Heat and cold he
bore with equal endurance; the cravings of nature, not the pleasure of the palate, determined the measure of his food and drink.
His waking and sleeping hours were not regulated by day and
night. Such time as business left him, he gave to repose; but it
was not on a soft couch or in stillness that he sought it. Many a
man often saw him wrapped in his military cloak, lying on the
ground amid the sentries and pickets. His dress was not one whit
superior to that of his comrades, but his accoutrements and horses
were conspicuously splendid. Among the cavalry or the infantry
he was by far the first soldier ; the first in battle, the last to leave
it when once begun.
These great virtues in the man were equaled by monstrous vices,
inhuman cruelty, a worse than Punic perfidy. Absolutely false

and irreligious, he had no fear of God, no regard for an oath, no scruples. With this combination of virtues and vices, he served three years under the command of Hasdrubal, omitting nothing which a man who was to be a great general ought to do or to see.

Hannibal had attacked Sa-gun'tum. Saguntum was a Spanish town on the E'bro. The question was to whom it belonged. Hannibal solved the question by laying siege to it and taking it. Rome, disturbed too late, sent envoys to Carthage. The Carthaginian senate must disavow the proceedings of Hannibal, or accept a state of war with Rome. Parley was attempted by the Carthaginians, but Quin'tus Fa'bi-us, in the fashion that became him as Roman, did—what Livy thus describes :

Upon this the Roman gathered his robe into a fold, and said: "Here we bring you peace and war; take which you please." Instantly on the word rose a shout as fierce: "Give us which you please." The Roman, in reply, shook out the fold, and spoke again: "I give you war." The answer from all was: "We accept it, and in the spirit with which we accept it, will we wage it."

Hannibal was, like Napoleon, a child of destiny. He had a dream which dominated him—a dream darkly prophetic of his future. Livy relates it with a "so the story goes," to save his own credit, at the same time that he saved an incident dear to his romantic taste and to his pictorial style. The vision came to Hannibal after he had resolved on crossing the Alps and descending upon Italy. Here is Livy's account :

He saw in a dream, so the story goes, a youth of godlike shape, who said that he had been sent by Jupiter to conduct the army of Hannibal into Italy; that he was, therefore, to follow and nowhere turn his eyes away from him. At first Hannibal followed trembling, neither looking around nor behind; after awhile, with the natural curiosity of the human mind, as he thought what it could be on which he was forbidden to look back, he could not restrain his eyes; he then saw behind him a serpent of marvelous size moving onward with a fearful destruction of trees and bushes; close after this followed a storm-cloud with crashing thunder. When he asked what was the monster and what the portent meant, he was told it was "the devastation of Italy; let him go straight on and ask no more questions, and leave the fates in darkness."

Pub'li-us Cor-ne'li-us Scipio, on the part of the Romans, advanced against advancing Hannibal. Hannibal was now just twenty-six years of age.

The battle that impended was not one of the great battles of the war; but when it finally was joined, it went against the Romans. Scipio, their general, was wounded. He was rescued by his son. That son was the great Scipio—to be surnamed Africanus, in honor of the decisive victory that he will hereafter win over Hannibal and the Carthaginians.

But where, it may be asked, did this hostile encounter occur? It was on the Italian side of the Alps. Hannibal had previously performed one of the greatest military feats on record, by crossing the Alps with his army. It will not quite do to let this exploit of his pass in silence. We however limit ourselves to giving a single feature only of the arduous undertaking. The Carthaginian army had now reached the "last and sharpest height" of their difficulty. Livy says:

At last, when both men and beasts were worn out with fruitless exertion, they encamped on a height, in a spot which with the utmost difficulty they had cleared; so much snow had to be dug out and removed. The soldiers were then marched off to the work of making a road through the rock, as there only was a passage possible. Having to cut into the stone, they heaped up a huge pile of wood from the great trees in the neighborhood, which they had felled and lopped. As soon as there was strength enough in the wind to create a blaze they lighted the pile, and melted the rocks, as they heated, by pouring vinegar on them. The burning stone was cleft open with iron implements, and then they relieved the steepness of the slopes by gradual winding tracks, so that even the elephants as well as the other beasts could be led down. Four days were spent in this rocky pass, and the beasts almost perished of hunger, as the heights generally are quite bare, and such herbage as grows is buried in snow. Amid the lower slopes were valleys, sunny hills, too, and streams, and woods beside them, and spots now at last more worthy to be the habitations of man. Here they sent the beasts to feed, and the men, worn out with the toil of road-making, were allowed to rest. In the next three days they reached level ground, and now the country was less wild, as was also the character of the inhabitants.

Such on the whole was the march which brought them to Italy, in the fifth month, according to some authors, after leaving New Carthage, the passage of the Alps having occupied fifteen days.

The whole description in Livy is powerful ; but it lacks the traits that would naturally mark description written by an eye-witness and sharer of the scenes and experiences described. It is conceived from the imagination alone, working with a few points given, rather than from the memory and imagination working together, with all the material at command. It contrasts in essential character with the lifelike delineations of Xenophon, for example, in the Anabasis, who saw all and was himself a great part. Livy's description is valuable, more perhaps as rhetoric than as history.

Military operations, attended with various fortune, more often favorable to the Carthaginians, followed that first battle in which the Romans were beaten. The great battle, or rather the great Roman disaster, of Thras-y-me'nus, was near. This celebrated action we must presently let Livy describe at full.

It is a marked feature of Roman history, as Roman history is written by Livy and by Tacitus, that chapters come in at intervals throughout their works, recording omens that occurred. The Romans were a profoundly superstitious people. They lived under as it were a shadow of the sinister supernatural all the time. We shall not be able to make a full due impression of the effect which these recurring lists of omens observed, produce on the mind of the reader of the original works. To do so would require the reproduction of a considerable number of these formidable and gloomy catalogues ; and that would occupy too much of our space. But it is the quantity, not less than the quality, of such material, together with what seems the periodicity of its return to view, that oppresses the imagination of one occupied in reading the full text of the native historians of Rome. We give at this point a single catalogue of omens which must stand as representative of its kind. The following passage occurs near the opening of the second book of that third decade of Livy, with which we are now concerned. The disaster of Thrasymenus (Tras-u-men'nus is the more recent orthography) impended for the Romans. The Romans meantime were oppressed with the gloomiest fears:

These fears were increased by the tidings of marvels which now came from many places at once. Some soldiers' spears in Sicily had burst into a blaze; so too in Sardinia had the staff which an officer held in his hand as he went his rounds inspecting the sentries on the wall; two shields had sweated blood; certain soldiers had been struck by lightning; there had been seen an eclipse of the sun; at Præ-nes'te blazing stones had fallen from the sky; at Arpi shields had been seen in the sky, and the sun had seemed to fight with the moon; at Capua two moons had risen in the daytime; the stream at Cæ're had flowed half blood; gouts of blood had been seen on the water that dripped from the spring of Hercules; reapers in the field near Antium had seen the ears fall all bloody into the basket; at Fa-le'ri-i the sky had seemed parted by a huge cleft, while an overpowering light shone forth from the opening; certain oracle tablets had spontaneously shrunk, and on one that fell out were the words, "MARS SHAKES HIS SPEAR"; at the same time at Rome, sweat came out on the statue of Mars that stands in the Appian Road by the images of the wolves; at Cap'u-a the sky had seemed to be on fire, and a moon to fall in the midst of a shower. Then men began to believe less solemn marvels. Some persons had had goats become sheep; a hen had changed into a cock, and a cock into a hen. The consul gave the whole story at length, as it had been told him, at the same time introducing into the senate those who vouched for it, and asked the opinion of the house on the religious aspect of the matter.

Readers will wish to see what the practical Romans considered ought to be done under such gruesome circumstances:

It was resolved that such expiation should be made as these portents demanded, with victims, some of which should be full-grown, some sucklings, that public prayers should be offered during three days at every shrine. Everything else was to be done after the College of the Ten had inspected the holy books, in such fashion as they might declare from the prophecies to be pleasing to the gods. They ordered that the first offering, of gold weighing fifty pounds, should be made to Jupiter, that to Juno and Mi-ner'va offerings of silver should be presented; that full-grown victims should be sacrificed to Juno the Queen on the Av'en-tine Hill, and to Juno the Preserver at La-nu'vi-um; that the matrons, collecting a sum of money, as much as it might be convenient for each to contribute, should carry it as an offering to Juno the Queen on the Aventine; that a religious feast should be held, and that even the very freedwomen should raise contributions accord-ing to their means for a gift to the goddess Feronia. After all this the College of the Ten sacrificed full-grown victims in the market place at Ardea. Last of all, as late as December, a sacrifice was made at the temple of Saturn in Rome; a religious feast was ordered (furnished by the senators) and a public banquet; and a festival of Saturn to last a day and a night proclaimed throughout Rome. This day the people were enjoined to keep and observe as a holiday forever.

All did not avail. The overhanging ruin fell.

Hannibal struggled forward in invasion against adverse circumstances that might well have cowed a less resolute spirit. Fla-min'i-us, the Roman consul in command, will presently afford the Carthaginian his coveted opportunity. Flaminius was a headstrong and fiery soul that could brook neither opposition nor delay. Defying every expostulation dissuasive from the plan, he resolved on giving Hannibal battle. His soldiers believed in Flaminius but too well. Their trust was their ruin and his own.

Fiercely from the council of war unanimous against him, the foolhardy Flaminius burst forth with orders to pluck up the standard and advance upon Hannibal. The sequel shall be told in Livy's own words:

Flaminius himself leapt upon his horse, when lo! in a moment the horse fell, throwing the consul over his head. Amid the terror of all who stood near—for this was an ill omen for the beginning of a campaign—came a message to say that the standard could not be wrenched from the ground, though the standard-bearer had ex-erted all his strength. Turning to the messenger, the consul said,

"Perhaps you bring me a dispatch from the senate, forbidding me to fight. Go tell them to dig the standard out, if their hands are so numb with fear that they cannot wrench it up." The army then began its march. The superior officers, not to speak of their having dissented from the plan, were alarmed by these two portents; the soldiers generally were delighted with their headstrong chief. Full of confidence, they thought little on what their confidence was founded.

Hannibal devastated, with all the horrors of war, the country between Cor-to'na and Lake Trasumennus, seeking to infuriate the Romans into avenging the sufferings of their allies. They had now reached a spot made for an ambuscade, where the lake comes up close under the hills of Cortona. Between them is nothing but a very narrow road, for which room seems to have been purposely left. Farther on is some comparatively broad, level ground. From this rise the hills, and here in the open plain Hannibal pitched a camp for himself and his African and Spanish troops only; his slingers and other light-armed troops he marched to the rear of the hills; his cavalry he stationed at the mouth of the defile, behind some rising ground which conveniently sheltered them. When the Romans had once entered the pass and the cavalry had barred the way, all would be hemmed in by the lake and the hills.

Flaminius had reached the lake at sunset the day before. On the morrow, without reconnoitering and while the light was still uncertain, he traversed the narrow pass. As his army began to deploy into the widening plain, he could see only that part of the enemy's force which was in front of him; he knew nothing of the ambuscade in his rear and above his head. The Carthaginian saw his wish accomplished. He had his enemy shut in by the lake and the hills and surrounded by his own troops. He gave the signal for a general charge, and the attacking columns flung themselves on the nearest points. To the Romans the attack was all the more sudden and unexpected because the mist from the lake lay thicker on the plains than on the heights, while the hostile columns on the various hills had been quite visible to each other, and had, therefore, advanced in concert. As for the Romans, with the shout of battle rising all around them, before they could see plainly, they found themselves surrounded, and fighting begun in their front and their flanks before they could form in order, get ready their arms, or draw their swords.

Amidst universal panic the consul showed all the courage that could be expected in circumstances so alarming. The broken ranks, in which every one was turning to catch the discordant shouts, he reformed as well as time and place permitted, and, as

far as his presence or his voice could reach, bade his men stand
their ground and fight. "It is not by prayers," he cried, "or
entreaties to the gods, but by strength and courage that you
must win your way out. The sword cuts a path through the midst
of the battle; and the less fear, there for the most part, the less
danger." But such was the uproar and confusion, neither en-
couragements nor commands could be heard; so far were the men
from knowing their standards, their ranks, or their places, that
they had scarcely presence of mind to snatch up their arms and
address them to the fight, and some found them an overwhelming
burden rather than a protection. So dense too was the mist that
the ear was of more service than the eye. The groans of the
wounded, the sound of blows on body or armor, the mingled
shouts of triumph or panic, made them turn this way and that
an eager gaze. Some would rush in their flight on a dense knot of
combatants and become entangled in the mass; others, returning
to the battle, would be carried away by the crowd of fugitives.
But after awhile, when charges had been vainly tried in every
direction, when it was seen that the hills and the lake shut them in
on either side, and the hostile lines in front and rear, when it was
manifest that the only hope of safety lay in their own right hands
and swords, then every man began to look to himself for guidance
and for encouragement, and there began afresh what was indeed a
new battle. No battle was it with its three ranks of combatants,
its vanguard before the standards, and its second line fighting
behind them, with every soldier in his own legion, cohort, or company: chance massed them together, and each man's impulse
assigned him his post, whether in the van or rear. So fierce was
their excitement, so intent were they on the battle, that not one of
the combatants felt the earthquake which laid whole quarters of
many Italian cities in ruins, changed the channels of rapid streams,
drove the sea far up into rivers, and brought down enormous land-
slips from the hills.

For nearly three hours they fought fiercely everywhere, but
with especial rage and fury round the consul. It was to him
that the flower of the army attached themselves. He, wherever he
found his troops pressed hard or distressed, was indefatigable in
giving help; conspicuous in his splendid arms, the enemy assailed
and his fellow-Romans defended him with all their might. At
last an Insubrian trooper (his name was Ducarius), recognizing
him also by his face, cried to his comrades, "See! this is the man
who slaughtered our legions, and laid waste our fields and our
city; I will offer him as a sacrifice to the shades of my countrymen
whom he so foully slew." Putting spurs to his horse, he charged
through the thickest of the enemy, struck down the armor-bearer

who threw himself in the way of his furious advance, and ran the consul through with his lance. When he would have stripped the body, some veterans thrust their shields between and hindered him.

Then began the flight of a great part of the army. And now neither lake nor mountain checked their rush of panic; by every defile and height they sought blindly to escape, and arms and men were heaped upon each other. Many finding no possibility of flight, waded into the shallows at the edge of the lake, advanced until they had only head and shoulders above the water, and at last drowned themselves. Some in the frenzy of panic endeavored to escape by swimming; but the endeavor was endless and hopeless, and they either sunk in the depths when their courage failed them, or they wearied themselves in vain till they could hardly struggle back to the shallows, where they were slaughtered in crowds by the enemy's cavalry which had now entered the water. Nearly six thousand of the vanguard made a determined rush through the enemy, and got clear out of the defile, knowing nothing of what was happening behind them. Halting on some high ground, they could only hear the shouts of men and clashing of arms, but could not learn or see for the mist how the day was going. It was when the battle was decided that the increasing heat of the sun scattered the mist and cleared the sky. The bright light that now rested on hill and plain showed a ruinous defeat and a Roman army shamefully routed. Fearing that they might be seen in the distance and that the cavalry might be sent against them, they took up their standards and hurried away with all the speed they could. The next day, finding their situation generally desperate, and starvation also imminent, they capitulated to Hannibal, who had overtaken them with the whole of his cavalry, and who pledged his word that if they would surrender their arms, they should go free, each man having a single garment. The promise was kept with Punic faith by Hannibal, who put them all in chains.

Such was the famous fight at Trasumennus, memorable as few other disasters of the Roman people have been. Fifteen thousand men fell in the battle; ten thousand, flying in all directions over Etruria, made by different roads for Rome. Of the enemy two thousand five hundred fell in the battle. Many died afterwards of their wounds. Other authors speak of a loss on both sides many times greater. I am myself averse to the idle exaggeration to which writers are so commonly inclined, and I have here followed, as my best authority, Fabius, who was actually contemporary with the war. Hannibal released without ransom all the prisoners who claimed Latin citizenship; the Romans he imprisoned. He had the corpses of his own men separated from the vast heaps of dead, and buried. Careful search was also made for the body of Flaminius, to which he wished to pay due honor, but it could not be found.

At Rome the first tidings of this disaster brought a terror-stricken and tumultuous crowd into the forum. The matrons wandered through the streets and asked all whom they met what was this disaster of which news had just arrived, and how the army had fared. A crowd, thick as a thronged assembly, with eyes intent upon the senate-house, called aloud for the magistrates, till at last, not long before sunset, the prætor, Mar'cus Pom-po'ni-us, said, "We have been beaten in a great battle." Nothing more definite than this was said by him; but each man had reports without end to tell his neighbor, and the news which they carried back to their homes was that the consul had perished with a great part of his troops, that the few who had survived were either dispersed throughout Etruria, or taken prisoners by the enemy.

The mischances of the beaten army were not more numerous than the anxieties which distracted the minds of those whose relatives had served under Flaminius. All were utterly ignorant how this or that kinsman had fared; no one even quite knew what to hope or to fear. On the morrow, and for some days after, there stood at the gates a crowd in which the women even outnumbered the men, waiting to see their relatives or hear some tidings about them. They thronged round all whom they met, with incessant questions, and could not tear themselves away, least of all leave any acquaintance, till they had heard the whole story to an end. Different indeed were their looks as they turned away from the tale which had filled them either with joy or grief, and friends crowded round to congratulate or console them as they returned to their homes. The women were most conspicuous for their transports and their grief. Within one of the very gates, a woman unexpectedly meeting a son who had escaped, died, it is said, in his embrace; another who had had false tidings of her son's death and sat sorrowing at home, expired from excessive joy when she caught sight of him entering the house. The prætors for some days kept the senate in constant session from sunrise to sunset, deliberating who was to lead an army, and what army was to be led against the victorious foe.

Other reverses to Roman arms followed close upon the overthrow of Trasumennus. A dictator was created, the dictator being Fabius Maximus. This is that memorable master of delay, destined at last to save Rome by a long course of strongly doing nothing.   He stood simply a rock on which Hannibal dashed himself to pieces—rather he was a yielding mountain of sand on which the sea sought in vain to deliver a shock.

Mar'cus Min-u'ci-us Rufus was joined to Fabius, as master of horse.   It was harnessing together in one team a restive and a restless steed—a steed that would not stir, and a steed that would not stand still.   The Romans, with all their practical genius for war and statesmanship, made, from the foundation of the Republic down to the foundation of the Empire, the singular, the almost inexplicable, blunder—such it seems to us now—of dividing administrative responsibility between two men, placed together at the head of affairs.

The policy, and the effects of the policy, adopted by Fabius Cunctator (Fabius Delayer), are thus sketched by Livy:

Always reconnoitering his ground most carefully, he advanced against the enemy, resolved nowhere to risk anything more than necessity might compel.   The first day that he pitched his camp in sight of the enemy (the place was not far from Arpi), Hannibal, without a moment's delay, led out his men and offered battle. When he saw that all was quiet in the Roman army, and that there was no sign of any stir in their camp, he returned to his quarters, loudly exclaiming that at last the martial spirit of Rome was broken—they had made open confession of defeat and yielded the palm of glory and valor.   But in his heart was a secret fear that he had now to deal with a general very different from Flaminius or Sempronius, and that, taught by disasters, the Romans had at last found a general equal to himself.   He felt at once afraid of the wariness of the new dictator; of his firmness he had not yet made trial, and so began to harass and provoke him by repeatedly moving his camp and wasting under his eyes the territory of the allies.   At one time he would make a rapid march and disappear; at another he would make a sudden halt, concealed in some winding road, where he hoped that he might catch his antagonist descending to the plain.   Fabius continued to move his forces along high ground, preserving a moderate distance from the enemy, neither letting him out of his sight nor encountering him.   He kept his soldiers within their camp, unless they were required for some necessary service.   When they went in quest of forage or wood, it was not in small parties or at random.   Pickets of cavalry and light troops were told off and kept in readiness to meet sudden alarms, a constant protection to his own troops, a constant terror to the vagrant marauders of the enemy. He refused to stake his all on the hazard of a general engagement, but slight encounters, of little importance with a refuge so near, could be safely ventured on; and a soldiery demoralized by former disasters were thus habituated to think more hopefully of their own courage and good luck.

The relation in which Rufus placed himself to Fabius is indicated by Livy in the following sentences :

But these sober counsels found an adversary not only in Hannibal but quite as much in his own master of the horse, who, headstrong and rash in counsel and intemperate in speech, was kept from ruining his country only by the want of power. First to a few listeners, then openly before the ranks of the army, he stigmatized his commander as more indolent than deliberate, more cowardly than cautious, fastening on him failings which were akin to his real virtues, and seeking to exalt himself by lowering his chief—a vile art, which has often thriven by a too successful practice.

Hannibal spread consternation among the Italian allies of Rome, but they stood fast in their loyalty. Their steadfastness inspires Livy to make the following patriotically self-complacent remark:

The truth was that they were under a righteous and moderate rule, and they yielded—and this is the only true bond of loyalty—a willing obedience to their betters.

Fabius had anything but a tranquil time of it in keeping resolutely quiet. Rufus was constantly a thorn in the side of his impassible commander. Livy invents for this man—your ideal demagogue he was, according to Livy—some very spirited harangues in character, from one of which we must have a representative sentence or two. The Roman army sitting still, while under their very eyes fire and sword in Carthaginian hands were wasting Roman allies, Rufus broke out:

" Have we come hither to see, as though it were some delightful spectacle, our allies wasted by fire and sword? . . . It is folly to think that the war can be finished by sitting still and praying.

You must take your arms; you must go down to the plain; you must meet the enemy man to man. It is by boldness and action that the power of Rome has grown, not by these counsels of indolence, which only cowards call caution."

The effect of seditious utterances like these from Rufus was vicious, but it served only to set the firmness of Fabius in stronger light.   Livy says :

Fabius had to be on his guard against his own men just as much as against the enemy, and made them feel that they could not conquer his resolution. Though he knew well that his policy of delay was odious, not only in his own camp, but also at Rome, yet he steadfastly adhered to the same plan of action, and so let the summer wear away.

Hannibal was a famous master of stratagem. Here is a specimen of his ready resource in that kind. The expedient described was adopted by Hannibal to extricate himself from a desperate situation in which he became involved, a situation much resembling the situation in which he had himself previously involved the Romans. Now Livy :

The deception was thus arranged.—Firewood was collected from all the country round, and bundles of twigs and dry fagots were fastened to the horns of oxen, of which he had many, from the plundered rural districts, both broken and unbroken to the plow. Upward of two thousand oxen were thus treated, and Hasdrubal was intrusted with the business of driving this herd, with their horns alight, on to the hills, more particularly, as he best could, to those above the passes occupied by the enemy.
In the dusk of evening, he silently struck his camp; the oxen were driven a little in front of the standards. When they reached the foot of the mountain, where the roads narrowed, the signal was immediately given to hurry the herd with their horns alight up the slope of the hills. They rushed on, goaded into madness by the terror of the flames which flashed from their heads, and by the heat which soon reached the flesh at the root of their horns. At this sudden rush all the thickets seemed to be in a blaze, and the very woods and mountains to have been fired ; and when the beasts vainly shook their heads, it seemed as if men were running about in every direction. The troops posted in the pass, seeing fires on the hill-tops and above them, fancied that they had been surrounded, and left their position. They made for the loftiest heights as being their safest route, for it was there that the fewest

flashes of light were visible; but even there they fell in with some
of the oxen which had strayed from their herd. When they saw
them at a distance, they stood thunderstruck at what seemed to be
the miracle of oxen breathing fire. As soon as it was seen to be
nothing but a human contrivance, they suspected some deep
stratagem and fled in wilder confusion than ever. They also
fell in with some of the enemy's light-armed troops, but both sides
were equally afraid in the darkness to attack, and so they remained until dawn. Meanwhile Hannibal had led his whole army
through the pass, cutting off, as he went, some of his opponents,
and pitched his camp in the territory of Allifæ.

Fabius did not conduct his command in a manner to suit
the wishes of Hannibal. In fact, Fabius did not suit anybody's wishes in his manner of carrying on the war. His own
soldiers chafed, and his countrymen at home were indignant
and restless. Hannibal artfully contrived to exasperate the
prevalent feeling against Fabius still more. What the Carthaginian wanted was a foe that would fight. He hoped by
making Fabius unpopular at Rome to have that general ousted
from his command. The chance then was that the senate
would send some general against him that he could entice
into battle. The following was the deep trick that Hannibal
played. Livy:

Deserters had pointed out to him the dictator's estate, and he had
given orders that, while everything round it was leveled to the
ground, it should be kept safe from fire and sword and all hostile
violence, hoping that this forbearance might be thought the consideration for some secret agreement.

But the virtue of Fabius was more than a match for the
cunning of Hannibal. That very estate of the Roman, so
insidiously spared by his crafty antagonist, became, without
design or consciousness perhaps on Fabius's part, the means of
his own complete vindication. There had been an exchange
of prisoners between the two armies. One stipulation was
that whichever party received back the greater number of
men, should pay money to the other, at the rate of two
pounds and a half of silver for every head in excess. Hanni-

bal brought Fabius in debt for the ransom of two hundred and forty-seven prisoners. The senate, taking offense, because not previously consulted, were slow to hand over the money. Fabius thereupon, through his son, sold the estate that Hannibal had spared and, thus enabled to do so, discharged the public obligation out of his own private fortune.

But the Commons of Rome added to the burden that Fabius was bearing for his country. A bill was passed, advancing the factious master of horse to equality in command with the dictator himself. Livy very finely describes the splendid serenity of conscious power and of conscious patriotism, with which, under the sting of this indignity inflicted by his countrymen upon him, Fabius pauselessly pursued his way back to his army from his visit to Rome :

All men, whether at Rome or in the army, whether friends or foes, took the bill as an intentional insult to the dictator. Not so the dictator himself. In the same dignified spirit in which he had borne the charges made against him before the populace, he now bore the wrong which the Commons inflicted in their rage. The dispatch from the senate announcing the equalization of military authority reached him on his way. Confident that the commander's skill could not be equalized along with the right to command, he returned to the army with a soul that neither his fellow-citizens nor the enemy could subdue.

If Rufus was delighted, not less delighted was Hannibal. The Roman army was divided, and two separate camps were formed. This latter idea was the preference of Rufus. Livy has few more eloquent passages than that in which he describes the result. The result was almost too striking to be true. It reads more like poetry than like history. Here it is in Livy's incomparable narrative :

Hannibal was now doubly delighted, and not a single movement of his foe escaped him. The deserters told him much, and he learnt much from his own spies. He would entrap in his own fashion the frank rashness of Minucius, while the experienced Fabius had lost half of his strength. There was some rising ground between the camp of Minucius and that of the Carthaginians, and it was clear that whoever should occupy it, would thereby make the enemy's position less favorable. It was not so much Hannibal's desire to gain this without fighting, though that would have been worth the attempt, as to find in it the occasion of a battle with Minucius, who would, he was quite sure, sally forth to oppose him. All the ground between them seemed at first sight useless for purposes of ambush. Not only had it no vestige of wood about it, but it was without even a covering of brambles. In reality, nature made it to conceal an ambush, all the more because no hidden danger could be feared in so bare a valley. In its windings were caverns, some of them large enough to hold two hundred armed men. Into these hiding places, wherever there was one which could be conveniently occupied, he introduced five thousand infantry and cavalry. Still in so exposed a valley the stratagem might be discovered by the incautious movement of a single soldier, or by the gleam of arms, and he therefore sent a few troops at early dawn to occupy the hill mentioned before, and so to distract the attention of the enemy. To see them was to conceive at once a contempt for their scanty numbers. Every man begged for the task of dislodging the enemy and occupying the place. Conspicuous among these senseless braggarts was the general himself, as he called his men to arms and assailed the enemy with idle threats. First he sent his light troops, then his cavalry in close array; at last seeing that the enemy were receiving re-enforcements, he advanced with his legions in order of battle.

Hannibal, too, as the conflict waxed fiercer and his troops were hard pressed, sent again and again infantry and cavalry to their support, till his line of battle was complete, and both sides were fighting with their whole strength. First of all the Roman light-armed troops, attacking, as they did, from below an elevation already occupied, were repulsed and thrust back, carrying panic with them into the cavalry behind and flying until they reached the standards of the legions. It was the infantry that alone stood firm amidst the route and seemed likely, if once they had had to fight a regular battle in face of the enemy, to be quite a match for him. The successful action of a few days before had given them abundance of courage; but the ambushed troops unexpectedly rose upon them, charged them on the flank and in the rear, and spread such confusion and panic that they lost all heart for fighting and all hope of escape.

Fabius first heard the cry of terror; then saw from afar the broken lines. "It is true," he cried, "disaster has overtaken rashness, but not sooner than I feared. They made him equal to Fabius, but he sees that Hannibal is his superior both in courage

and in good fortune. Another time, however, will do for angry
reproof and censure; now advance the standards beyond the
rampart. Let us wring from the enemy his victory, from our
countrymen the confession of error."

Many had already fallen and many were looking for the chance
to fly, when the army of Fabius, as suddenly as if it had dropped
from heaven, appeared to help them. Before javelins were thrown
or swords crossed it checked the Romans in their headlong flight,
the enemy in the fierce eagerness of their attack. Where the
ranks had been broken and the men scattered hither and thither,
they hurried from all sides to the unbroken lines; larger bodies
had retreated together, these now wheeled round to face the enemy
and formed square, sometimes slowly retiring, sometimes standing in firm and close array. By the time that the beaten army and
the unbroken army had all but combined into a single force and
were advancing against the enemy, Hannibal gave the signal for
retreat, thus openly confessing that, as he had conquered Minucius,
so he had himself been worsted by Fabius.

Returning to the camp late on this day of checkered fortune,
Minucius assembled his troops. "Soldiers," he said, " I have
often heard that the best man is he who can tell us himself what is
the right thing; that next comes he who listens to good advice;
and that he who cannot advise himself or submit to another,
has the meanest capacity of all. Since the best blessing of heart
and understanding has been denied us, let us hold fast that next
best gift which is between the two, and, while we learn to rule,
make up our minds to obey the wise. Let us join our camp to the
camp of Fabius. When we have carried our standards to his head-
quarters, and I have given him the title of parent, so well deserved
by the service which he has done us, and by his high position, ycu,
my soldiers, will salute as the authors of your freedom the men
whose right hands and swords lately saved you. So this day will
give us, if nothing else, yet at least the credit of having grateful
hearts."

The signal was given, and proclamation made to collect the camp
equipage. Then they started and marched in regular array to the
dictator's camp, much to his wonder and that of those who stood
round him. When the standards were set up before the hustings,
the master of the horse stepped forward and called Fabius by the
name of " father," while the whole array saluted as "authors of
their freedom" the soldiers as they stood grouped around their
commander. "Dictator," he said, "I have put thee on a level with
my parents by this name, and it is all that speech can do; but while
I owe to them life only, to thee I owe the safety of myself and of all
these. Therefore I am the first to reject and repeal that decree

which has been to me a burden rather than an honor, and praying that this act may be prospered to thee and me and to these thy armies, the preserver and the preserved alike, I put myself again under thy command and fortunes, and restore to thee these standards and legions. Forgive us, I pray, and allow me to keep my mastership of the horse, and each of these his several rank."

There was a general clasping of hands; and when the assembly was dismissed, the soldiers were kindly and hospitably invited by strangers as well as friends. Thus a day which but a few hours before had been full of sorrow and almost of unspeakable disaster became a day of merriment. In Rome, as soon as the news of this incident arrived, followed and confirmed by letters, not only from the generals but from many persons in either army, every one joined in extolling Maximus to the skies. Hannibal and the Carthaginians equally admired him. They felt at last that it was with Romans and in Italy that they were fighting. For the last two years they had so despised both the generals and the soldiers of Rome that they could scarcely believe themselves to be fighting with that same people of whom they had heard so terrible a report from their fathers. Hannibal, too, they say, exclaimed, as he was returning from the field, " At last the cloud which has been dwelling so long upon the hills, has burst upon us in storm and rain."

For our specimen extracts from Livy we use the version made in partnership by Messrs. Church and Brodribb, respectively of Oxford and Cambridge Universities in England. This is a version worthy to be compared for workmanship with the best English transcripts in existence from the ancient classics, Latin or Greek. The same accomplished translators have given us Tacitus also in a style equally admirable.

The six months' dictatorship of Fabius is now nearing its close. The savior of his country hands over his army to the consuls, who pursue the policy of the dictator for the rest of that campaign.

Consuls Paulus and Varro were yoked together like Fabius and Rufus. Repetition of the folly thus committed will be followed by repetition of the punishment to Rome. Cannæ is now close at hand. The two consuls bicker, but Varro the rash has support instead of Paulus the prudent. Now for a good stretch of Livy again ;

The judgment of the majority prevailed, and the army moved out to make Cannæ, for so destiny would have it, famous forever for a great Roman defeat. Hannibal had pitched his camp near that village, so as not to face the wind called Vul-tur'nus, which, blowing across plains parched with drought, carries with it clouds of dust. The arrangement was most convenient for the camp, and was afterwards found to be of similar advantage when they marshaled their troops for battle. Their own faces were turned away and the wind did but blow on their backs, while the enemy with whom they were to fight was blinded by volumes of dust.

The consuls, after duly reconnoitering the roads, followed the Carthaginians till they reached Cannæ, where they had the enemy in sight. They then intrenched and fortified two camps, separating their forces by about the same distance as before at Ger-e-o'ni-um. The river Au'fi-dus, which flowed near both camps, furnished water to both armies, the soldiers approaching as they most conveniently could, not, however, without some skirmishing. From the smaller camp, which had been pitched on the farther side of the Aufidus, the Romans procured water with less difficulty, as the opposite bank was not held by any hostile force. Hannibal saw his hope accomplished, that the consuls would offer battle on ground made for the action of cavalry, in which arm he was invincible. He drew up his men, and sought to provoke his foe by throwing forward his Numidian troopers. Then the Roman camp was once more disturbed by mutiny among the troops and disagreement between the consuls. Paulus taunted Varro with the rashness of Sempronius and Flaminius; Varro reproached Paulus with copying Fabius, an example attractive to timid and indolent commanders, and called both gods and men to witness that it was no fault of his if Hannibal had now a prescriptive possession of Italy. "I," said he, "have my hands tied and held fast by my colleague. My soldiers, furious and eager to fight, are stripped of their swords and arms." Paulus declared that if any disaster befell the legions recklessly thrown and betrayed into battle without deliberation or forethought, he would share all their fortunes, while holding himself free from all blame. " Let Varro look to it that they whose tongues were so ready and so bold, had hands equally vigorous in the day of battle."

While they thus wasted the time in disputing rather than in deliberating, Hannibal, who had kept his lines drawn up till late in the day, called back the rest of his troops into his camp, but sent forward the Numidian cavalry across the river to attack the water-parties from the smaller of the two Roman camps. Coming on with shouting and uproar they sent the undisciplined crowd flying before they had even reached the bank, and rode on till they came on an outpost stationed before the rampart and close to the very camp-gates. So scandalous did it seem that a Roman camp should be alarmed by some irregular auxiliaries that the only circumstance which hindered the Romans from immediately crossing the river and forming their line of battle was, that the supreme command that day rested with Paulus. But the next day Varro, without consulting his colleague, gave the signal to engage, and drawing up his forces led them across the river. Paulus followed him; he could withhold his sanction from the movement, but not his support. The river crossed, they joined to their own the forces retained by them in the smaller camp, and then formed their lines. On the right wing (the one nearer to the river) they posted the Roman cavalry and next the infantry. On the extreme flank of the left wing were the allied cavalry, next the allied infantry, side by side with the Roman legions in the center. Slingers and other light-armed auxiliaries made up the first line. Paulus commanded the left wing; Varro the right; Ge-min'i-us Ser-vil'i-us had charge of the center.

At dawn Hannibal, sending in advance his slingers and light-armed troops, crossed the river, assigning each division its position as it crossed. His Gallic and Spanish cavalry he posted near the river bank on the left wing, facing the Roman horse; the right wing was assigned to the Numidian cavalry; the center showed a strong force of infantry, having on either side the African troops, with the Gauls and Spaniards between them. These Africans might have been taken for a Roman force; so largely were they equipped with weapons taken at Trebia, and yet more at Trasumennus. The Gauls and Spaniards had shields of very nearly the same shape, but their swords were widely different in size and form, the Gauls having them very long and pointless, while the Spaniards, who were accustomed to assail the enemy with thrusts rather than with blows, had them short, handy, and pointed. These nations had a specially terrible appearance, so gigantic was their stature and so strange their look. The Gauls were naked above the navel; the Spaniards wore tunics of linen bordered with purple, of a whiteness marvelously dazzling. The total number of the infantry who were that day ranged in line was forty thousand, that of the cavalry ten thousand. Hasdrubal commanded the left wing; Maharbal the right; Hannibal himself, with his brother Mago, was in the center. The sun—whether the troops were purposely so placed, or whether it was by chance—fell very conveniently sideways on both armies, the Romans facing the south, the Carthaginians the north. The wind (called Vulturnus by the natives of those parts) blew straight against the Romans and whirled clouds of dust into their faces till they could see nothing.

With a loud shout the auxiliaries charged, the light troops thus beginning the battle. Next the Gallic and Spanish horse of the left wing encountered the right wing of the Romans. The fight was not at all like a cavalry engagement; they had to meet face to face; there was no room for maneuvering, shut in as they were by the river on one side and the lines of infantry on the other. Both sides pushed straightforward till, with their horses brought to a stand and crowded together in a mass, each man seized his antagonist and strove to drag him from his seat. The struggle now became mainly a struggle of infantry; but the conflict was rather fierce than protracted. The Roman cavalry were defeated and put to flight. Just before the encounter of the cavalry came to an end, the fight between the infantry began. The two sides were well matched in strength and courage, as long as the Gauls and Spaniards kept their ranks unbroken; at last the Romans, after long and repeated efforts, sloped their front and broke, by their deep formation, the enemy's column, which, advanced as it was from the rest of the line, was shallow and therefore weak. Pursuing the broken and rapidly retreating foe, they made their way without a halt through the rout of panic-stricken fugitives till they reached, first, the center of the line, and then, meeting with no check, the reserves of the African troops. These had been stationed on the wings which had been somewhat retired, while the center, where the Gauls and Spaniards had been posted, was proportionately advanced. As that column fell back, the line became level; when they pushed their retreat, they made a hollow in the center. The Africans now overlapped on either side, and as the Romans rushed heedlessly into the intervening space, they first outflanked them and then, extending their own formation, actually hemmed in their rear. Upon this the Romans, who had fought one battle to no purpose, quitted the Gauls and Spaniards, whose rear they had been slaughtering, and began a new conflict with the Africans, a conflict unfair, not only because they were shut in with foes all round them, but because they were wearied, while the enemy was fresh and vigorous.

On the left wing of the Romans the cavalry of the allies had been posted against the Numidians. Here, too, battle had been joined, though with little spirit for a time, the first movement being a Carthaginian stratagem. Nearly five hundred Numidians who, besides their usual armor and missiles had swords hidden under their cuirasses, rode out from their own line with their shields slung behind their backs as though they had been deserters, leaped in haste from their horses and threw their shields and javelins at the feet of the Romans. They were received into the center of the line, taken to the extreme rear, and bidden to keep their place behind. While the battle spread from place to place they remained motionless; but as soon as all eyes and thoughts were intent on the conflict, they seized the shields which lay scattered everywhere among the piles of dead, and fell on the Roman line from the rear. They wounded the backs and legs of the men, and while they made a great slaughter, spread far greater panic and confusion. While there was terror and flight on the right, and in the center an obstinate resistance, though with little hope, Hasdrubal, who was in command in this quarter, withdrew the Numidians from the center, seeing that they fought with but little spirit, and having sent them in all directions to pursue the enemy, re-enforced with the Spanish and Gallic cavalry the African troops, wearied as they now were with slaughter rather than with fighting.

Paulus was on the other side of the field. He had been seriously wounded at the very beginning of the battle by a bullet from a sling, but yet he repeatedly encountered Hannibal with a compact body of troops, and at several points restored the fortune of the day. He was protected by the Roman cavalry, who at last sent away their horses when the consul became too weak to manage his charger. Some one told Hannibal that the consul had ordered the cavalry to dismount. "He might better hand them over to me bound hand and foot," said he. The horsemen fought on foot as men were likely to fight, when, the victory of the enemy being beyond all doubt, the vanquished preferred dying where they stood to flight, and the victors, furious with those who delayed their triumph, slaughtered the foes whom they could not move. Move them, however, they did—that is, a few survivors, exhausted with wounds and fatigue. All were then scattered, and such as were able sought to recover their horses and fly. Cn. [Cne'i-us] Len'tu-lus, as he galloped by, saw the consul sitting on a stone and covered with blood. "Lucius Æmilius," he cried, "the one man whom heaven must regard as guiltless of this day's calamity, take this horse while you have some strength left, and I am here to be with you, to lift you to the saddle, and to defend you. Do not make this defeat yet sadder by a consul's death. There is weeping and sorrow enough without this." The consul replied, "'Tis a brave thought of thine, Cn. Cornelius; but waste not the few moments you have for escaping from the enemy in fruitless pity. My public message to the senators is that they must fortify Rome and make its garrison as strong as may be before the victorious enemy arrives. My private message to Quintus Fabius is that Lucius Æmilius remembered his teaching in life and death. As for me, let me breathe my last among my slaughtered soldiers. I would not again leave my consulship to answer for my life, nor would I stand up to accuse my colleague, and by accusing another protect my own innocence."

While they thus talked together, they were overtaken, first by a crowd of Roman fugitives and then by the enemy. These last buried the consul under a shower of javelins, not knowing who he was. Lentulus galloped off in the confusion. The Romans now fled wildly in every direction. Seven thousand men escaped into the smaller, ten thousand into the larger camp, ten thousand more into the village of Cannæ itself. These last were immediately surrounded by Car'tha-lo and the cavalry, for no fortification protected the place. The other consul, who, whether by chance or of set purpose, had not joined any large body of fugitives, fled with about five hundred horsemen to Ve-nu'si-a. Forty-five thousand five hundred infantry, two thousand seven hundred cavalry, and almost as many more citizens and allies are said to have fallen. Among these were the quæstors of both consuls, Lucius Atilius and Furius Bi-bac'u-lus, twenty-nine tribunes of the soldiers, and not a few ex-consuls, ex-prætors, and ex-ædiles (among them Cn. Servilius and Marcus Minucius, who the year before had been the master of the horse, and consul some years before that), eighty who were either actual senators or had filled such offices as made them eligible for the senate, and who had volunteered to serve in the legions. In this battle three thousand infantry and one thousand five hundred cavalry are said to have been taken prisoners.

Such was the battle of Cannæ, as famous as the disaster at the Allia, and though less serious in its consequences, thanks to the inaction of the enemy, yet in loss of men still more ruinous and disgraceful. The flight at the Allia lost the city but saved the army; at Cannæ the consul who fled was followed by barely fifty men; with the consul who perished, perished nearly the whole army.

Livy perhaps was mistaken, but, according to Livy, Hannibal did not quite prove a match to the greatness of his own triumph—the excess of his victory defeated him. Livy thus relates what one can only guess how he knew:

Round the victorious Hannibal crowded his officers with congratulations and entreaties that now that this mighty war was finished he should take what remained of that day and the following night for rest, and give the same to his wearied soldiers. Maharbal, the general of his cavalry, thought that there should be no pause. "Nay," he cried, "that you may know what has been achieved by this victory, you shall hold a conqueror's feast within five days in the Capitol. Pursue them; I will go before you with my cavalry, and they shall know that you are come before. they know that you are coming." Hannibal felt that his success was too great for him to be able to realize it at the moment. "He commended," he said, "Maharbal's zeal, but he must take time to deliberate." Maharbal replied, "Well, the gods do not give all gifts to one man. Hannibal, you know how to conquer; not how to use a conquest." That day's delay is believed to have saved Rome and its empire.

Scipio, destined to be Scipio Af-ri-ca'nus, now makes a grand theatric entrance upon the scene—amid the general dismay the one figure at Rome that rose greater than the greatness of the ruin around him. Always equal to his most Roman occasion, Livy thus shows "Scipio, the highth of Rome," striding out into the blaze of history, like a triumphant tragedian saluting his audience from behind the footlights upon the boards where he reigns:

The supreme command was unanimously assigned to Scipio, who was a very young man, and to Claudius. They were holding council with a few friends about the state of affairs, when Publius Furius Philus, whose father was an ex-consul, said that it was idle for them to cling to utterly ruined hopes. The State, he declared, was given over for lost. Certain young nobles with Lu'ci-us Cæ-cil'i-us Me-tel'lus at their head, were thinking of flying beyond sea and deserting their country for the service of some foreign king. In face of a peril, terrible in itself, and coming with fresh force after so many disasters, all present stood motionless in amazement and stupefaction. They proposed that a council should be called to consider the matter, but the young Scipio, Rome's predestined champion in this war, declared that it was no time for a council. "We must dare and act," he said, "not deliberate, in such awful calamity. Let all who desire the salvation of their country, come armed with me. No camp is more truly a camp of the enemy than that in which men have such thoughts." He immediately started with a few followers for the house of Metellus; there he found a gathering of the youths of whom he had heard. Drawing his sword over the heads of the conspirators, "It is my fixed resolve," he cried, "as I will not myself desert the commonwealth of Rome, so not to suffer any other Roman citizen to desert it; if I knowingly fail therein, almighty and merciful Jupiter, smite me, my house, and fortunes with utter destruction. I insist that you, Lucius Cæcilius, and all others present, take this oath .

after me. Whoever takes it not may be sure this sword is drawn against him." They were as frightened as if they saw the victorious Hannibal before them, and to a man they swore and delivered themselves to the custody of Scipio.

Was not this Scipio a born master of men? Or, if he was not really such, did not Livy nobly imagine him such?

Some small remnant of the Roman force escaped from the destruction at Cannæ. But (Livy again now, in description of the state of things existing in the capital):

At Rome report said that no such mere remnant of citizens and allies survived, but that the army with the two consuls had been utterly destroyed, and that the whole force had ceased to exist. Never before, with Rome itself still safe, had there been such panic and confusion within our walls. I shall decline the task of attempting a lengthened description which could not but be far inferior to the truth. The year before a consul with his army had perished at Trasumennus; it was not wound after wound, but multiplied disasters that were announced. Two consuls and the armies of two consuls had perished. Rome had now no camp, no general, no soldiers. Hannibal was master of Apulia, of Samnium, of nearly the whole of Italy. Certainly there was not a nation in the world which would not have been overwhelmed by such a weight of calamity. Compare, for instance, the blow which the Carthaginians received in the sea-fight at the Æ-ga′tes Islands, a blow which made them evacuate Sicily and Sardinia and allow themselves to be burdened with indemnity and tribute; compare again the defeat in Africa, by which Hannibal himself was subsequently crushed. In no respect are they comparable with Cannæ, except because they were borne with less courage.

How Livy rejoices to pluck a garland of glory for Rome off the very acme and summit of her utmost disaster! And unquestionable fact abundantly justifies the historian's audacity. Rome was truly a wonderful nation—the very incarnation of virtue, as she conceived virtue, and as virtue, under the tuition of her conquering power, came, in pagan antiquity, to be universally conceived. The sound itself, of her name, is a spell to call up the idea of such character.

The allies of Rome began to forsake her. Livy gives a formidable list of these losses to Rome. He then loftily adds:

Yet all these disasters and defections never made the Romans so much as mention peace, either before the consul returned to Rome, or after his return had renewed the remembrance of the terrible loss sustained. On this latter occasion, indeed, such was the high spirit of the country, that when the consul returned after this great disaster of which he had himself been the chief cause, all classes went in crowds to meet him, and he was publicly thanked because "he had not despaired of the commonwealth."

Livy contrasts, with all confidence certainly, and probably with truth, what, in a different case, would have befallen the consul :

Had he been a Carthaginian general, they knew that there was no torture which he would not have had to suffer.

We have now got to the end of the second book of Livy's third decade. But we shall not fairly have presented the state of things created at Rome by the disaster of Cannæ, without mention of the fact that there were fearful omens observed by the Romans and fearful expiations accomplished to the gods. Livy seems to shudder rhetorically as he gives his account of the latter :

In obedience to the books of Fate, some unusual sacrifices were offered. Among them were a man and a woman of Gaul, and a man and a woman of Greece, who were buried alive in the Ox-market in a stone-vaulted chamber, not then for the first time polluted by what Roman feeling utterly abhorred, human sacrifice.

The rest of the story of Hannibal stretches out too long for us to give it here in any detail. He has now reached the height of his prosperity. It remains for him henceforth to the end of his protracted career to display his greatness under adversity. He was tried, in every vicissitude of fortune, by every experiment of situation, and he was seldom, perhaps never, found wanting. He was more than simply a great general. He was a truly great man.

From Italy the war at length was, by Scipio's motion and under his conduct, transferred into Africa. Carthage, who would not support her illustrious son abroad, now summoned that son to her own support at home. Hannibal loyally came at the call of his country and joined, with his brilliant antagonist, Scipio, the great battle of Za'ma. Scipio conquered, and Carthage was at the mercy of Rome. Hannibal, without an army, and a fugitive from land to land, was still formidable to his ancient foe. But the stars in their courses fought against the indomitable Carthaginian. What—after having first sought in vain to inspire the stolid mercantile oligarchy of Carthage with his own spirit of patriotic hostility to Rome, and then in vain to make An-ti'o-chus of Asia let him demonstrate how Rome might yet be conquered—what, we say, after all this, Hannibal finally attempted and suffered, we may hope many of our readers will be incited to learn for themselves, exploring in the full text of Livy translated.

In the course of doing this, they will find that Livy supplied to his countrymen, in his story of Rome, an unsurpassed text-book of lofty example, of nobly inspiring national and individual tradition.

CHAPTER VIII.

A very different writer of history from Livy, is Tacitus.
Tacitus, however, though different, is not less interesting than
Livy. He has an equally entertaining story to tell, and he tells
his story every whit as admirably. It is not romance, it is
history, with Tacitus. The color is not rose any longer. It
is stern, often livid, likeness to life. If Livy is Claude Lor-
raine, Tacitus is Salvator Rosa: if Livy is Titian, Tacitus is
Rembrandt. You read Livy, and you are inspired. You read
Tacitus, and you are oppressed. But the oppression somehow
at length leaves you, by reaction, braced; while the inspiration somehow at length leaves you, as if through too much
elixir, languid. For the inspiration is the effect of romance,
and the oppression is the effect of reality. Reality is generally
much more somber than romance, and Tacitus is far more
somber than Livy.

When Livy wrote, the Roman Empire was young. It had
the halo of uncertain hope about it. Augustus had brought
back peace to a distracted commonwealth, and Livy wrote in
the sunrise of a new era that perhaps would be glorious.
When Tacitus wrote, the aureole was gone, for the empire
was now a hundred years old. There had been Tiberius,
Caligula, Claudius, Nero. No wonder if now, for the writing
of Roman history, grim realism took the place of blithe
romance.

Of Caius Cornelius Tacitus himself we know very little.

We do not know where he was born. We do not know when
he was born. He was probably born about the year 50 of the
Christian era.   A town in Umbria is named as his birthplace.
Pliny was a younger friend, a loyal and affectionate admirer,
of the historian. From Pliny we derive what knowledge we
possess concerning his elder and more illustrious compeer;
except, indeed, that Tacitus himself makes us know that he
held public office in a constantly ascending scale under Ves-
pasian, under Titus, and under Domitian. Later, Tacitus was
consul; for there was still a titular consulship, even under
the empire. He was also senator; for there was still a titular
senate. With the accession of Trajan, the political activity of
Tacitus seems to have terminated. That great prince was too
strong for individual subjects under his sway to enjoy much
freedom of political action. But he was also too strong to feel
any necessity of greatly abridging his subjects' freedom of
speech. Romans might say what pleased themselves, on the
simple condition that they would do what pleased their emperor. Tacitus accordingly turned now decisively from politics to
literature ; and well it is for us that he did so. Near two centuries from his time will pass, and there will then ascend the
throne of the world an emperor who, bearing the same name,
the name of Tacitus, will fondly trace his lineage back to this
prince in literature, so to derive for himself a prouder than
imperial ancestry.

Tacitus had probably, before Trajan's accession, already produced his Dialogue on Oratory. Shortly after Trajan's accession, he published his life of Agricola, his own father-in-law.
His tract on Germany, we may suppose, soon followed. The
principal historical works of Tacitus are two ; the History, or
Histories, distinctively so called, and the Annals. The Annals,
though subsequent in composition, treat of an earlier period
than the History. The History Tacitus seems never to have
completed according to his original design for that work. He

alludes to projects in history entertained by him, of which, if he ever fulfilled them, we have utterly lost the fulfillment. But on the basis of that which survives of writing actually accomplished by him, Tacitus stands forth to-day an historian confessedly without superior in the republic of letters. If he does not flash like Livy, he burns as steady and as strong as Thucydides. No more weighty, no more serious, no more penetrating, no sounder, truer, manlier mind than Tacitus, perhaps, ever wrote history.

We shall chiefly draw from the Annals, to give our readers their taste of the quality of Tacitus. But first from the great other work of his hand let us show the majestic sentences in which, at the beginning of the work, the historian sets forth the object proposed by him, and passes in rapid review the whole course of the history. The reader will find it very interesting and suggestive to compare the opening of Macaulay's History of England. Tacitus:

I am entering on the history of a period rich in disasters, frightful in its wars, torn by civil strife, and even in peace full of horrors. Four emperors perished by the sword. There were three civil wars; there were more with foreign enemies; there were often wars that had both characters at once. There was success in the East, and disaster in the West. There were disturbances in Illyricum; Gaul wavered in its allegiance; Britain was thoroughly subdued and immediately abandoned; the tribes of the Suevi and the Sarmatæ rose in concert against us; the Dacians had the glory of inflicting as well as suffering defeat; the armies of Parthia were all but set in motion by the cheat of a counterfeit Nero. Now, too, Italy was prostrated by disasters either entirely novel, or that recurred only after a long succession of ages; cities in Campania's richest plains were swallowed up and overwhelmed; Rome was wasted by conflagrations, its oldest temples consumed, and the Capitol itself fired by the hands of citizens. Sacred rites were profaned; there was profligacy in the highest ranks; the sea was crowded with exiles, and its rocks polluted with bloody deeds. In the capital there were yet worse horrors. Nobility, wealth, the refusal or the acceptance of office, were grounds for accusation, and virtue insured destruction. The rewards of the informers were no less odious than their crimes; for while some seized on consulships

and priestly offices, as their share of the spoil, others on procurator-
ships, and posts of more confidential authority, they robbed and
ruined in every direction amid universal hatred and terror. Slaves
were bribed to turn against their masters, and freedmen to betray
their patrons: and those who had not an enemy were destroyed by
friends.

Yet the age was not so barren in noble qualities, as not also to exhibit examples of virtue. Mothers accompanied the flight of their
sons; wives followed their husbands into exile; there were brave
kinsmen and faithful sons-in-law; there were slaves whose fidelity
defied even torture; there were illustrious men driven to the last
necessity, and enduring it with fortitude; there were closing
scenes that equaled the famous deaths of antiquity. Besides
the manifold vicissitudes of human affairs, there were prodigies in
heaven and earth, the warning voices of the thunder, and other intimations of the future, auspicious or gloomy, doubtful or not to be
mistaken. Never, surely, did more terrible calamities of the
Roman people, or evidence more conclusive, prove that the gods
take no thought for our happiness, but only for our punishment.

I think it proper, however, before I commence my purposed
work, to pass under review the condition of the capital, the temper
of the armies, the attitude of the provinces, and the elements
of weakness and strength which existed throughout the whole empire, that so we may become acquainted, not only with the vicissitudes and the issues of events, which are often matters of chance,
but also with their relations and their causes.

The clause, " with their relations and their causes," reveals
a feature of the method of Tacitus in which he differs from
Livy. Livy is a romantic, whereas Tacitus is a philosophical,
historian. History, in the handling of Tacitus, becomes philosophy teaching by example. History, in the handling of
Livy, was largely the imagination delighting by pictures,
whether pictures of fact or of fancy. The pathetic gravity,
the sententious density, of the foregoing passage from Tacitus,
would be better appreciated by the reader who could turn
back to it, and peruse it again, after having first gone through
the details which it compresses in that marvelous brevity
of statement. The preface thus prefixed to the History will
be found to fit the Annals nearly as well.

We said that Tacitus has a story to tell not less entertaining than the story told by Livy. This is true whether understood of his History or of his Annals. Tacitus himself, however, felt that he wrote at disadvantage, as contrasted with preceding historians, because his subject was less heroic, less glorious. He was at heart an aristocrat of the elder times. The degeneracy of the senate of his own days, he bewailed, as one kindred in spirit with that proud oligarchy of which, a hundred years before Livy had sung in lyric prose his "passionate· ballad, gallant and gay." Still Tacitus was, under the circumstances that he found existing, a good enough imperialist. Doubtless he thought the new order, that had established itself, better than the old order which, because it was no longer worthy, had lapsed. You hear, however, the undertone of pathos for the long-gone and irrecoverable past, mingled with superb disdain for the ignoble present, running through the whole course of the history of Tacitus. Indignant pessimism is the keynote everywhere to his writing.

The Annals, a work, as already said, to be distinguished from the History, embraced the interval between the years 14 and 68 of the Christian era. The concluding part, that is, the part covering the last three years of the reign of Nero, is lost. Parts also in the midst of the work have perished. The whole narrative is depressing. It is a melancholy monotony of misery and crime. But Tacitus writes with such art that you are fascinated to read it from beginning to end. He holds you with his glittering eye.

The story of Nero is, perhaps, the part most familiar of all to the modern reader. This might seem a reason for choosing some other part, some part more novel, to be presented here. But the evil tale of Nero is the most familiar, because it is the most interesting. We should commit a mistake, to be deterred from it by that very fact about it which proves it the most attractive. Let us then, undoubtingly, make choice of Nero for the hero of what we draw here from the Annals of

Tacitus.   There will be found, by intelligent readers, a considerable compensation for the sense of familiarity experienced, in the satisfaction they will derive from the consciousness of having now to do with an original source of information on the subject treated.

The story of Nero, as told by Tacitus, is a long story.   Let us take a plunge at once into the midst of things.   There are three associate personages of the plot, to share, almost equally with Nero, the interest of the reader.   These three are Burrus, Seneca, and, above all, A-grip-pi′na, the emperor's mother.   Of A-fra′ni-us Burrus and An-næ′us Seneca—this is the famous philosopher—Tacitus says :

These two men guided the emperor's youth with a unity of purpose seldom found where authority is shared, and though their accomplishments were wholly different, they had equal influence. Burrus, with his soldier's discipline and severe manners, Seneca, with lessons of eloquence and a dignified courtesy, strove alike to confine the frailty of the prince's youth, should he loathe virtue, within allowable indulgences.   They had both alike to struggle against the domineering spirit of Agrippina.

One of the earliest among the public acts of the youthful emperor Nero, was to pronounce a funeral oration on his predecessor, Claudius.   Tacitus's account of this, with characteristic comment of his own interspersed, lets out some secrets of Nero's disposition and of the current temper of the time—not less, perhaps, also, of the historian's own individual humor :

On the day of the funeral the prince pronounced Claudius's panegyric, and while.he dwelt on the antiquity of his family and on the consulships and triumphs of his ancestors, there was enthusiasm both in himself and his audience.   The praise of his graceful accomplishments, and the remark that during his reign no disaster had befallen Rome from the foreigner, were heard with favor.   When the speaker passed on to his foresight and wisdom, no one could refrain from laughter, though the speech, which was composed by Seneca, exhibited much elegance, as indeed that famous man had an attractive genius which suited the popular ear of the time.   Elderly men, who amuse their leisure with comparing the past and the present, observed that Nero was the first emperor who needed another man's eloquence. The dictator Cæsar rivaled the greatest orators, and Augustus had an easy and fluent way of speaking, such as became a sovereign. Tiberius, too, thoroughly understood the art of balancing words, and was sometimes forcible in the expression of his thoughts, or else intentionally obscure. Even Caius Cæsar's disordered intellect did not wholly mar his faculty of speech. Nor did Claudius, when he spoke with preparation, lack elegance. Nero from early boyhood turned his lively genius in other directions; he carved, painted, sang, or practiced the management of horses, occasionally composing verses which showed that he had the rudiments of learning.

Nero began apparently well. He promised to restore to the senate something of its ancient prerogative, and Tacitus says he was true to his word. But the evil presiding spirit of his mother resisted the young emperor. It is almost incredible, but, according to Tacitus, the senators used to be summoned to the imperial palace in order that she, Agrippina, "might stand close to a hidden door behind them screened by a curtain which was enough to shut her out of sight but not out of hearing." Nero was scarcely more than seventeen years of age. It seems a cruelty of fortune that, at such an age, still under the tuition of such a mother, this pampered boy should have been forced into the most dangerous and the most conspicuous position in the world. The passions of a young man were of course not wanting to a young emperor. He fell in love with a freedwoman and got two fashionable young fellows to act as his panders. What Tacitus tells of this, and of Nero's relation to his mother, is fraught with sad instruction :

Without the mother's knowledge, then in spite of her opposition, they [the two young fellows just referred to] had crept into his favor by debaucheries and equivocal secrets, and even the prince's older friends did not thwart him, for here was a girl who without harm to any one gratified his desires, when he loathed his wife Octavia, high born as she was, and of approved virtue, either from some fatality, or because vice is overpoweringly attractive. . .

Agrippina, however, raved with a woman's fury about having a freedwoman for a rival, a slave girl for a daughter-in-law, with like expressions. Nor would she wait till her son repented or wearied of his passion. The fouler her reproaches, the more powerfully did they inflame him, till, completely mastered by the strength of his desire, he threw off all respect for his mother, and put himself under the guidance of Seneca, one of whose friends, Annæus Serenus, had veiled the young prince's intrigue in its beginning by pretending to be in love with the same woman, and had lent his name as the ostensible giver of the presents secretly sent by the emperor to the girl. Then Agrippina, changing her tactics, plied the lad with various blandishments, and even offered the seclusion of her chamber for the concealment of indulgences which youth and the highest rank might claim. She went further; she pleaded guilty to an ill-timed strictness, and handed over to him the abundance of her wealth, which nearly approached the imperial treasures, and from having been of late extreme in her restraint of her son, became now, on the other hand, lax to excess. The change did not escape Nero; his most intimate friends dreaded it, and begged him to beware of the arts of a woman who was always daring and was now false.

But mother and son were equally, for both of them were supremely, selfish, and they could not be solidly reconciled with each other. The breach between them soon became open and wide. The mother bethought herself of a resource against her son. There was Claudius's son, Bri-tan'ni-cus, younger step-brother to Nero. Britannicus had the blood of a Cæsar in his veins. Nero was Agrippina's son by a former husband, not by Claudius. He was, therefore, not natural heir to the empire. Tacitus relates:

Agrippina rushed into frightful menaces, sparing not the prince's ears her solemn protest "that Britannicus was now of full age, he who was the true and worthy heir of his father's sovereignty, which a son, by mere admission and adoption, was abusing in outrages on his mother. She shrank not from an utter exposure of the wickedness of that ill-starred house, of her own marriage, to begin with, and of her poisoner's craft. All that the gods and she herself had taken care of was that her stepson was yet alive; with him she would go to the camp, where on one side should be heard the daughter of Germanicus; on the other, the crippled Burrus and the exile Seneca, claiming, forsooth, with disfigured hand, and a pedant's tongue, the government of the world." As she spoke, she raised her hand in menace and heaped insults on him, as she appealed to the deified Claudius, to the infernal shades of the Silani, and to those many fruitless crimes.

The "fruitless crimes" were crimes of Agrippina's own committing—fruitless, since the obstinacy of her own boy balked her of her purpose in committing them. She had meant to be empress of the world. But Nero unexpectedly had developed a liking for the game, as well as the name, of emperor. He now, stung by the taunts and threats of his mother, entered headlong on his unparalleled career of crime. Tacitus:

Nero was confounded at this, and as the day was near on which Britannicus would complete his fourteenth year, he reflected, now on the domineering temper of his mother, and now again on the character of the young prince, which a trifling circumstance had lately tested, sufficient however to gain for him wide popularity. During the feast of Saturn, amid other pastimes of his playmates, at a game of lot-drawing for king, the lot fell to Nero, upon which he gave all his other companions different orders, and such as would not put them to the blush; but when he told Britannicus to step forward and begin a song, hoping for a laugh at the expense of a boy who knew nothing of sober, much less of riotous, society, the lad with perfect coolness commenced some verses which hinted at his expulsion from his father's house and from supreme power. This procured him pity, which was the more conspicuous, as night with its merriment had stripped off all disguise. Nero saw the reproach and redoubled his hate. Pressed by Agrippina's menaces, having no charge against his brother and not daring openly to order his murder, he meditated a secret device and directed poison to be prepared through the agency of Julius Pollio, tribune of one of the prætorian cohorts, who had in his custody a woman under sentence for poisoning, Locusta by name, with a vast reputation for crime. That every one about the person of Britannicus should care nothing for right or honor, had long ago been provided for. He actually received his first dose of poison from his tutors and passed it off his bowels, as it was either rather weak or so qualified as not at once to prove deadly. But Nero, impatient at such slow progress in crime, threatened the tribune and ordered the poisoner to execution for prolonging his anxiety while they were thinking of the popular talk and planning their own defense. Then they promised that death should be as sudden as if it were the hurried work of the dagger, and a rapid poison of previously tested ingredients was prepared close to the emperor's chamber.

It was customary for the imperial princes to sit during their meals with other nobles of the same age, in the sight of their kinsfolk, at a table of their own, furnished somewhat frugally. There Britannicus was dining, and as what he ate and drank was always tested by the taste of a select attendant, the following device was contrived, that the usage might not be dropped or the crime betrayed by the death of both prince and attendant. A cup as yet harmless, but extremely hot and already tasted, was handed to Britannicus; then, on his refusing it because of its warmth, poison was poured in with some cold water, and this so penetrated his entire frame that he lost alike voice and breath. There was a stir among the company; some, taken by surprise, ran hither and thither, while those whose discernment was keener, remained motionless, with their eyes fixed on Nero, who, as he still reclined in seeming unconsciousness, said that this was a common occurrence, from a periodical epilepsy, with which Britannicus had been afflicted from his earliest infancy, and that his sight and senses would gradually return. As for Agrippina, her terror and confusion, though her countenance struggled to hide it, so visibly appeared, that she was clearly just as ignorant as was Octavia, Britannicus's own sister. She saw, in fact, that she was robbed of her only remaining refuge, and that here was a precedent for parricide. Even Octavia, notwithstanding her youthful inexperience, had learned to hide her grief, her affection, and indeed every emotion. And so after a brief pause the company resumed its mirth.

"Of all things human," remarks Tacitus, "the most precarious and transitory is a reputation for power which has no strong support of its own." This he says on occasion of the disgrace of Agrippina, whom her son now sent away from the palace and deprived of her military guard. The wretched woman, in her weakness, did not fail of enemies to accuse her to her son. One accusation, naturally to her son the heaviest, was that she was plotting against his emperorship. A certain Plautus, so the accusation ran, was encouraged by Agrippina to pretend to the throne of the Cæsars. Against him and the emperor's mother, one Paris was found a willing informer. Tacitus now (let readers not miss the indications incidentally dropped by the historian, as to his method in treating his authorities):

Night was far advanced and Nero was still sitting over his cups, when Paris entered, who was generally wont at such times to heighten the emperor's enjoyments, but who now wore a gloomy expression. He went through the whole evidence in order, and so frightened his hearer as to make him resolve not only on the destruction of his mother and of Plautus, but also on the removal of Burrus from the command of the guards, as a man who had been promoted by Agrippina's interest, and was now showing his gratitude. We have it on the authority of Fabius Rusticus that a note was written to Cæ-ci'na Tuscus, intrusting to him the charge of the prætorian cohorts, but that through Seneca's influence that distinguished post was retained for Burrus. According to Plinius and Cluvius, no doubt was felt about the commander's loyalty. Fabius certainly inclines to the praise of Seneca, through whose friendship he rose to honor. Proposing as I do to follow the consentient testimony of historians, I shall give the differences in their narratives under the writers' names. Nero, in his bewilderment and impatience to destroy his mother, could not be put off till Burrus answered for her death, should she be convicted of the crime, but "any one," he said, "much more a parent, must be allowed a defense. Accusers there were none forthcoming, they had before them only the word of a single person from an enemy's house, and this the night with its darkness and prolonged festivity and every thing savoring of recklessness and folly, was enough to refute."

Having thus allayed the prince's fears, they went at day-break to Agrippina, that she might know the charges against her, and either rebut them or suffer the penalty. Burrus fulfilled his instructions in Seneca's presence, and some of the freedmen were present to witness the interview. Then Burrus, when he had fully explained the charges with the authors' names, assumed an air of menace. Instantly Agrippina, calling up all her high spirit, exclaimed, "I wonder not that Silana, who has never borne offspring, knows nothing of a mother's feelings. Parents do not change their children as lightly as a shameless woman does her paramours. . . . Only let the man come forward who can charge me with having tampered with the prætorian cohorts in the capital, with having sapped the loyalty of the provinces, or, in a word, with having bribed slaves and freedmen into any wickedness. Could I have lived with Britannicus in the possession of power? And if Plautus or any other were to become master of the State so as to sit in judgment on me, accusers forsooth would not be forthcoming to charge me not merely with a few incautious expressions prompted by the eagerness of affection, but with guilt from which a son alone could absolve me."

There was profound excitement among those present, and they even tried to soothe her agitation, but she insisted on an interview with her son. Then, instead of pleading her innocence, as though she lacked confidence, or her claims on him by way of reproach, she obtained vengeance on her accusers and rewards for her friends.

Agrippina enjoyed her momentary triumph. But her dreadful doom was only postponed.

Nero was well on the downward road. *Facilis descensus*, and the rate of descent already was swift. Read the record (remember that still there was the titular consulship, and that still, as of old, the years of the empire were reckoned by the names of the consuls):

In the consulship of Quintus Vo-lu'si-us and Publius Scipio, there was peace abroad, but a disgusting licentiousness at home on the part of Nero, who in a slave's disguise, so as to be unrecognized, would wander through the streets of Rome, to brothels and taverns, with comrades, who seized on goods exposed for sale and inflicted wounds on any whom they encountered, some of these last knowing him so little that he even received blows himself and showed the marks of them in his face. When it was notorious that the emperor was the assailant, and the insults on men and women of distinction were multiplied, other persons, too, on the strength of a license once granted under Nero's name, ventured with impunity on the same practices, and had gangs of their own, till night presented the scenes of a captured city.

Julius Mon-ta'nus, a senator, but one who had not yet held any office, happened to encounter the prince in the darkness, and because he fiercely repulsed his attack and then on recognizing him begged for mercy, as though this was a reproach, was forced to destroy himself. Nero was for the future more timid, and surrounded himself with soldiers and a number of gladiators, who, when a fray began on a small scale and seemed a private affair, were to let it alone, but, if the injured persons resisted stoutly, they rushed in with their swords.

"Was forced to destroy himself." Compulsory suicide became the favorite form of executing a capital sentence issuing from the arbitrary will of the emperor. Tacitus is full of instances which vary the monotony of imperial murder with every conceivable permutation of incident. Pathetically instructive it is, to come, as one glances along these pages dense with tragedy, upon occasional sentences like the following: "Still there yet remained some shadow of a free State." Again, disdaining to do more than merely mention the erection of a great amphitheater, Tacitus says: "We have learned that it suits the dignity of the Roman people to reserve history for great achievements, and to leave such details to the city's daily register." Such expressions as the preceding from Tacitus strikingly reveal the character of their author.

The climax of Nero's wickedness, as the general opinion rates it, was his conspiracy to murder his mother. This crime is now near at hand. A woman was the immediate cause. That woman was the infamous Pop-pæ′a. Let Tacitus sketch her for us:

Poppæa had everything but a right mind. Her mother, who surpassed in personal attractions all the ladies of her day, had bequeathed to her alike fame and beauty. Her fortune adequately corresponded to the nobility of her descent. Her conversation was charming and her wit anything but dull. She professed virtue, while she practiced laxity. Seldom did she appear in public, and it was always with her face partly veiled, either to disappoint men's gaze or to set off her beauty. Her character she never spared, making no distinction between a husband and a paramour, while she was never a slave to her own passion or to that of her lover. Wherever there was a prospect of advantage, there she transferred her favors.

Poppæa was married and had a son, but this did not prevent her intriguing, and intriguing successfully, for the hand of Otho, that favorite of Nero's. She now had what she needed in order to get what she wanted, which was—power over Nero. Through Otho, used as tool or as accomplice, she got access to the emperor. Her shameless arts of seduction, and her cool triangulation toward her object, are thus described by Tacitus:

Poppæa won her way by artful blandishments, pretending that she could not resist her passion and that she was captivated by Nero's person. Soon as the emperor's love grew ardent she would change and be supercilious, and [artfully tantalizing her infatuated imperial lover] would say again and again that she was a married woman and could not give up her husband, attached as she was to Otho by a manner of life which no one equaled. "His ideas and his style were grand; at his house everything worthy of the highest fortune was ever before her eyes. Nero, on the contrary, with his slave-girl mistress, tied down by his attachment to Acte, had derived nothing from his slavish associations but what was low and degrading."

The historian, with judicial impartiality, makes commendatory notes of certain equitable measures adopted by Nero for the administration of the empire, adding that they "for a short time were maintained and were subsequently disregarded." It seems to have been Tacitus's feeling that Nero should have—he certainly needed—all the credit that belonged to good attempts on his part, of any kind, however momentary.

The fourteenth book of the Annals covers a period of three years, from 59 A. D. to 62. The beginning of the book is occupied with narration and description too absorbingly interesting to be much abridged or interrupted. We transfer a long passage, which will not seem long, to these pages. (We need to forewarn readers that here, as occasionally elsewhere in Tacitus, they will come upon things said and suggested by the historian which, for an exercise of reading aloud in a mixed company, would require to be touched upon very lightly. Such things we should gladly have omitted; but we could not, omitting them altogether, even hint, adequately, what Tacitus is, and what is the dreadful story that Tacitus had it for his mission to tell. It will be noted that he always describes vice after the manner of a man strongly siding with virtue.)

In the year of the consulship of Caius Vip-sta'nus and Caius

Fon-te'i-us, Nero deferred no more a long-meditated crime. Length of power had matured his daring, and his passion for Poppæa daily grew more ardent. As the woman had no hope of marriage for herself or of Octavia's divorce while Agrippina lived, she would reproach the emperor with incessant vituperation and sometimes call him in jest a mere ward who was under the rule of others, and was so far from having empire that he had not even his liberty. "Why," she asked, "was her marriage put off? Was it, forsooth, her beauty and her ancestors, with their triumphal honors, that failed to please; or her being a mother, and her sincere heart? No; the fear was that as a wife at least she would divulge the wrongs of the Senate, and the wrath of the people at the arrogance and rapacity of his mother. If the only daughter-in-law Agrippina could bear was one who wished evil to her son, let her be restored to her union with Otho. She would go anywhere in the world, where she might hear of the insults heaped on the emperor, rather than witness them, and be also involved in his perils."

These and the like complaints, rendered impressive by tears and by the cunning of an adulteress, no one checked, as all longed to see the mother's power broken, while not a person believed that the son's hatred would steel his heart to her murder.

Cluvius relates that Agrippina in her eagerness to retain her influence went so far that more than once at midday, when Nero, even at that hour, was flushed with wine and feasting, she presented herself attractively attired to her half-intoxicated son. . . . When kinsfolk observed wanton kisses and caresses, portending infamy, it was Seneca who sought a female's aid against a woman's fascinations, and hurried in Acte, the freed-girl, who alarmed at her own peril, and at Nero's disgrace, told him that the incest was notorious, as his mother boasted of it, and that the soldiers would never endure the rule of an impious sovereign. Fabius Rusticus tells us that it was not Agrippina, but Nero who lusted for the crime, and that it was frustrated by the adroitness of that same freed-girl. Cluvius's account, however, is also that of all other authors, and popular belief inclines to it, whether it was that Agrippina really conceived such a monstrous wickedness in her heart, or perhaps because the thought of a strange passion seemed comparatively credible in a woman, who in her girlish years had allowed herself to be seduced by Lepidus in the hope of winning power, had stooped with a like ambition to the lust of Pallas, and had trained herself for every infamy by her marriage with her uncle.

Nero accordingly avoided secret interviews with her, and when she withdrew to her gardens or to her estates at Tusculum and Antium, he praised her for courting repose. At last, convinced that she would be too formidable, wherever she might dwell, he resolved to destroy her, merely deliberating whether it was to be accomplished by poison, or by the sword, or by any other violent means. Poison at first seemed best, but, were it to be administered at the imperial table, the result could not be referred to chance after the recent circumstances of the death of Britannicus. Again, to tamper with the servants of a woman who, from her familiarity with crime, was on her guard against treachery, appeared to be extremely difficult, and then, too, she had fortified her constitution by the use of antidotes. How again the dagger and its work were to be kept secret, no one could suggest, and it was feared too that whoever might be chosen to execute such a crime would spurn the order.

An ingenious suggestion was offered by An-i-ce'tus, a freedman, commander of the fleet at Mi-se'num, who had been tutor to Nero in boyhood and had a hatred of Agrippina which she reciprocated. He explained that a vessel could be constructed, from which a part might by a contrivance be detached, when out at sea, so as to plunge her unawares into the water. "Nothing," he said, "allowed of accidents so much as the sea, and should she be overtaken by shipwreck, who would be so unfair as to impute to crime an offense committed by the winds and waves? The emperor would add the honor of a temple and of shrines to the deceased lady, with every other display of filial affection."

Nero liked the device, favored as it also was by the particular time, for he was celebrating Minerva's five days' festival at Bai'æ. Thither he enticed his mother by repeated assurances that children ought to bear with the irritability of parents and to soothe their tempers, wishing thus to spread a rumor of reconciliation and to secure Agrippina's acceptance through the feminine credulity, which easily believes what gives joy. As she approached, he went to the shore to meet her (she was coming from Antium), welcomed her with outstretched hand and embrace, and conducted her to Bauli. This was the name of a country house, washed by a bay of the sea, between the promontory of Misenum and the lake of Baiæ. Here was a vessel distinguished from others by its equipment, seemingly meant, among other things, to do honor to his mother; for she had been accustomed to sail in a trireme, with a crew of marines. And now she was invited to a banquet, that night might serve to conceal the crime. It was well known that somebody had been found to betray it, that Agrippina had heard of the plot, and in doubt whether she was to believe it, was conveyed to Baiæ in her litter. There some soothing words allayed her fear; she was graciously received, and seated at table above the emperor.

Nero prolonged the banquet with various conversation, passing from a youth's playful familiarity to an air of constraint, which seemed to indicate serious thought, and then, after protracted festivity, escorted her on her departure, clinging with kisses to her eyes and bosom, either to crown his hypocrisy or because the last sight of a mother on the eve of destruction caused a lingering even in that brutal heart.

A night of brilliant starlight with the calm of a tranquil sea was granted by heaven, seemingly, to convict the crime. The vessel had not gone far, Agrippina having with her two of her intimate attendants, one of whom, Cre-pe-re'ius Gallus, stood near the helm, while A-cer-ro'ni-a, reclining at Agrippina's feet as she reposed herself, spoke joyfully of her son's repentance and of the recovery of the mother's influence, when at a given signal the ceiling of the place, which was loaded with a quantity of lead, fell in, and Crepereius was crushed and instantly killed. Agrippina and Acerronia were protected by the projecting sides of the couch, which happened to be too strong to yield under the weight. But this was not followed by the breaking up of the vessel; for all were bewildered, and those too, who were in the plot, were hindered by the unconscious majority. The crew then thought it best to throw the vessel on one side and so sink it, but they could not themselves promptly unite to face the emergency, and others, by counteracting the attempt, gave an opportunity of a gentler fall into the sea. Acerronia, however, thoughtlessly exclaiming that she was Agrippina, and imploring help for the emperor's mother, was dispatched with poles and oars, and such naval implements as chance offered. Agrippina was silent and was thus the less recognized; still, she received a wound in her shoulder. She swam, then met with some small boats which conveyed her to the Lucrine lake, and so entered her house.

There she reflected how for this very purpose she had been invited by a lying letter and treated with conspicuous honor, how also it was near the shore, not from being driven by winds or dashed on rocks, that the vessel had in its upper part collapsed, like a mechanism anything but nautical. She pondered too the death of Acerronia; she looked at her own wound, and saw that her only safeguard against treachery was to ignore it. Then she sent her freedman A-ger-i'nus to tell her son how by heaven's favor and his good fortune she had escaped a terrible disaster; that she begged him, alarmed, as he might be, by his mother's peril, to put off the duty of a visit, as for the present she needed repose. Meanwhile, pretending that she felt secure, she applied remedies to her wound, and fomentations to her person. She then ordered search to be made for the will of Acerronia, and her property to be sealed, in this alone throwing off disguise.

Nero, meantime, as he waited for tidings of the consummation of the deed, received information that she had escaped with the injury of a slight wound, after having so far encountered the peril that there could be no question as to its author. Then, paralyzed with terror and protesting that she would show herself the next moment eager for vengeance, either arming the slaves or stirring up the soldiery, or hastening to the senate and the people, to charge him with the wreck, with her wound, and with the destruction of her friends, he asked what resource he had against all this, unless something could be at once devised by Burrus and Seneca. He had instantly summoned both of them, and possibly they were already in the secret. There was a long silence on their part; they feared they might remonstrate in vain, or believed the crisis to be such that Nero must perish, unless Agrippina were at once crushed. Thereupon Seneca was so far the more prompt as to glance back on Burrus, as if to ask him whether the bloody deed must be required of the soldiers. Burrus replied "that the prætorians were attached to the whole family of the Cæsars, and remembering Ger-man'i-cus would not dare a savage deed on his offspring. It was for Anicetus to accomplish his promise."

Anicetus, without a pause, claimed for himself the consummation of the crime. At those words, Nero declared that that day gave him empire, and that a freedman was the author of this mighty boon. "Go," he said, "with all speed and take with you the men readiest to execute your orders." He himself, when he had heard of the arrival of Agrippina's messenger, Agerinus, contrived a theatrical mode of accusation, and, while the man was repeating his message, threw down a sword at his feet, then ordered him to be put in irons, as a detected criminal, so that he might invent a story how his mother had plotted the emperor's destruction; and in the shame of discovered guilt had, by her own choice, sought death.

Meantime, Agrippina's peril being universally known and taken to be an accidental occurrence, everybody, the moment he heard of it, hurried down to the beach. Some climbed projecting piers; some the nearest vessels; some, again, stood with outstretched arms, while the whole shore rung with wailings, with prayers and cries, as different questions were asked and uncertain answers given. A vast multitude streamed to the spot with torches, and as soon as all knew that she was safe they at once prepared to wish her joy, till the sight of an armed and threatening force scared them away. Anicetus then surrounded the house with a guard, and having burst open the gates, dragged off the slaves who met him, till he came to the door of her chamber, where a few still stood, after the rest had fled in terror at the attack. A small lamp was in the room, and one slave-girl with Agrippina, who grew more and more anxious, as no messenger came from her son, not even Agerinus, while the appearance of the shore was changed, a solitude one moment, then sudden bustle and tokens of the worst catastrophe. As the girl rose to depart, she exclaimed, "Do you, too, forsake me?" and looking round saw Anicetus, who had with him the captain of the trireme, Her-cu-le'ius, and O-bar'i-tus, a centurion of marines. "If," said she, "you have come to see me, take back word that I have recovered, but if you are here to do a crime, I believe nothing about my son; he has not ordered his mother's murder."

The assassins closed in round her couch, and the captain of the trireme first struck her head violently with a club. Then, as the centurion bared his sword for the fatal deed, presenting her person, she exclaimed, "Smite my womb," and with many wounds she was slain. . . .

But the emperor, when the crime was at last accomplished, realized its portentous guilt. The rest of the night, now silent and stupefied, now and still oftener starting up in terror, bereft of reason, he awaited the dawn as if it would bring with it his doom. He was first encouraged to hope by the flattery addressed to him, at the prompting of Burrus, by the centurions and tribunes, who again and again pressed his hand and congratulated him on his having escaped an unforeseen danger and his mother's daring crime. Then his friends went to the temples, and, an example having once been set, the neighboring towns of Campania testified their joy with sacrifices and deputations. He himself, with an apposite phase of hypocrisy, seemed sad, and almost angry, at his own deliverance, and shed tears over his mother's death. But as the aspects of places change not, as do the looks of men, and as he had ever before his eyes the dreadful sight of that sea with its shores (some, too, believed that the notes of a funeral trumpet were heard from the surrounding heights, and wailings from the mother's grave), he retired to Neapolis, and sent a letter to the Senate, the drift of which was that Agerinus, one of Agrippina's confidential freedmen, had been detected with the dagger of an assassin, and that in the consciousness of having planned the crime she had paid its penalty.

He even revived the charges of a period long past, how she had aimed at a share of empire, and at inducing the prætorian cohorts to swear obedience to a woman, to the disgrace of the Senate and people; how, when she was disappointed, in her fury with the soldiers, the Senate, and the populace, she opposed the usual donative and largess, and organized perilous prosecutions against distinguished citizens. What efforts had it cost him to hinder her from bursting into the Senate-house and giving answers to foreign nations! He glanced, too, with indirect censure at the days of Claudius, and ascribed all the abominations of that reign to his mother, thus seeking to show that it was the State's good fortune which had destroyed her. For he actually told the story of the shipwreck; but who could be so stupid as to believe that it was accidental, or that a shipwrecked woman had sent one man with a weapon to break through an emperor's guards and fleets? So now it was not Nero, whose brutality was far beyond any remonstrance, but Seneca, who was in ill-repute, for having written a confession in such a style.

Still there was a marvelous rivalry among the nobles in decreeing thanksgivings at all the shrines, and the celebration with annual games of Minerva's festival, as the day on which the plot had been discovered; also, that a golden image of Minerva, with a statue of the emperor by its side, should be set up in the Senate-house, and that Agrippina's birthday should be classed among the inauspicious days. Thrasea Pætus, who had been used to pass over previous flatteries in silence or with brief assent, then walked out of the Senate, thereby imperiling himself, without communicating to the other senators any impulse toward freedom.

Can anything be conceived of more incredible than such wickedness as Nero's? Yes. The baseness exhibited in view of Nero's wickedness, by the senate, and by the people of Rome, was more incredible still. Tacitus:

While Nero was lingering in the towns of Campania, doubting how he should enter Rome, whether he would find the Senate submissive and the populace enthusiastic, all the vilest courtiers, and of these never had a court a more abundant crop, argued against his hesitation, by assuring him that Agrippina's name was hated, and that her death had heightened his popularity. "He might go without a fear," they said, "and experience in his person men's veneration for him." They insisted at the same time on preceding him. They found greater enthusiasm than they had promised, the tribes coming forth to meet him, the Senate in holiday attire, troops of their children and wives arranged according to sex and age, tiers of seats raised for the spectacle, where he was to pass, as a triumph is witnessed. Thus elated and exulting over his people's slavery, he proceeded to the Capitol, performed the thanksgiving, and then plunged into all the excesses, which, though ill-restrained, some sort of respect for his mother had for awhile delayed.

"Some sort of respect for his mother"! There follows immediately now from the hand of Tacitus as dreadful a picture of omnipotent and frolicsome despotism as ever was drawn. It is almost an adequate punishment of the infamy, to have the infamy thus pitilessly damned to everlasting contempt:

He had long had a fancy for driving a four-horse chariot, and a no less degrading taste for singing to the harp, in a theatrical fashion, when he was at dinner. This he would remind people was a royal custom, and had been the practice of ancient chiefs; it was celebrated too in the praises of poets and was meant to show honor to the gods. Songs, indeed, he said, were sacred to Apollo, and it was in the dress of a singer that that great and prophetic deity was seen in Roman temples as well as in Greek cities. He could no longer be restrained, when Seneca and Burrus thought it best to concede one point that he might not persist in both. A space was inclosed in the Vatican valley where he might manage his horses, without the spectacle being public. Soon he actually invited all the people of Rome, who extolled him in their praises, like a mob which craves for amusements and rejoices when a prince draws them the same way. However, the public exposure of his shame acted on him as an incentive instead of sickening him, as men expected. Imagining that he mitigated the scandal by disgracing many others, he brought on the stage descendants of noble families, who sold themselves, because they were paupers. As they have ended their days, I think it due to their ancestors not to hand down their names. And indeed the infamy is his who gave them wealth to reward their degradation rather than to deter them from degrading themselves. He prevailed too on some well-known Roman knights, by immense presents, to offer their services in the amphitheater; only pay from one who is able to command carries with it the force of compulsion.

Still, not yet wishing to disgrace himself on a public stage, he instituted some games under the title of "juvenile sports," for which people of every class gave in their names. Neither rank nor age nor previous high promotion hindered any one from practicing the art of a Greek or Latin actor, and even stooping to gestures and songs unfit for a man. Noble ladies too actually played disgusting parts, and in the grove, with which Augustus had surrounded the lake for the naval fight, there were erected places for meeting and refreshment, and every incentive to excess was offered for sale.

Money, too, was distributed, which the respectable had to spend under sheer compulsion and which the profligate gloried ·in squandering. Hence a rank growth of abomination and of all infamy. Never did a more filthy rabble add a worse licentiousness to our long corrupted morals. Even with virtuous training, purity is not easily upheld; far less amid rivalries in vice could modesty or propriety or any trace of good manners be preserved. Last of all, the emperor himself came on the stage, tuning his lute with elaborate care and trying his voice with his attendants. There were also present, to complete the show, a guard of soldiers with centurions and tribunes, and Burrus, who grieved and yet applauded. Then it was that Roman knights were first enrolled under the title of Augustani, men in their prime and remarkable for their strength, some from a natural frivolity, others from the hope of promotion. Day and night they kept up a thunder of applause, and applied to the emperor's person and voice the epithets of deities. Thus they lived in fame and honor, as if on the strength of their merits.

Nero, however, that he might not be known only for his accomplishments as an actor, also affected a taste for poetry, and drew round him persons who had some skill in such compositions, but not yet generally recognized. They used to sit with him, stringing together verses prepared at home, or extemporized on the spot, and fill up his own expressions, such as they were, just as he threw them off. This is plainly shown by the very character of the poems, which have no vigor or inspiration, or unity in their flow.

He would also bestow some leisure after his banquets on the teachers of philosophy, for he enjoyed the wrangles of opposing dogmatists. And some there were who liked to exhibit their gloomy faces and looks, as one of the amusements of the court.

It is some relief to the long monotony of shame which draws out in Tacitus the story of Nero, to read of distant wars and expeditions that meanwhile continued the great career of the empire. Cor'bu-lo is a Roman general, destined to a tragical end, who, till near the close of Nero's reign, figured conspicuously as conqueror in the East. We have here no room for more than this mere mention of Corbulo's name. The name of London, scarcely disguised as Londinium, catches the eye. The place is spoken of as "much frequented by a number of merchants and trading vessels." Little did the Roman historian dream that, one day, his history would be read by Londoners who could justly claim that their town was a city greater than Rome at its height ever was. The British queen, Bo-ä-di-ce′a, careers for a moment into the pages of Tacitus :

Boädicea, with her daughters before her in a chariot, went up to tribe after tribe, protesting that it was indeed usual for Britons to fight under the leadership of women. "But now," she said, "it is not as a woman descended from noble ancestry, but as one of the people, that I am avenging lost freedom, my scourged body, the outraged chastity of my daughters. Roman lust has gone so far that not our very persons, nor even age or virginity, are left un-polluted. But heaven is on the side of a righteous vengeance; a legion which dared to fight has perished; the rest are hiding them-selves in their camp, or are thinking anxiously of flight. They will not sustain even the din and the shout of so many thousands, much less our charge and our blows. If you weigh well the strength of the armies, and the causes of the war, you will see that in this battle you must conquer or die. This is a woman's re-solve; as for men, they may live and be slaves."

Burrus makes his figure in the pages of Tacitus, rather through the praises bestowed upon him by the historian, than through any recital of things that he achieved. His end was not without accompaniment of tragedy. The tale is, with that suggestion of pathos so characteristic of Tacitus, and in him so effective, thus briefly told by the historian :

While the miseries of the State were daily growing worse, its supports were becoming weaker. Burrus died, whether from illness or from poison was a question. It was supposed to be illness from the fact that from the gradual swelling of his throat inwardly and the closing up of the passage he ceased to breathe. Many positively asserted that by Nero's order his throat was smeared with some poisonous drug under the pretense of the application of a remedy, and that Burrus, who saw through the crime, when the emperor paid him a visit, recoiled with horror from his gaze, and merely replied to his question, "I indeed am well." Rome felt for him a deep and lasting regret, because of the remembrance of his worth, because too of the merely passive virtue of one of his successors and the very flagrant iniquities of the other.

The fall from power of Seneca was as graceful, decorous, and dignified a piece of acting, as a scene well presented out of the French classic drama of the seventeenth century. Readers will think of Wolsey and King Henry the Eighth. Tacitus:

The death of Burrus was a blow to Seneca's power, for virtue had not the same strength when one of its champions, so to say, was removed, and Nero too began to lean on worse advisers. They assailed Seneca with various charges, representing that he continued to increase a wealth which was already so vast as to be beyond the scale of a subject, and was drawing to himself the attachment of the citizens, while in the picturesqueness of his gardens and the magnificence of his country-houses he almost surpassed the emperor. They further alleged against him that he claimed for himself alone the honors of eloquence, and composed poetry more assiduously, as soon as a passion for it had seized on Nero. "Openly inimical to the prince's amusements, he disparaged his ability in driving horses, and ridiculed his voice whenever he sang. When was there to be an end of nothing being publicly admired but what Seneca was thought to have originated! Surely Nero's boyhood was over, and he was all but in the prime of youthful manhood. He ought to shake off a tutor, furnished as he was with sufficiently noble instructors in his own ancestors."

Seneca meanwhile, aware of these slanders, which were revealed to him by those who had some respect for merit, coupled with the fact that the emperor more and more shunned his intimacy, besought the opportunity of an interview. This was granted, and he spoke as follows:

"It is fourteen years ago, Cæsar, that I was first associated with your prospects, and eight years since you have been emperor. In the interval you have heaped on me such honors and riches that nothing is wanting to my happiness but a right use of it. I will refer to great examples taken not from my own but from your position. Your great-grandfather Augustus granted to Marcus Agrippa the calm repose of Mit-y-le'ne, to Caius Mæcenas what was nearly equivalent to a foreign retreat in the capital itself. One of these men shared his wars; the other struggled with many laborious duties at Rome; both received rewards which were indeed splendid, but only proportioned to their great merits. For myself, what other recompense had I for your munificence than a culture nursed, so to speak, in the shade of retirement, and to which a glory attaches itself, because I thus seemed to have helped on the early training of your youth, an ample reward for the service.

"You on the other hand have surrounded me with vast influence and boundless wealth, so that I often think within myself, Am I, who am but of an equestrian and provincial family, numbered among the chief men of Rome? Among nobles who can show a long succession of glories, has my new name become famous? Where is the mind once content with an humble lot? Is this the man who is building up his garden terraces, who paces grandly through the suburban parks, and revels in the affluence of such broad lands and such widely spread investments? Only one apology occurs to me, that it would not have been right in me to have thwarted your bounty.

"And yet we have both filled up our respective measures, you in giving as much as a prince can bestow on a friend, and I in receiving as much as a friend can receive from a prince. All else only fosters envy, which, like all things human, sinks powerless beneath your greatness, though on me it weighs heavily. To me relief is a necessity. Just as I should implore support if exhausted by warfare or travel, so in this journey of life, old as I am and unequal even to the lightest cares, since I cannot any longer bear the burden of my wealth, I crave assistance. Order my property to be managed by your agents and to be included in your estate. Still I shall not sink myself into poverty, but having surrendered the splendors which dazzle me, I will henceforth again devote to my mind all the leisure and attention now reserved for my gardens and country houses. You have yet before you a vigorous prime, and that on which for so many years your eyes were fixed, supreme power. We, your older friends, can answer for our quiet behavior. It will likewise redound to your honor that you have raised to the highest places men who could also bear moderate fortune."

Nero's reply was substantially this: "My being able to meet your elaborate speech with an instant rejoinder is, I consider, primarily your gift, for you taught me how to express myself not only after reflection but at a moment's notice. My greatgrandfather Augustus allowed Agrippa and Mæcenas to enjoy rest after their labors, but he did it at an age carrying with it an authority sufficient to justify any boon, of any sort, he might have bestowed. But neither of them did he strip of the rewards he had given. It was by war and its perils they had earned them; for in these the youth of Augustus was spent. And if I had passed my years in arms, your sword and right hand would not have failed me. But, as my actual condition required, you watched over my boyhood, then over my youth, with wisdom, counsel, and advice. And indeed your gifts to me will, as long as life holds out, be lasting possessions; those which you owe to me, your parks, investments, your country houses, are liable to accidents. Though they seem much, many far inferior to you in merit have obtained more.   I am ashamed to quote the names of freedmen who parade a greater wealth.   Hence I actually blush to think that, standing as you do first in my affections, you do not as yet surpass all in fortune.

"Yours too is still a vigorous manhood, quite equal to the labors of business and to the fruit of those labors; and, as for myself, I am but treading the threshold of empire. But perhaps you count yourself inferior to Vitellius, thrice a consul, and me to Claudius. Such wealth as long thrift has procured for Volusius, my bounty, you think, cannot fully make up to you. Why not rather, if the frailty of my youth goes in any respect astray, call me back and guide yet more zealously with your help the manhood which you have instructed?   It will not be your moderation, if you restore me your wealth, not your love of quiet, if you forsake your emperor, but my avarice, the fear of my cruelty, which will be in all men's mouths.   Even if your self-control were praised to the utmost, still it would not be seemly in a wise man to get glory for himself in the very act of bringing disgrace on his friend."

To these words the emperor added embraces and kisses; for he was formed by nature and trained by habit to veil his hatred under delusive flattery.   Seneca thanked him, the usual end of an interview with a despot. But he entirely altered the practices of his former greatness; he kept the crowds of his visitors at a distance, avoided trains of followers, seldom appeared in Rome, as though weak health or philosophical studies detained him at home.

It is quite impossible, within the space at our command, to make anything like an adequate impression of the dreadful and shameful tragedy that drags itself interminably along, through all the pages of Tacitus that tell the story of Nero. Shame after shame, crime after crime, file before your eyes in ghastly procession.   You shudder, but you are fascinated to gaze.

Marie Antoinette had in some respects her ancient counterpart in Octavia, the fair young wife of Nero. Poppæa was intolerant of any rival to her claim of absolute power over the emperor. Octavia must be driven from Nero's side, that Poppæa may marry him. For this purpose, an infamous accusation of intrigue on her part with a slave, is brought against Octavia. Her slave-girls were tortured to make them swear against their mistress. But one of them bravely swore that her mistress's person was purer than the mouth of the man who accused her. Octavia could not be condemned; but the emperor could divorce her. Divorced she was, and banished. The common people muttered dangerously in her favor, and the coward tyrant was fain to take her back. But the populace proved imprudent friends to Octavia. They flung down the statues of Poppæa and decked the images of the empress. They even rioted into the palace, with menacing shouts of joy. The soldiers dispersed them thence. But the popular triumph had already been carried too far. The reaction was fatal to Octavia.

A new crime was charged upon her. The emperor summoned Anicetus, the man that before had helped make away with his mother, and suborned him to confess an intrigue with Octavia. He should be secured from evil consequence and be well rewarded; if he refused, he should die. Anicetus was not wanting to the emperor's wish. Tacitus, with that condensed pessimistic sarcasm of his, simply adds: "He [Anicetus] was then banished to Sardinia, where he endured exile without poverty and died a natural death." One is reminded of Juvenal's kindred remark concerning an infamous exile, prospering in spite of his crimes, that he "basked in the wrath of heaven."

Octavia was branded adulteress by the false husband's own perjury, and sent in exile to an obscure island. Tacitus, with noble restrained pathos, says:

No exile ever filled the eyes of beholders with tears of greater compassion. Some still remembered Agrippina, banished by Tiberius, and the yet fresher memory of Julia, whom Claudius exiled, was present to men's thoughts. But they had life's prime for their stay; they had seen some happiness, and the horror of the moment was alleviated by recollections of a better lot in the past. For Octavia, from the first, her marriage-day was a kind of funeral, brought, as she was, into a house where she had nothing but scenes of mourning, her father and, an instant afterward, her brother, having been snatched from her by poison; then, a slave-girl raised above the mistress; Poppæa married only to insure a wife's ruin, and, to end all, an accusation more horrible than any death.

The brief sequel is unspeakably sad:

And now the girl, in her twentieth year, with centurions and soldiers around her, already removed from among the living by the forecast of doom, still could not reconcile herself to death. After an interval of a few days she received an order that she was to die, although she protested that she was now a widow and only a sister, and appealed to their common ancestors, the Germanici, and finally to the name of Agrippina, during whose life she had endured a marriage, which was miserable enough indeed, but not fatal. She was then tightly bound with cords, and the veins of every limb were opened; but as her blood was congealed by terror and flowed too slowly, she was killed outright by the steam of an intensely hot bath. To this was added the yet more appalling horror of Poppæa beholding the severed head which was conveyed to Rome.

If there were wanting anything to complete the shame and horror of such deeds, the servile senate supplied the deficiency. Tacitus, now, speaking with a scorn too scornful to condescend to express itself explicitly:

And for all this offerings were voted to the temples. I record the fact with a special object. Whoever would study the calamities of that period in my pages or those of other authors, is to take it for granted that as often as the emperor directed banishments or executions, so often was there a thanksgiving to the gods, and what formerly commemorated some prosperous event, was then a token of public disaster. Still, if any decree of the Senate was marked by some new flattery, or by the lowest servility, I shall not pass it over in silence.

Foils to the indescribable baseness of the senate, and reliefs to the indescribable depravity of the emperor, are provided by Tacitus, not only in the names of Burrus and Seneca, but also in the name of now and then a solitary example of surviving Roman virtue, like Memmius, Reg'u-lus, Thra-se'a. The whole effect resulting is scarcely more than to deepen a little the dark of the picture by contrast of bright. Corbulo likewise moves with the air of antique Roman grandeur, through that part of the imperial drama which meantime is enacted in the East. The reverberation of his wars reaches Rome like the sound of "thunder heard remote." We have no space in these pages to introduce the nobler background against which, on the canvas of Tacitus, Nero's effeminacy and depravity show conspicuous with a shame the more fatal to his memory. But consider in mercy—what boy ever came to " that heritage of woe," supreme despotic power, under auspices blacker than those which frowned on the youth of this imperial wretch ?

The destruction of Pompeii (pe′-yi) is thus briefly narrated :

An earthquake too demolished a large part of Pompeii, a populous town in Campania.

Nero had a daughter born to him by Poppæa. The little creature's life happily was brief, but the eager servility of the senate, and the drunken pride of the despot, alike at her birth and at her death, appear in strong colors. Tacitus :

The place of Poppæa's confinement was the colony of Antium, where the emperor himself was born. Already had the Senate commended Poppæa's safety to the gods, and had made vows in the State's name, which were repeated again and again and duly discharged. To these was added a public thanksgiving, and a temple was decreed to the goddess of fecundity, as well as games and contests after the type of the ceremonies commemorative of Actium, and golden images of the two Fortunes were to be set up on the throne of Jupiter of the Capitol. Shows too of the circus were to be exhibited in honor of the Claudian and Domitian families at Antium, like those at Bo-vil′læ in commemoration of the Ju′li-i. Transient distinctions all of them, as within four months the infant died. Again there was an outburst of flattery, men voting the honors of deification, of a shrine, a temple, and a priest.

The emperor, too, was as excessive in his grief as he had been in his joy. It was observed that when all the Senate rushed out to Antium to honor the recent birth, Thrasea was forbidden to go, and received with fearless spirit an affront which foreboded his doom. Then followed, as rumor says, an expression from the emperor, in which he boasted to Seneca of his reconciliation with Thrasea, on which Seneca congratulated him. And now henceforth the glory and the peril of these illustrious men grew greater.

There still recur at intervals those interludes of distant thunder muttered on the frontier of the empire, in the warlike operations of Corbulo. Frequently the eye is caught with dense and weighty sayings of the historian, which the temptation is great to transfer to these pages. But the effect would be, of course, much impaired by removal from the setting in which they originally appear. Of Corbulo's manner in public discourse Tacitus—himself, let it be remembered, of the highest repute as an orator—says, "He spoke with much impressiveness, which in him, as a military man, was as good as eloquence." Macaulay might have said that of the Duke of Wellington.

Nero took the pleasures of empire with a boyish delight that was not far off from malignity. It was perhaps an emotion as much malicious as insane, the gratification he experienced in making the proud patricians of Rome applaud him while he disgraced himself in their eyes by appearing, in private and in public, as a singer. (It was now the year 64, and Nero was a young fellow of about twenty-six.) But Tacitus says of Nero, that "even amid his pleasures there was no cessation to his crimes." It is only because the limits of our space forbid, that we omit to tell how instance after instance occurs of Romans, the most conspicuous for virtue, forced under imperial pressure to make away with themselves by suicide—the preferred method of which suicide was to open the veins, or the arteries, and bleed to death.

Thus is related the famous infamy of the burning of Rome under Nero, with its horrible sequel:

A disaster followed, whether accidental or treacherously contrived by the emperor, is uncertain, as authors have given both accounts, worse, however, and more dreadful than any which have ever happened to this city by the violence of fire. It had its beginning in that part of the circus which adjoins the Palatine and Cælian hills, where, amid the shops containing inflammable wares, the conflagration both broke out and instantly became so fierce and so rapid from the wind that it seized in its grasp the entire length of the circus. For here there were no houses fenced in by solid masonry, or temples surrounded by walls, or any other obstacle to interpose delay. The blaze in its fury ran first through the level portions of the city, then rising to the hills, while it again devastated every place below them, it outstripped all preventive measures; so rapid was the mischief and so completely at its mercy the city, with those narrow winding passages and irregular streets, which characterized old Rome. Added to this were the wailings of terror-stricken women, the feebleness of age, the helpless inexperience of childhood, the crowds who sought to save themselves and others, dragging out the infirm or waiting for them, and by their hurry in the one case, by their delay in the other, aggravating the confusion. Often, while they looked behind them, they were intercepted by flames on their side or in their face. Or if they reached a refuge close at hand, when this too was seized by the fire, they found, that even places which they had imagined to be remote, were involved in the same calamity. At last, doubting what they should avoid or whither betake themselves, they crowded the streets or flung themselves down in the fields, while some who had lost their all, even their very daily bread, and others out of love for their kinsfolk, whom they had been unable to rescue, perished, though escape was open to them. And no one dared to stop the mischief, because of incessant menaces from a number of persons who forbade the extinguishing of the flames, because again others openly hurled brands, and kept shouting that there was one who gave them authority, either seeking to plunder more freely, or obeying orders.

Nero at this time was at Antium, and did not return to Rome until the fire approached his house, which he had built to connect the palace with the gardens of Mæcenas. It could not, however, be stopped from devouring the palace, the house, and every thing around it. However, to relieve the people, driven out homeless as they were, he threw open to them the Campus Martius and the public buildings of Agrippa, and even his own gardens, and raised temporary structures to receive the destitute multitude. Supplies of food were brought up from Ostia and the neighboring towns, and the price of corn was reduced to three sesterces a peck. These acts, though popular, produced no effect, since a rumor had gone forth every where that, at the very time that the city was in flames, the emperor appeared on a private stage and sang of the destruction of Troy, comparing present misfortunes with the calamities of antiquity.

At last, after five days, an end was put to the conflagration at the foot of the Esquiline hill, by the destruction of all buildings on a vast space, so that the violence of the fire was met by clear ground and open sky. But before people had laid aside their fears, the flames returned, with no less fury this second time, and especially in the spacious districts of the city. Consequently, though there was less loss of life, the temples of the gods, and the porticoes which were devoted to enjoyment, fell in a yet more wide-spread ruin. And to this conflagration there attached the greater infamy because it broke out on the Æmilian property of Tigellinus, and it seemed that Nero was aiming at the glory of founding a new city and calling it by his name. Rome, indeed, is divided into fourteen districts, four of which remained uninjured, three were leveled to the ground, while in the other seven were left only a few shattered, half-burnt relics of houses.

Tacitus relates that Nero "availed himself of his country's desolation, and erected a mansion in which the jewels and gold, long familiar objects, quite vulgarized by our extravagance, were not so marvelous as the fields and lakes, with woods on one side to resemble a wilderness, and, on the other, open spaces and extensive views." Many audacious public works were undertaken, some of them in absolute defiance of the laws of nature. The city was splendidly rebuilt, and the gods were elaborately propitiated—in vain. Tacitus says—and here occurs the sole mention deemed necessary by the historian to be made, of a certain religious sect, destined, however little he dreamed it, to multiply, and to endure, untold centuries after that imperial Rome of which he wrote should have become a name and a memory—Tacitus says :

All human efforts, all the lavish gifts of the emperor, and the propitiations of the gods, did not banish the sinister belief that the conflagration was the result of an order. Consequently, to get rid of the report, Nero fastened the guilt and inflicted the most exquisite tortures on a class hated for their abominations, called Christians by the populace. Christus, from whom the name had its origin, suffered the extreme penalty during the reign of Tiberius at the hands of one of our procurators, Pon'ti-us Pi-la'tus, and a most mischievous superstition, thus checked for the moment, again broke out not only in Judæa, the first source of the evil, but even in Rome, where all things hideous and shameful from every part of the world find their center and become popular. Accordingly, an arrest was first made of all who pleaded guilty; then, upon their information, an immense multitude was convicted, not so much of the crime of firing the city, as of hatred against mankind. Mockery of every sort was added to their deaths. Covered with the skins of beasts, they were torn by dogs and perished, or were nailed to crosses, or were doomed to the flames and burnt, to serve as a nightly illumination, when daylight had expired.

Nero offered his gardens for the spectacle, and was exhibiting a show in the circus, while he mingled with the people in the dress of a charioteer or stood aloft on a car. Hence, even for criminals who deserved extreme and exemplary punishment, there arose a feeling of compassion; for it was not, as it seemed, for the public good, but to glut one man's cruelty, that they were being destroyed.

The world now was ransacked and plundered to glut the passion of the emperor for profuse expenditure. The temples of the gods did not escape. Seneca felt that his own person was in danger, should he stick at committing sacrilege at the beck of the emperor. He, therefore—"it was said," as Tacitus cautiously relates it—:

To avert from himself the obloquy of sacrilege, begged for the seclusion of a remote rural retreat, and, when it was refused, feigning ill health, as though he had a nervous ailment, would not quit his chamber. According to some writers, poison was prepared for him at Nero's command by his own freedman, whose name was Cleonnicus. This Seneca avoided through the freedman's disclosure, or his own apprehension, while he used to support life on the very simple diet of wild fruits, with water from a running stream when thirst prompted.

Wantonness of despotism, such as Nero's, could not but provoke conspiracy against the despot. Tacitus gives a circumstantial account of a plot which, having gone near to success, failed, at the critical point, through the perfidy of a freedman. The fidelity unto death of a freedwoman affords a striking contrast. Tacitus thus admiringly describes this woman's conduct:

Nero, meanwhile, remembering that E-pich'a-ris was in custody

on the information of Vo-lu'si-us Proc'u-lus, and assuming that a
woman's frame must be unequal to the agony, ordered her to be
torn on the rack.   But neither the scourge nor fire, nor the fury of
the men as they increased the torture that they might not be a
woman's scorn, overcame her positive denial of the charge.   Thus
the first day's inquiry was futile.   On the morrow, as she was
being dragged back on a chair to the same torments (for with her
limbs all dislocated she could not stand), she tied a band, which
she had stript off her bosom, in a sort of noose to the arched back
of the chair, put her neck in it, and then straining with the whole
weight of her body, wrung out of her frame its little remaining
breath.   All the nobler was the example set by a freedwoman at
such a crisis in screening strangers and those whom she hardly
knew, when freeborn men, Roman knights, and senators, yet un-
scathed by torture, betrayed, every one, his dearest kinsfolk.

Following the exposure of the plot, comes a sickening list of
horrors in revenge, enacted under order of Nero. These involve the doom, now no longer to be postponed, of Seneca, the
philosopher. Seneca was not a convicted conspirator. He
was, perhaps, not even seriously suspected of conspiring.
But Nero hated him, and would at all cost be rid of him.
Seneca was reported to have said, ambiguously and darkly,
concerning a man involved in the plot: "I will not talk with
him, but my own safety is bound up in his." This was
enough. Seneca was given the opportunity, at his option, to
acknowledge or to repudiate the language attributed to him.
He answered proudly and bravely. Nero, on receiving the
report of his answer, asked, "Is he meditating suicide?" The
officer said he saw in Seneca no signs of fear and no signs
of low spirits. He was bidden go back and tell Seneca to
make away with himself. Now Tacitus:

Seneca, quite unmoved, asked for tablets on which to inscribe
his will, and, on the centurion's refusal, turned to his friends,
protesting that as he was forbidden to requite them, he bequeathed
to them the only, but still the noblest, possession yet remaining to
him, the pattern of his life, which, if they remembered, they
would win a name for moral worth and steadfast friendship. At
the same time [braced, beyond doubt, by the remembered example
of Socrates], he called them back from their tears to manly resolu-

tion, now with friendly talk, and now with the sterner language of rebuke. "Where," he asked again and again, "are your maxims of philosophy, or the preparation of so many years' study against evils to come? Who knew not Nero's cruelty? After a mother's and a brother's murder, nothing remains but to add the destruction of a guardian and a tutor."

Having spoken these and like words, meant, so to say, for all, he embraced his wife; then softening awhile from the stern resolution of the hour, he begged and implored her to spare herself the burden of perpetual sorrow, and, in the contemplation of a life virtuously spent, to endure a husband's loss with honorable consolations. She declared, in answer, that she too had decided to die, and claimed for herself the blow of the executioner. Thereupon Seneca, not to thwart her noble ambition, from an affection too which would not leave behind him for insult one whom he dearly loved, replied: "I have shown you ways of smoothing life; you prefer the glory of dying. I will not grudge you such a noble example. Let the fortitude of so courageous an end be alike in both of us, but let there be more in your decease to win fame."

Then by one and the same stroke they sundered with a dagger the arteries of their arms. Seneca, as his aged frame, attenuated by frugal diet, allowed the blood to escape but slowly, severed also the veins of his legs and knees. Worn out by cruel anguish, afraid too that his sufferings might break his wife's spirit, and that, as he looked on her tortures, he might himself sink into irresolution, he persuaded her to retire into another chamber. Even at the last moment his eloquence failed him not; he summoned his secretaries, and dictated much to them which, as it has been published for all readers in his own words, I forbear to paraphrase.

Seneca's wife was not thus to die with her husband. She must survive him ; and must so incur a reaction of suspicion against herself, that will cloud the fame of her courage. Nero, not hating her, and not wishing to aggravate with the people the odium of his cruelty, forbade her to die. Tacitus again :

At the soldiers' prompting her slaves and freedmen bound up her arms, and stanched the bleeding, whether with her knowledge is doubtful. For as the vulgar are ever ready to think the worst, there were persons who believed that, as long as she dreaded Nero's relentlessness, she sought the glory of sharing her husband's death, but that after a time, when a more soothing prospect presented itself, she yielded to the charms of life. To this she added a few subsequent years, with a most praiseworthy remembrance of her husband, and with a countenance and frame white to a degree of pallor which denoted a loss of much vital energy.

The historian returns to finish the slow suicide of Seneca :

Seneca meantime, as the tedious process of death still lingered on, begged Sta'ti-us An-næ'us, whom he had long esteemed for his faithful friendship and medical skill, to produce a poison with which he had some time before provided himself, the same drug which extinguished the life of those who were condemned by a public sentence of the people of Athens. It was brought to him and he drank it in vain, chilled as he was throughout his limbs, and his frame closed against the efficacy of the poison. At last he entered a pool of heated water, from which he sprinkled the nearest of his slaves, adding the exclamation, "I offer this liquid as a libation to Jupiter the Deliverer." He was then carried into a bath, with the steam of which he was suffocated, and he was burned without any of the usual funeral rites. So he had directed in a codicil of his will, when even in the height of his wealth and power he was thinking of his life's close.

Rumor could not fail to breed plentifully in the teeming ferment of such crime and such tragedy. Subrius Flavus was a chief conspirator from among the soldiers of Nero, while Piso was the figure-head put forward as pretender to the empire in Nero's room. Now let Tacitus give us, in his own words, a popular rumor affecting these two men, in connection with Seneca :

There was a rumor that Subrius Flavus had held a secret consultation with the centurions, and had planned, not without Seneca's knowledge, that when Nero had been slain by Piso's instrumentality, Piso also was to be murdered, and the empire handed over to Seneca, as a man singled out for his splendid virtues by all persons of integrity. Even a saying of Flavus was popularly current, "that it mattered not as to the disgrace if a harp-player were removed and a tragic actor succeeded him." For as Nero used to sing to the harp, so did Piso in the dress of a tragedian.

Subrius Flavus did not escape. But he died at last with a scornful bravery that has immortalized his fame. Tacitus :

Questioned by Nero as to the motives which had led him on to forget his oath of allegiance, "I hated you," he replied; "yet

not a soldier was more loyal to you while you deserved to be loved.
I began to hate you when you became the murderer of your
mother and your wife, a charioteer, an actor, and an incendiary."
I have given the man's very words, because they were not, like
those of Seneca, generally published, though the rough and vigorous sentiments of a soldier ought to be no less known.

Throughout the conspiracy nothing, it was certain, fell with more
terror on the ears of Nero, who was as unused to be told of the
crimes he perpetrated as he was eager in their perpetration. The
punishment of Flavus was intrusted to Ve-ia'ni-us Niger, a
tribune. At his direction, a pit was dug in a neighboring field.
Flavus, on seeing it, censured it as too shallow and confined,
saying to the soldiers around him, "Even this is not according to
military rule." When bidden to offer his neck resolutely, "I
wish," said he, "that your stroke may be as resolute." The
tribune trembled greatly, and having only just severed his head at
two blows, vaunted his brutality to Nero, saying that he had slain
him with a blow and a half.

The opportunity seemed favorable to Nero for clearing off
at once the score of his personal hatreds. Ves-ti'nus, the
consul, could not be brought under any show of suspicion.
But the emperor hated him as a boon companion "who often
bantered him with that rough humor which [an observation
showing the historian wise in human nature], when it draws
largely on facts, leaves a bitter memory behind it." Nero
used his imperial reserve of outright and peremptory despotism, for the destruction of Vestinus. The soldiers came upon
the consul in the midst of a banquet, at which he was entertaining friends in his own house. The tribune announced his
sentence. Now Tacitus :

He rose without a moment's delay, and every preparation was at
once made. He shut himself into his chamber; a physician was at
his side; his veins were opened; with life still strong in him,
he was carried into a bath, and plunged into warm water, without
uttering a word of pity for himself. Meanwhile the guards surrounded those who had sat at his table, and it was only at a late
hour of the night that they were dismissed, when Nero, having
pictured to himself and laughed over their terror at the expectation
of a fatal end to their banquet, said that they had suffered enough
punishment for their consul's entertainment.

The poet Lucan, author of the " Pharsalia," an epic poem on the civil war between Cæsar and Pompey, was another victim. He died at twenty-seven years of age, with theatric circumstance well befitting the type of his genius. Tacitus:

As the blood flowed freely from him, and he felt a chill creeping through his feet and hands, and the life gradually ebbing from his extremities, though the heart was still warm and he retained his mental power, Lu-ca'nus recalled some poetry he had composed in which he had told the story of a wounded soldier dying a similar kind of death, and he recited the very lines. These were his last words.

The abjectness of Rome amid this carnival of blood passes belief. " One after another," so Tacitus relates, " on the destruction of a brother, a kinsman, or a friend, would return thanks to the gods, deck his house with laurels, prostrate himself at the knees of the emperor, and weary his hand with kisses."

" Poppæa died," so Tacitus relates, " from a casual outburst of rage in her husband, who felled her with a kick when she was pregnant." Nero eulogized her publicly from the rostra.

We break into the gloomy catalogue of imperial crimes recounted by Tacitus, to give the story, surpassing in tragedy, of the threefold associate death of Lucius Vetus, of Sextia, his mother-in-law, and of Pollutia, his daughter. Pollutia was the widow of a man formerly murdered by Nero. She interceded in vain with the emperor on her father's behalf. Tacitus says :

He was at the same time informed that judicial proceedings in the Senate and a dreadful sentence were hanging over him. Some there were who advised him to name the emperor as his chief heir, and so secure the remainder for his grandchildren. But he spurned the notion, and unwilling to disgrace a life which had clung to freedom by a final act of servility, he bestowed on his slaves all his ready money, and ordered each to convey away for himself whatever he could carry, leaving only three couches for the last scene. Then in the same chamber, with the same weapon, they sundered their veins, and speedily hurried into a bath, covered each, as delicacy required, with a single garment, the father gazing intently on his daughter, the grandmother on her grandchild, she again on both, while with rival earnestness they prayed that the ebbing life might have a quick departure, each wishing to leave a relative still surviving, but just on the verge of death. Fortune preserved the due order; the oldest died first, then the others according to priority of age. They were prosecuted after their burial, and the sentence was that "they should be punished in ancient fashion." Nero interposed his veto, allowing them to die without his interference. Such were the mockeries added to murders already perpetrated.

Storms accompanied, and pestilence, to signalize, more gloomily still, this year of shameful human deeds. Tacitus interrupts himself, amid his narrative of horrible things, to say :

Even if I had to relate foreign wars and deaths encountered in the service of the State with such a monotony of disaster, I should myself have been overcome by disgust, while I should look for weariness in my readers, sickened as they would be by the melancholy and continuous destruction of our citizens, however glorious to themselves. But now a servile submissiveness and so much wanton bloodshed at home fatigue the mind and paralyze it with grief. The only indulgence I would ask from those who will acquaint themselves with these horrors is, that I be not thought to hate men who perished so tamely. Such was the wrath of heaven against the Roman State that one may not pass over it with a single mention, as one might the defeat of armies and the capture of cities. Let us grant this privilege to the posterity of illustrious men, that just as in their funeral obsequies such men are not confounded in a common burial, so in the record of their end they may receive and retain a special memorial.

A singular case of gay and gallant greeting to compulsory death occurred—without mention of which, our picture of the time would want something of proper contrast to make it complete. Of this incident, Caius Pe-tro′ni-us was the hero. A certain literary interest attaches to the name of Petronius. He was putative author of a phrase that is one of the most familiar commonplaces of literature—" curious felicity," as it is transferred, rather than translated, from the original Latin, *curiosa felicitas.* The words thus combined were meant to express the idea of that perfection in phrase which is the result of great care, joined to excellent good luck, in the choice of language to match your thought. Tacitus says:

With regard to Caius Petronius, I ought to dwell a little on his antecedents. His days he passed in sleep, his nights in the business and pleasures of life. Indolence had raised him to fame, as energy raises others, and he was reckoned not a debauchee and spendthrift, like most of those who squander their substance, but a man of refined luxury. And indeed his talk and his doings, the freer they were and the more show of carelessness they exhibited, were the better liked, for their look of a natural simplicity. Yet as proconsul of Bithynia, and soon afterward as consul, he showed himself a man of vigor and equal to business. Then falling back into vice, or affecting vice, he was chosen by Nero to be one of his few intimate associates, as a critic in matters of taste, while the emperor thought nothing charming or elegant in luxury unless Petronius had expressed to him his approval of it. Hence jealousy on the part of Tigellinus, who looked on him as a rival and even his superior in the science of pleasure. And so he worked on the prince's cruelty, which dominated every other passion, charging Petronius with having been the friend of Scævi'nus, bribing a slave to become informer, robbing him of the means of defense, and hurrying into prison the greater part of his domestics.

It happened at the time that the emperor was on his way to Campania, and that Petronius, after going as far as Cumæ, was there detained. He bore no longer the suspense of fear or hope. Yet he did not fling away life with precipitate haste, but having made an incision in his veins and then, according to his humor, bound them up, he again opened them, while he conversed with his friends, not in a serious strain or on topics that might win for him the glory of courage. And he listened to them as they repeated, not thoughts on the immortality of the soul or on the theories of philosophers, but light poetry and playful verses. To some of his slaves he gave liberal presents, a flogging to others. He dined, indulged himself in sleep, that death, though forced on him, might have a natural appearance. Even in his will he did not, as did many in their last moments, flatter Nero or Tigellinus or any other of the men in power. On the contrary, he described fully the prince's shameful excesses, with the names of his male and female companions and their novelties in debauchery, and sent the account under seal to Nero. Then he broke his signet-ring, that it might not be subsequently available for imperiling others.

One cannot help indulging a transient admiration of something in the dying of this Roman exquisite, of an evil time, that goes toward redeeming the ignoble of his life.

Thra-se'a is almost as much the chosen historical favorite of Tacitus, as William of Orange notoriously was of Macaulay. The story of the end of this "noblest Roman of them all" the historian begins with this impressive preface: "Nero, after having butchered so many illustrious men, at last aspired to extirpate virtue itself by murdering Thrasea Pætus and Ba-re'a So-ra'nus."

How Thrasea died is thus related by Tacitus:

As evening approached, the consul's quæstor was sent to Thrasea, who was passing his time in his garden. He had had a crowded gathering of distinguished men and women, giving special attention to Demetrius, a professor of the Cynic philosophy. With him, as might be inferred from his earnest expression of face and from words heard when they raised their voices, he was speculating on the nature of the soul and on the separation of the spirit from the body, till Domitius Cæ'cil-i-a'nus, one of his intimate friends, came to him and told him in detail what the Senate had decided. When all who were present wept and bitterly complained, Thrasea urged them to hasten their departure and not mingle their own perils with the fate of a doomed man. Arria too who aspired to follow her husband's end and the example of Arria, her mother, he counseled to preserve her life, and not rob the daughter of their love of her only stay.

Then he went out into a colonnade, where he was found by the quæstor, joyful rather than otherwise, as he had learned that Hel-vid'i-us, his son-in-law, was merely excluded from Italy. When he heard the Senate's decision, he led Helvidius and Demetrius into a chamber, and having laid bare the arteries of each arm, he let the blood flow freely, and, as he sprinkled it on the ground, he called the quæstor to his side and said: "We pour out a libation to Jupiter the Deliverer. Behold, young man, and may the gods avert the omen, but you have been born into times in which it is well to fortify the spirit with examples of courage." Then as the slowness of his end brought with it grievous anguish, turning his eyes on Demetrius. . . .

The "Annals" of Tacitus, as they exist to moderns, end abruptly thus, on a sentence unfinished, with Thrasea in the unfinished act of dying.   The rest of Nero's reign, a period of two years, we lose from the incomparable record of Tacitus. That living bulwark of the empire, Corbulo, fell a victim to the jealousy of the emperor, being met at Corinth on his return from the East with the imperial sentence to suicide. In A. D. 68, Nero, risen against by his subjects, and himself now under sentence of death from the senate, died wretchedly at last by his own hand.

A Rome how different from the Rome of Livy, is the Rome that Tacitus describes ! But the degeneracy, so great, of later Rome was, after all, only a ripeness in the fruit, of a disease that lurked from the first in the heart of the flower.

CHAPTER IX.

WE put Plautus and Terence together in treatment, both because we have not room to treat them separately, and because they are naturally associated, as being to us the two sole surviving representatives of the ancient Roman drama. Plautus was the elder. Plautus, in fact, is the very eldest Roman writer known to moderns by any complete work remaining from his hand. He was not many years before Terence; but Terence, by something more modern in his manner, seems two or three literary generations nearer to our time.

Plautus as well as Terence borrowed freely from the Greek. By a curious fortune in survival, the Greek Menander lives now only, or almost only, in the reproductions of his works proceeding from these two Roman borrowers. Menander was a very different writer of comedy from Aristophanes. The colossal drollery, the personal hard-hitting, the illimitable freedom, of Aristophanes, were in Menander exchanged for something much nearer to that decent raillery at current morals and manners which is the prevailing character of modern comedy. The "New Comedy," Menander's school was called, to distinguish it from the school of Aristophanes, which was called the "Old," in contrast. We have in part to guess how much Plautus and Terence owed to Menander. It seems clear that, as between the two, Plautus contributed more than did Terence, of the personal, and more, likewise, of the national, element, to qualify his adaptations from the Greek. In both cases alike, however, the result is a mixed product, rather puzzling to our natural sense of fitness and consistency. The Roman play had its scene laid somewhere in Hellas, the names of persons were chiefly Greek, the life represented was rather Greek than Roman; and yet Roman civil institutions and Roman traits of manners were introduced, quite as if the comic writer were unconscious of unkindly mixing things that differed; or else as if this very mixing itself were trusted to by him for enhancing his comic effect. Probably both writer and spectator were sufficiently uncritical, neither, on the one hand, to be disturbed by the incongruity, nor, on the other hand, distinctly to enjoy the incongruity, as an element of humor. We know from Terence that his audience was difficult; but it was by no means to their being over-critical that the difficulty of his audience was due. Quite to the contrary. They were childish and frisky to a degree. Terence, in one of his comedies, begs his audience to give him a chance with them. They had, it would seem, those half-civilized Romans, a reprehensible habit of flinging out of the playhouse upon occasion, in the midst of the play—if, for example, they happened to hear the sound outside of anything going forward (boxing, it might be, rope-dancing, a gladiatorial show, a procession in the street) that promised diversion at less cost to them of brain than the comedy in progress required. So the comedist of Terence's time had his trials.

Plautus was of the people. Terence was cultivated somewhat away from the people. There is a considerably stronger smack of real Roman character and life in Plautus than in Terence. Plautus lived to old age, and produced a good many plays. Terence died young, and brought out only six plays in all. Plautus had to work for his daily bread. Terence became the favorite of the great and lived very much at his ease. Neither poet was a native Roman. Plautus was of the

district of Umbria, in Italy. Terence is said to have been
a Carthaginian. Plautus is a nickname, meaning "flatfoot."
The name Terence—Te-ren'tius is the Latin form—was prob-
ably given to the bearer from the name of his patron, the
Roman patrician that freed him. For Terence was either born
slave, or else had become slave by fortune of war. Titus
Mac'ci-us Plautus was the full name of the one—Publius
Terentius A'fer [African] of the other.

Plautus was a natural dramatist. He is full of movement
and life. There is in his comedies an incessant bustle of
change going forward. The plot may stand still, but the play
does not. There is at least activity, if there is no action.
Your attention is never suffered for a moment to flag.

Terence, on the other hand, depends more upon what the
eye cannot see. There is an element of reflection introduced.
Terence, herein, as we guess, more nicely responds, than does
Plautus, to the genius and method of their common Greek
original, Menander. Both writers are sufficiently coarse; but
Plautus, as more Roman, is coarser than Terence. Neither
seems to care for any moral lesson to be enforced. Each seeks
to amuse, not at all to amend, his audience. There can be
little doubt that the practical tendency of both alike was to
deprave the moral tone of Roman character. The influence
exerted for bane by such importations from Greece as Plautus
and Terence purveyed for the amusement of Rome, may be
likened to the influence exerted by licentious French ballets
and licentious French operas, working, through English
adaptations, to debauch the taste and morals of England or
America. It was an evil hour for Rome, when she began to be
accustomed to see reverend old age flouted in the comic theater, and to laugh there at trickeries and knaveries, practiced at
the expense of everything that was holy in home life and
in the conjugal relation. It is a sad lesson in enlightened
pagan manners, the lesson that we learn from Plautus and

Terence. The canker is in them somewhat opened to view, that secretly worked beneath the gallant show of full-flowering Roman life and character.

We are limited in our choice from among the works of Plautus and Terence, by the inseparable moral character of their comedies. Hardly, indeed, could any single play out of the whole number be presented here entire. We must use care in choosing, and then we must also expurgate with care. On the whole, we shall go pretty safely, if, for Plautus, we take the play selected some time ago for representation by the young ladies of Washington University, in St. Louis. This is "Rudens," or "The Shipwreck," as the name sometimes is given. *Rudens* means "rope." A fisherman's rope plays an important part in the action. A violent tempest at sea occurs, whence the title "Shipwreck." One almost ventures to be reminded of The Tempest of Shakespeare. (By permission, we here use the Washington University translation, throughout the play.)

The speaker of the prologue is Arc-tu'rus, a star, supposed to bode wind and storm. Probably the actor who personated Arcturus displayed a decoration in the form of a brilliant star. The appointments of the comic theater in Rome were simple and rude. In the time of Plautus and Terence, there was not even a permanent building devoted to theatric representation. A wooden structure, hastily thrown together, and temporary in its design, was made to answer the purpose. Not until Pompey's time was there a durable theater of stone. Imagine, then, an actor designated and illustrated with a star, perhaps on his forehead, appearing before the expectant audience, and, at the beginning of the representation, delivering himself of the following prologue :

> Splendid and glowing, a subject am I
> Of the king of the bright constellations,
> Rising as pleases my own sovereign will,

Both on earth and above in the heavens.
Nightly I shine in the clear azure sky,
And there with celestials hold converse;
Daily I walk midst the dwellings of men,
And am worshiped on earth as Arcturus.
Now I will show you the reason I came,
And will tell you the plot of this story.
Diph'i-lus wished that the name of this town
(To the right of you here) be Cyrene.
Here in this villa o'erlooking the sea,
Dwells one Dæmones, exiled from Athens.
Not on account of his own wicked deeds,
But through services rendered to others,
Lost he his fortune and lost he his home,
And grows gray here in want and in sorrow.
Once a young daughter had smoothed from his brow
Every wrinkle that care might have wrought there;
She in her youth had been stolen away,
And been sold to a wicked slave-dealer.
Fate had ordained that the girl should be brought
To this town near the home of her father.
Here, while returning one day from her school,
She was seen by the youth Ples-i-dip'pus;
Beauty and grace gave her wonderful charms,
And in haste to her master he hurried,
Purchased the girl for himself with bright gold,
And bound with an oath the slave-dealer.
This one, however, did shame to his trade,
If he cared e'en a straw for his pledges.
He had a guest, a Sicilian old man,
Who had fled from his home, Ag-ri-gen'tum:
This one declares that the place in the world,
Which is best for his host and his business,
Sicily, home of his youth and his crime,
Is the market for slaves and slave-dealers.
Soon he obtains the vile master's consent,
And they hire a ship, but in secret;
That which is needed by night they convey
To the ship, and make ready for starting.
Vows to the temple of Venus, he says
To the youth, are the cause of his going.
(This is the temple at which he pretends
He is going to pay his devotions.)
Thither he asks that the youth will soon come,
And invites him to join him at breakfast.

> Others make clear to the youth what this means,
> That the scoundrel has only deceived him.
> He, when he comes to the harbor, perceives
> That the ship is quite lost in the distance.
> I, since I know that the girl has by fraud
> Been taken away from Cyrene,
> Raise a great storm that both brings her swift aid,
> And destruction at once to her master,
> He and his guest are thrown out by the waves,
> And barely escape death by swimming.
> She and a hand-maid leap into a skiff,
> And are driven ashore by the tempest,
> Here by the house of her father unknown,
> Whose tiling the storm-wind has injured.
> This is his slave who is just coming out,
> And the youth Plesidippus, the lover,
> Soon will appear. Fare you well, and be strong,
> That your enemies all may be vanquished.

The "Argument" prefixed to the play is further helpful to the understanding of the dramatic design :

"A fisherman drew up from the sea with his net a wallet, which contained the trinkets of his master's daughter, who having been stolen in her youth, was now owned by a slave-dealer. Thrown ashore in a shipwreck, she came, without her knowledge, under the protection of her own father. She was recognized and married to her lover, Ples-i-dip'pus."

Sce-par'nio is a slave of Dæ'mon-es. Dæmones is the man to whom the lost girl of the play will be restored, as his daughter. Sceparnio, with Dæmones, stands on the shore watching the fortunes of a skiff struggling in the surf. His description of what he sees is life-like. It is a very good specimen of dramatic vision. "What is it you see?" asks Dæmones. Sceparnio replies :

Sceparnio. Two women seated alone in a skiff! Poor wretches! how they are tossed about! Well done! Well done! First-rate! The wave has turned the skiff from the rock toward the shore! No pilot could have done better. I never saw higher waves. They're all right, if they avoid those waves. Now! now, look out! See how one of them is thrown out! But she's in shallow water.

She will easily swim out. Well done! She's all right. She has got out of the water. Now she's on the shore. The other one has jumped from the skiff into the water. See her fall on her knees in the water! There, she is up! If she turns this way, she's safe. If she goes to the right, she'll be badly off! She'll wander around to-day, I guess.

Dæmones. What difference does it make to you, Sceparnio?

Sc. If she falls down from that rock whither she is going, she'll shorten her wandering.

Dæ. If you're going to dine with them to-day, Sceparnio, look after them, of course; but if you are going to eat with me, I wish you'd attend to me.

Sc. That's only fair.

Dæ. Then follow me.

Sc. All right.

The cool indifference exhibited by the master Dæmones is well contrasted against the lively interest, of sympathy, or of curiosity, shown by the slave Sceparnio. If readers find provincialisms in the English rendering, such provincialisms they may take to represent the unconventional freedom of the original Latin.

The two women—one of whom is Pa-læs'tra, the lost daughter, still claimed by the slave-dealer La'brax as his property—finally get safe to land, but separately, each thinking the other is drowned. The coming together of the two must have been a very amusing representation, as managed by the playwright and the scene-master between them. A ledge or cliff of rock kept the two women from seeing each other, while still they could hear each the other's voice. The audience, meantime, could see both the two persons of the action. Each has been soliloquizing aloud, within hearing of the other—when Palæstra speaks:

Palæstra. Whose voice sounds near me?

Ampelisca. I am afraid; who is talking here?

Pa. Good Hope, I beg you come to my aid.

Am. It is a woman; a woman's voice reaches my ears. Wont you free me, wretch that I am, from this dread?

Pa. Surely it's a woman's voice I hear. Is it Am-pe-lis'ca, pray?

Am. Do I hear you, Palæstra?

Pa. Why don't I call her by her name, so that she'll know me? Ampelisca!

Am. Hem! Who is it?

Pa. It is I.

Am. Is that you, Palæstra?

Pa. Yes.

Am. Where are you?

Pa. By Pollux, in the greatest evil.

Am. I'm no better off myself. But I long to see you.

Pa. And I you.

Am. Let's follow the voice with the footsteps. Where are you?

Pa. Here I am. Come this way.

Am. I'm coming as well as I can.

Pa. Give me your hand.

Am. Here it is.

Pa. Are you alive? Speak, pray.

Am. You make me want to live, now that I have you. I can scarcely believe that I do have you. Embrace me, my love. How you relieve me of all my troubles.

Pa. That was what I was going to say.

The humor of the foregoing passage, of course, lies in the situation rather than in the dialogue. The success of it with an audience would depend upon the scenery and the acting. Still the merit of the conception—whatever that merit may be—belongs to the original inventor. Who the original inventor was, nobody knows. Perhaps Plautus himself, perhaps Menander, Diph'i-lus, or some other Greek now nameless.

The two girls make their way to a temple of Venus not far off, where they are kindly welcomed by the priestess.

There are some gaps in the text of Plautus, and, besides this, the translators whom we follow, very judiciously make, as we have said, omissions here and there. The scene now to be given is on the border-line between proper and improper; but it will afford an instructive hint of what Roman comedists purveyed for their audience. Ampelisca, Palæstra's companion in shipwreck and in hair-breadth escape, has been despatched by the priestess of Venus to fetch water from the house of Dæmones. She raps at the door and is answered by our friend the slave Sceparnio.

Sceparnio. Who's making such a racket at our door?

Ampelisca. I am.

Sc. Ha! What good fortune is this? By Pollux, what a pretty woman!

Am. Good morning, young man.

Sc. You're welcome, my lady.

Am. I'm coming to your house.

Sc. I'll receive you hospitably; but what do you want, my pretty one?

Am. O, you're too familiar. (*He chucks her under the chin.*)

Sc. Immortal gods! she's the very image of Venus! What lovely eyes! What a pretty figure! She's quite dark—I mean to say, a handsome brunette.

Am. I'm no dish for the village. Take your hands off me!

Sc. Can't one touch you prettily, my pretty one?

Am. At another time I'll give you opportunity for a flirtation. Now I'd like you to say yes or no to the errand I'm sent on.

Sc. What do you want?

Am. Any one with good sense would know by what I carry.

Sc. And any one with good sense would know my errand by my attire.

Am. The priestess of Venus told me to ask for water here.

Sc. But I'm of royal descent, and wont give you a drop unless you beg me. We dug this well at our own risk and with our own tools. You wont get a drop from me without a great deal of coaxing.

Am. Why are you so stingy with your water, which even an enemy gives an enemy?

Sc. And why are you so stingy with your love, which a citizen gives a citizen?

Am. Well, my darling, I'll do everything you wish.

Sc. Good! I'm all right now; she calls me her darling. I'll give you water; you sha'n't love me in vain; give me your pitcher.

Am. Take it. Hasten, pray, and bring it back.

Sc. Wait; I'll soon be back, my dear. (*Exit Sceparnio.*)

While Sceparnio is gone for the water—to Ampelisca's dismay, Labrax, the slave-dealer, appears on the shore. Ampelisca had thought he was happily drowned and out of the way. She runs off, and Sceparnio coming back finds her gone. He had been chuckling to himself over his luck in

having a chance to flirt with Ampelisca.   When he reappears
with the water, he is speaking aloud :

Sc. O, immortal gods! I never believed there was so much
pleasure in drawing water; with how much delight I drew it.
The well never seemed so shallow; why, I got it up without a
bit of trouble. Haven't I been a fool never to have fallen in
love before! Here's your water, my beauty. There, I want you
to carry it off with as much pleasure as I bring it; so that you may
please me. But where are you, my dear? Take this water, if you
please. Where are you? I believe she's in love with me! She's
hiding. Where are you? Wont you take this pitcher? Where
are you? (*Gets more earnest.*) You play nicely, but now really be
serious. Wont you take the pitcher? (*Begins to get angry.*) Where
in the world are you? I don't see her anywhere; by Hercules,
she's making game of me! (*In a rage.*) I'll put this pitcher right
down in the middle of the road. (*Starts off but comes back slowly,
reflecting.*)   But what if some one should carry off this sacred urn
of Venus? It might get me into trouble. By Hercules, I fear lest
this woman has laid some plot that I may be caught with the
sacred urn of Venus in my possession. The officers would, very
justly, make me die in prison, if any one should see me have this.
(*Examines it more closely.*) For here's an inscription on it; this
tells whose it is! Now, by Hercules, I'll call the priestess of
Venus out of doors to take the pitcher. (*Goes up and knocks at the
temple.*) Halloo! Ptol-e-mo-cra'tia! If you please, come and
take this pitcher. Some woman or other brought it to me. It must
be carried in. (*Aside.*) I have found work enough, if I'm to carry
water in to them. (*Goes into the temple.*)

One can hear the roars of Roman laughter with which this
scene would be greeted. The drollery is broad enough to
be appreciated by everybody, as the acting would bring the
points sharply out.

There is a scene now between Labrax, the slave-dealer,
and his friend Char'mi-des. These worthies, having lost
everything, bemoan themselves and chide each other. Labrax had had a wallet that contained all his valuables. This
is gone now, and the two pretty slave-girls are gone. Labrax
is wretched. Slave-dealer we have called this fellow, but he
in truth was slave-dealer of a particular sort, a sort especially
infamous even with the ancients. He was a procurer.

Sceparnio, coming out of the temple, meets Labrax and Charmides. There is some racy talk between him and them, in which Sceparnio vents his ill-humor amusingly at their expense. But he lets out the secret that Labrax's slave-girls are in sanctuary within.

We have thus got through two acts of the comedy. The third act introduces another set of characters. Plesidippus, Palæstra's lover, a young Athenian, appears upon the scene— first, however, by proxy, in the person of his confidential slave Tra-cha′lio. Trachalio raises an uproarious hue and cry in the street. Cyrenians all are adjured to render help. The incoherent alarum of his outcry engages the attention of Dæmones. Very diverting is the back and forth between these two, while Dæmones tries to learn from Trachalio what the pother is all about. The upshot is that several slaves of Dæmones rush into the temple to rescue the girls and to thrash Labrax. The sound of this is heard outside. The girls meantime issue from the temple and Trachalio seeks to reassure them. There follows a long scene of brisk dialogue, with Dæmones, Trachalio, and Labrax for interlocutors. It is a triangular contest of menace, abuse, and braggadocio. The frank brutality of it would no doubt be highly refreshing to the groundlings of the ancient comic theater. The flavor is rich and strong. Of course, Labrax has, on the whole, the worst of it. He gives up getting his slave property by force.

Plesidippus is now at hand in person. Labrax, in vain imploring help, spurned as he is from every quarter, is dragged off to be tried for fraud committed by him in taking earnest-money from Plesidippus for Palæstra, and then running off with her to sea. The lively dialogue through which the foregoing result is reached, brings out contrasted character admirably. Plautus is a true dramatist.

The fourth act hints the approaching denouement. Gripus, fisherman, makes his appearance. Gripus has fished up Labrax's lost wallet with its valuable contents. This wallet will turn out to contain the keepsake trinkets proving Palæstra the long-lost daughter of Dæmones. Gripus is in the act of hiding his treasure-trove, all the while purring aloud to himself over his good luck, when Trachalio comes up. There is an amusing confabulation between the two men, too long drawn out for us to print here, but animated and very racy of character. The result is that Trachalio, having caught sight of Gripus's find, succeeds, by dint of threat and persistency, in getting that fisherman to submit the question of ownership in the wallet to Dæmones, as convenient arbiter. Gripus is well content to have it so—Dæmones, although the other does not know this, being Gripus's indulgent master. The scene that ensues, when the matter is referred to Dæmones, has interest enough, both of dramatic dialogue and of dramatic development, to be shown our readers. It will very well illustrate the lively bustle of movement that fills a comedy of Plautus. The cruel relation of master and slave has a grateful relief—probably true to many instances of real life—in the representation of Gripus's freedom of manner with Dæmones. The kindliness happily then as now inborn in some natures, was not always quite spoiled by the evil influence of despotic power, such as the master possessed over his slave.

Dæmones is just answering the appeal of the shipwrecked girls, as the fourth scene of the fourth act opens. At the self-same moment, the contestants, Gripus and Trachalio, arrive. It is a duel between these two, which of them shall get the ear of Dæmones. Now the text of the play, condensed :

Gr. Hail, master !
Dæ. Hail, what's going on ?
Tr. Is this fellow your slave ?
Gr. He's not ashamed of it.
Tr. I'm not talking to you.
Gr. Then go away from here, I beg.

Tr. Pray, answer, old gentleman, is this your slave?

Dæ. He is.

. . . .

Gr. Really, if you had any shame, you'd go away from here.

Dæ. Gripus, pay attention, and be silent.

Gr. And he speak first?

Dæ. (*To Gripus*) Listen. (*To Trachalio*) You speak.

Gr. Will you let another's slave speak before your own?

Tr. Pshaw! how hard it is to check that fellow. As I began to say, this one has the wallet of the slave-dealer whom you thrust out of the temple of Venus a short time ago.

Gr. If I caught it in the sea with my net, how is it more yours than mine?

Tr. Until the first speaker gets through, silence this fellow, pray, if he's yours.

Gr. What, you wish that inflicted on me which your master is accustomed to administer to you? If he's used to checking you that way, not so my master.

Dæ. He's got ahead of you in that speech. What do you want now? Tell me.

Tr. There is in that wallet a little casket belonging to this woman, who, I lately said, had been free. . . . Those trinkets, which she had long ago as a child, are in the casket. That slave of yours has no use for this, and it will afford help to that wretched girl, if he will give her that by which she may find her parents.

Dæ. I'll make him give it up; be quiet.

Gr. By Hercules, I'm not going to give anything to him.

Tr. I demand nothing but the casket and the trinkets.

Gr. What, if these are golden?

Tr. What is that to you? Gold will be given for gold, silver for silver.

Gr. Let me see the gold; then I'll let you see the casket.

Dæ. (*To Gripus*) Take care and hold your tongue. (*To Trachalio*) You proceed as you began.

Tr. I ask of you one thing, that you pity this woman, if this is the wallet of that slave-dealer, as I suspect. I do not affirm this as a certainty, but I think it is.

Gr. Do you see how the villain is laying his snares?

Tr. Permit me to speak, as I began. If this wallet belongs to that rascal whom I have named, the articles can be identified; order him to show them to these girls.

Gr. What do you say? To show them?

Dæ. He asks but what is just—that the wallet be shown.

Gr. Nay, by Hercules, it is flagrantly unjust.

Dæ. Why, pray?

Gr. Because, if I show it, straightway they will declare that they recognize it.

Tr. Source of villainy, do you judge all men by yourself? Fount of perjury!

Gr. I can grin and bear your abuse, if only my master sides with me.

Tr. But now he's on the other side; he will get the truth out of the wallet.

Dæ. (*To Gripus*) Gripus, pay attention. (*To Trachalio*) State briefly what you want.

Tr. I have said truly; but if you didn't understand I'll say it again. Both of these girls, as I said a short time ago, ought to be free. This maiden, when a child, was stolen from Athens.

    .   .   .   .

Gr. May Jupiter and the gods destroy you! What are you saying, hangman? What, are those girls dumb, that they can't speak for themselves? . . . (*To Dæmones*) Pray, am I to talk at all to-day?

Dæ. If you say one word more, I'll break your head.

Tr. As I began to say, old gentleman, I beg you would order this slave to return the casket to them.   If he asks any reward for this, it shall be given.   Whatever else there is in it he can have for himself.

Gr. Now, at length, you say that, since you see it is my right. A while ago you claimed half.

Dæ. Can't I check you without a beating?

Gr. If he is silent, I will be silent; if he speaks, let me speak in my own behalf.

Dæ. Give me now the wallet, Gripus.

Gr. I will trust it to you, but on the condition that if none of those things are in it, it shall be returned. ˙

Dæ. It shall be returned.

Gr. Take it. (*He gives Dæmones the wallet.*)

Dæ. Hear now, Palæstra and Ampelisca, what I say: Is this the wallet in which he said your casket was?

Pa. I will easily make this thing clear to you. There must be in this matter a wooden casket. I will call over the names of every thing therein; you will show nothing to me. If I shall speak falsely, I shall speak to no purpose. Then you will have for yourself whatever there is in it. But if I speak the truth, then I beg you, that my property may be returned to me.

Dæ. That pleases me. I think you speak fairly.

Gr. By Hercules, I think she speaks very unfairly. What, if she is a sorceress or a witch, and shall mention truly the names of all things therein? Shall the witch have it?

Dæ. She'll not take it off, unless she speaks the truth. She'll act the witch in vain. Open the wallet, then, that as soon as possible I may know the truth.

Gr. He has it; it is open. Ah, I am lost! I see the casket.

Dæ. Is this it? (*Dæmones takes out the casket.*)

Pa. It is. O, my parents, here I hold you inclosed. Here I have my hope and means of finding you stored away.

Gr. Then the gods should be angry with you, whoever you are, for having boxed your parents up in such a narrow place.

Dæ. Gripus, come here; your interests are at stake. You, maiden, tell from where you are, what is within this, and of what appearance it is; mention everything. If, by Hercules, you shall make a mistake, you'll not be able hereafter to rectify it; you will lose your labor in the attempt.

Gr. You ask simple justice.

Tr. (*To Gripus*) By Pollux, he doesn't ask it of you, for you are unjust.

Dæ. Speak, now, girl. Gripus, pay attention and be quiet.

Pa. There are trinkets in it.

Dæ. Yes, I see them.

Gr. I am killed by the first shot; hold on, don't show them.

Dæ. Of what sort are they? answer in order.

Pa. First, a little golden sword engraved with letters.

Dæ. Tell me now what letters are on that sword.

Pa. The name of my father. Next was a small two-edged battle-ax, likewise golden, and also engraved. On the little ax was my mother's name.

Dæ. Stay. Tell me, what is the name of your father on this sword.

Pa. Dæmones.

Dæ. Immortal gods, where are my hopes?

Gr. Nay, rather, by Pollux, where are mine?

Dæ. Continue, I beg you, at once.

Gr. Softly, or go to perdition.

Dæ. Speak, what is your mother's name on the little battle-ax?

Pa. Dædalis.

Dæ. The gods desire my safety.

Gr. But my destruction.

Dæ. This must be my daughter, Gripus.

Gr. She may be, for all I care. (*To Trachalio*) May the gods destroy you who saw me to-day, and myself, fool that I was, not to look around a hundred times to take care that none saw me, before I drew this from the water.

Pa. Then a little silver sickle and two little hands joined, and a windlass.

Gr. Confound you with your pigs and swine,

Pa. And a golden bulla that my father gave me on my birthday.

Dœ. It is she, truly. I cannot be restrained from embracing her. Hail, my daughter! I am your father; I am Dæmones; and here within is your mother, Dædalis.

Pa. Hail, my unlooked-for father!

Dœ. Hail! with what pleasure I embrace you.

Tr. It is pleasant that your piety has met its reward.

Dœ. Come, Trachalio, carry in the wallet.

Tr. See the knavery of Gripus; since you've had bad luck, I congratulate you, Gripus.

Dœ. Come, my daughter, let us go to your mother. She can more minutely examine the matter, for she took care of you, and knows all about you.

Tr. Let us all go within, since we give joint assistance.

Pa. Follow me, Ampelisca.

Am. It is a pleasure to me that the gods befriend you.

The fifth act has little to do but to wind up the play, with the happiest results accruing all around to the parties concerned. Gripus learns that his master is minded to restore the wallet to the slave-dealer.   Here is a bit of the colloquy about it between master and slave:

Gr. That's the reason you're poor, because you're too awfully honest.

Dœ. O, Gripus, Gripus! shall I conceal what's brought to me, when I know it belongs to somebody else? Our Dæmones can't do that sort of thing anyhow. It is proper for wise men always to look out for this, not to be partners in guilt with their slaves. I care nothing for money, except when I'm gaming.

Gr. I've seen actors in just that very way get off wise saws and be applauded, when they recommended these fine morals to the people. But when afterwards everybody went home, no one acted in the way they advised.

Dœ. Go into the house; don't be bothersome; hold your tongue, I'll not give you anything; don't you be mistaken.

Gr. Then I pray the gods, that whatever there is in that wallet, whether gold or silver, it may all go to the dogs.

This free-spoken slave had, for the purpose at least of that petulant moment, a low opinion of the teaching power of the drama. His petulance did not, perhaps, in this case lead him widely astray.

Gripus is by no means at the end of his shifts to make something yet out of that wallet. He meets Labrax and drives with him a sharp bargain, according to which, for a handsome consideration in gold, he on his own part engages to get the lost wallet restored to its owner ; Gripus will thus profit by his master's declared purpose to make the restitution. He binds Labrax by a tremendous oath to make the promised payment of money. Labrax, however, though he swore with his lips, kept his mind unsworn. Having got back his wallet and, in voluntary requital to Dæmones, relinquished all claim on Palæstra, he snaps his fingers at Gripus,. refusing to pay that party in interest any fraction of what he had promised. Dæmones overhears the two bandying words in altercation, and intervenes to get justice done. The way in which all is accomplished affords good dramatic opportunity for entertaining dialogue and lively exhibition of character. Gripus is kept in suspense, but even he says " All right " at last :

Dæ. Did you promise money to this slave ?

La. I confess, I did.

Dæ. What you promised my slave ought to belong to me. Slave-dealer, don't you think you can use a slave-dealer's faith here; you can't do it.

Gr. Now do you think you have found a man whom you can cheat? Good money must be paid to me; I'll give it over to this one right off, that he may set me free.

Dæ. Inasmuch, therefore, as I have been liberal to you, and these things have been saved to you through my aid—

Gr. Nay, by Hercules, through mine, don't you say yours!

Dæ. (*Aside to Gripus*) If you're sharp, you'll keep still. (*To Labrax*) Then it is only fair for you to be liberal to me, well deserving it.

La. Are you forsooth seeking my rights?

Dæ. It 's a wonder I don't seek from you your rights at your own peril.

Gr. I'm safe, the rascal 's wavering; I foresee my freedom.

Dæ. This one here found your wallet; he is my slave. Furthermore, I have preserved this for you with a great sum of money.

La. I am grateful to you ; and as for that talent which I swore to this fellow here, there 's no reason but that you should have it.

Gr. Here you, give it to me, then, if you're wise.

Dæ. Will you keep still or not?

Gr. You are just pretending to plead my suit. By Hercules, you sha'n't cheat me out of this, if I did have to lose the rest of the find.

Dæ. You shall have a beating if you add another word.

Gr. By Hercules, you may kill me! I'll never be silenced in any other way than by a talent.

La. (*To Gripus*) Indeed, he is aiding you, keep still.

Dæ. Come this way, slave-dealer.

La. All right.

Gr. Do this business openly now, I don't want any muttering nor whispering.

Dæ. Tell me, how much did you pay for that other little woman of yours, Ampelisca?

La. A thousand didrachms.

Dæ. Are you willing for me to make you a handsome offer?

La. Certainly.

Dæ. I'll divide a talent—

La. All right.

Dæ. And you keep half for this other woman, that she may be free, and give half to this boy here.

La. Very good. (*Pays Dæmones a half talent.*)

Dæ. For that half I'll free Gripus, through whom you found your wallet, and I my daughter.

La. You do well, I thank you much.

Gr. How soon, then, is the money going to be given to me?

Dæ. The affair is settled, Gripus, I've got the money.

Gr. Yes, I know you've got it, but I want it, by Hercules!

Dæ. Nothing of this goes to you, and don't expect it. I want that you should give him a release from his oath.

Gr. By Hercules, I'm done for! Unless I hang myself, I'm lost. Never shall you cheat me again after this day.

Dæ. Sup here to-day, slave-dealer.

La. All right; I'm delighted with the invitation.

Dæ. Follow me within. Spectators, I would invite you also to supper, if I had anything to give, and there was enough at home for a feast, and I did not believe you had been invited elsewhere to supper. But if you are willing to give kind applause to this play, then do you all come and banquet with me sixteen years hence. You two shall sup here to-night.

Gr. All right.

  All. Farewell, dear friends, now give applause,
    And happy live by fate's fixed laws.

A very satisfactory upshot to the action of the comedy, we are sure all readers will admit.

Of Terence very brief presentation must suffice. Let us take for our specimen the play entitled "The Brothers." For this play, we have the good fortune to possess a translation in verse by George Colman the elder. Though now near a hundred years old, it is free from archaic quality, and it runs off with smoothness and ease.

The prologue is a signally honest piece of writing. The frank-spokenness of it propitiates one. The author, who outright thus proclaims his own borrowing, is at least no sneak of a plagiarist. It will be observed that Terence's prologue differs from Plautus's in not explaining, as that did, the plot of the play. The anonymous allusion to Scipio, as reported collaborator with Terence in production of comedy, will not escape the attention of the reader:

> The bard, perceiving his piece cavill'd at
> By partial critics, and his adversaries
> Misrepresenting what we're now to play,
> Pleads his own cause: and you shall be the judges,
> Whether he merits praise or condemnation.
>   The *Synapothnescontes* is a piece
> By Diphilus, a comedy which Plautus,
> Having translated, call'd COMMORIENTES.
> In the beginning of the Grecian play
> There is a youth, who rends a girl perforce
> From a procurer: and this incident,
> Untouch'd by Plautus, render'd word for word,
> Has our bard interwoven with his *Brothers*—
> The new piece which we represent to-day.
> Say then if this be theft, or honest use
> Of what remained unoccupied. For that
> Which malice tells, that certain noble persons
> Assist the bard, and write in concert with him;
> That which they deem a heavy slander, he
> Esteems his greatest praise: that he can please
> Those who please you, who all the people please;
> Those who in war, in peace, in council, ever
> Have rendered you the dearest services,
> And ever borne their faculties so meekly.
>   Expect not now the story of the play:
> Part the old men, who first appear, will open;

Part will in act be shown. Be favorable;
And let your candor to the poet now
Increase his future earnestness to write!

We give an explication of the plot, in the words of an "Introduction" prefixed to the play as printed for the use of the students in the University of Michigan when these enterprising young men represented the piece in Latin:

"Its name, 'The Brothers,' is derived from the two pairs of brothers with whose fortunes the play is chiefly concerned; Mi'ci-o, a town-bred, good-natured old bachelor; De'me-a, a thrifty farmer and stern parent, and the two sons of the latter. One of these, Æs'chi-nus, adopted by Micio, had been allowed by his indulgent uncle to fall into all kinds of excesses; the other, Ctes'i-pho, brought up on the farm, was believed by his rigorous father to be a pattern of all virtues, but had, in fact, fallen in love with a music-girl in the city. Æschinus, whose fondness for his brother is one of the happiest touches in the play, in order to put the girl in Ctesipho's possession and shield him from exposure, removes her by force from the slave-merchant's house. It is at this point of time that the play begins. Demea, who has just heard the story of the abduction, meets Micio and lays upon him the blame of Æschinus's misdeeds. At the same time Sostrata, hearing the rumor, infers that he has deserted her daughter Pamphila, whom he had promised to marry, and appeals to Hegio, an old friend of the family, to see that Æschinus is brought to a sense of his duty. Demea, on his way back to the farm, learns from Hegio of Æschinus's relations with Pamphila, and returning to find Micio, is sent on a fool's errand to various parts of the city by the cunning slave Syrus. Upon his return to the house of Micio he finds that the latter has given his consent to the marriage of Æschinus with Pamphila, and also discovers, to his great astonishment, that Ctesipho has outwitted him, and has been all the time at his uncle's. In the fifth act Demea becoming convinced that his brother is in the right, suddenly changes character, becomes the most indulgent of fathers, and the comedy ends, as all comedies should, with the marriage of the parties most interested."

We shall not be able here to follow the course of the action throughout. The play is pitched on a low key of morality. No doubt the fashion of its time is truly mirrored in it. The spirit in which the Greek authors wrote is that of easy-going, rather good-hearted, Epicureanism. The philosophy of life recommended is 'Make the best of things about as they are; do not worry yourself trying to improve them.' Roman strictness was already in the way of sadly relaxing its tone, when it could contentedly listen and see, while such maxims of conduct were set forth. We shall no doubt best serve our readers by presenting to them at once, with little retrenchment, the fifth, the closing, act of the comedy.

Demea, the country churl, of the two brothers, is represented as becoming at last an out-and-out convert to the smiling wisdom of Micio, the dweller in the city. The suddenness and the completeness of the conversion, but especially, too, the startlingly aggressive propagandist, or missionary, phase which the conversion takes on, are an essential element in the comic effect. Demea soliloquizes and resolves to adopt his popular brother's universal complaisance. Those who have grown used to only surliness from Demea, are amazed at the change. A sentence of very worldly wisdom from Micio seems to have done the business for Demea. 'Demea,' says Micio, in effect, 'the boys will come out right when they grow up. Spendthrift youth quite naturally becomes miserly old age. That is the law.'

> O my dear Demea, in all matters else
> Increase of years increases wisdom in us;
> This only vice age brings along with it;
> 'We're all more worldly-minded than there's need:'
> Which passion age, that kills all passions else,

> Will ripen in your sons, too.

Demea resists at the moment, but the words work in his mind, as seems to show the following soliloquy, opening the fifth act:

> Never did man lay down so fair a plan,
> So wise a rule of life, but fortune, age,
> Or long experience, made some change in it;
> And taught him, that those things he thought he knew
> He did not know, and what he held as best,
> In practice he threw by.   .   .   .
> Striving to make a fortune for my sons,
> I have worn out my prime of life and health:
> And now, my course near finished, what return
> Do I receive for all my toil?   Their hate.
> Meanwhile, my brother, without any care,
> Reaps all a father's comforts.   Him they love.
> —Well, then, let me endeavor in my turn
> To teach my tongue civility, to give
> With open-handed generosity,
> Since I am challeng'd to 't!—and let me, too,
> Obtain the love and reverence of my children!
> And if 'tis bought by bounty and indulgence,
> I will not be behindhand.   Cash will fail:
> What 's that to me, who am the eldest born?

Demea has prompt opportunity to put his new scheme of conduct into operation. Syrus, the sly slave, who has, with his tricks, cost Demea so much bootless trouble, comes in, bringing a message from Micio to his brother. Demea swallows a great qualm of loathness and greets the knavish fellow fair:

Demea.   Who's there?
> What, honest Syrus! save you: how is 't with you?
> How goes it?
  Syrus.   Very well, sir.
    De. (*Aside*)   Excellent!
> Now for the first time I, against my nature,
> Have added these three phrases, "Honest Syrus!
> How is 't?—How goes it!"—(*To Syrus*) You have proved
>   yourself
> A worthy servant.   I'll reward you for it.
    Sy. I thank you, sir.

De.   I will, I promise you;
And you shall be convinc'd on 't very soon.

Geta, another slave, not Demea's own (as also Syrus was
not), is the next surprised person. He has just respectfully
saluted Demea, when, Demea replying, the following passage
between them, spiced to spectators with asides from the
strangely modified man, occurs:

De.   Geta, I this day have found you
To be a fellow of uncommon worth:
For sure that servant's faith is well approv'd
Who holds his master's interest at heart,
As I perceived that you did, Geta!   Wherefore,
Soon as occasion offers I'll reward you.
(*Aside*)   I am endeavoring to be affable,
And not without success.
Ge.   'Tis kind in you
To think of your poor slave, sir.
De. (*Aside*)   First of all,
I court the mob, and win them by degrees.

Æschinus, the scrapegrace son of Demea—spoiled, as the
father thinks, through the indulgence of the uncle who has
brought him up—now takes his turn of being astonished at
Demea's new humor.   Æschinus is impatiently waiting to be
married:

Æschinus. They murder me with their delays; and while
They lavish all this pomp upon the nuptials,
They waste the live-long day in preparation.
Demea. How does my son?
Æ.   My father! Are you here?
De. Ay, by affection, and by blood your father,
Who love you better than my eyes. But why
Do you not call the bride?
Æ.   'Tis what I long for:
But wait the music and the singers.
De.   Pshaw!
Will you for once be rul'd by an old fellow?
Æ. Well?
De.   Ne'er mind singers, company, lights, music;
But tell them to throw down the garden wall,
As soon as possible. Convey the bride
That way, and lay both houses into one.

> Bring, too, the mother, and whole family,
> Over to us.
> _Æ._   I will. O charming father!
> _De._ (_Aside_) Charming! See there! he calls me _charming_ now.
>   —My brother's house will be a thoroughfare;
>   Throng'd with whole crowds of people; much expense
>   Will follow; very much; what's that to me?
>   I am called _charming_, and get into favor.
>   Ho! order Babylo immediately
>   To pay him twenty minæ. Prithee, Syrus,
>   Why don't you execute your orders?
> _Sy._   What?
> _De._ Down with the wall! (_Exit Syrus_)—You, Geta, go and
>   bring
>   The ladies over.
> _Ge._   Heaven bless you, Demea,
>   For all your friendship to our family! (_Exit Geta._)
> _De._ They're worthy of it.—What say you to this? (_to
>   Æschinus._)
> _Æ._ I think it admirable.
> _De._   'Tis much better
>   Than for a poor soul, sick and lying-in,
>   To be conducted through the street.
> _Æ._   I never
>   Saw anything concerted better, sir.
> _De._ 'Tis just my way.—But here comes Micio.

Perhaps the most wonder-stricken man of all, was Micio hearing of Demea's extravagant proposal for the nuptials. Micio is destined, however, to be still further impressed; for Demea, in the overflow of his vicarious universal benevolence, is even going to make his bachelor brother marry the mother of Æschinus's bride. The following scenes show this matrimonial charity successfully enforced upon Micio's consent (the lady in the case not being consulted at all), with a comic profusion of other kindnesses scattered freely about, at the instance of the whimsically altered Demea; wherewithal—the audience, be sure, sympathetically amused and delighted—the comedy ends:

> _Micio._ (_At entering_) My brother order it, d'ye say? Where is
>   he?
>   —Was this your order, Demea?
> _De._   'Twas my order;
>   And by this means, and every other way,

I would unite, serve, cherish, and oblige,
And join the family to ours!
Æ. (*To Micio*)   Pray do, sir.
Mi. I don't oppose it.
De.   Nay, but 'tis our duty.
First, there 's the mother of the bride—
Mi.   What then?
De. Worthy and modest.
Mi.   So they say.
De.   In years.
Mi. True.
De.   And so far advanced that she is long
Past child-bearing, a poor lone woman too,
With none to comfort her.
Mi.   What means all this?
De. This woman 'tis your place to marry, brother;
And yours (*to Æschinus*) to bring him to 't.
Mi.   I marry her?
De. You.
Mi.   I?
De.   Yes, you, I say.
Mi.   Ridiculous!
De. (*To Æschinus*) If you're a man, he'll do 't.
Æ. (*To Micio*)   Dear father!
Mi.   How!
Do you then join him, fool?
De.   Nay, don't deny.
It can't be otherwise.
Mi.   You've lost your senses!
Æ. Let me prevail upon you, sir!
Mi.   You're mad.
Away!
De.   Oblige your son.
Mi.   Have you your wits?
I a new-married man at sixty-five!
And marry a decrepid poor old woman!
Is that what you advise me?
Æ.   Do it, sir!
I've promis'd them.
Mi.   You've promised them, indeed!
Prithee, boy, promise for yourself.
De.   Come, come!
What if he asked still more of you?
Mi.   As if
This was not even the utmost.
De.   Nay, comply!

Æ. Be not obdurate!

De.   Come, come, promise him.

Mi. Won't you desist?

Æ.   No, not till I prevail.

Mi. This is mere force.

De.   Nay, nay, comply, good Micio!

Mi. Though this appears to me absurd, wrong, foolish,
And quite repugnant to my scheme of life,
Yet, if you're so much bent on 't, let it be!

Æ. Obliging father, worthy my best love!

De. (*Aside*) What now? This answers to my wish. What
   more?
Hegio 's their kinsman, (*to Micio*) our relation, too,
And very poor. We should do him some service.

Mi. Do what?

De.   There is a little piece of ground,
Which you let out near town. Let's give it him
To live upon.

Mi.   So little, do you call it?

De. Well, if 'tis large, let 's give it. He has been
Father to her; a good man; our relation.
It will be given worthily. In short,
That saying, Micio, I now make my own,
Which you so lately and so wisely quoted:
" It is the common failing of old men,
To be too much intent on worldly matters: "
Let us wipe off that stain. The saying 's true,
And should be practiced.

Mi.   Well, well, be it so,
If he requires it. (*Pointing to Æschinus.*)

Æ.   I beseech it, father.

De. Now you're indeed my brother, soul and body.

Mi. I'm glad to find you think me so.

De. (*Aside*)   I foil him
At his own weapons.

SCENE VI.

(*To them Syrus.*)

Syrus.   I have executed
Your orders, Demea.

De.   A good fellow!—Truly,
Syrus, I think, should be made free to-day.

Mi. Made free! He?—Wherefore?

De.   O, for many reasons.

Sy. O Demea, you're a noble gentleman,

I've taken care of both your sons from boys;
Taught them, instructed them, and given them
The wholesomest advice that I was able.

De. The thing 's apparent: and these offices:
To cater;—bring a wench in, safe and snug;—
Or in midday prepare an entertainment;—
All these are talents of no common man.

Sy. O, most delightful gentleman!

De.   Besides,
He has been instrumental, too, this day,
In purchasing the music-girl.   He manag'd
The whole affair.   We should reward him for it.
It will encourage others.—In a word,
Your Æschinus would have it so.

Mi.   Do you
Desire it?

Æ.   Yes, sir.

Mi.   Well, if you desire it—
Come hither, Syrus!—Be thou free!

(SYRUS *kneels:* MICIO *strikes him, being the ceremony of manu-
mission, or giving a slave his freedom.*)

Sy.   I thank you:
Thanks to you all; but most of all, to Demea!

De. I'm glad of your good fortune.

Æ.   So am I.

Sy. I do believe it; and I wish this joy
Were quite complete, and I might see my wife,
My Phrygia, too, made free, as well as I.

De. The very best of women!

Sy.   And the first
That suckled my young master's son, your grandson.

De. Indeed! the first who suckled him!—Nay, then,
Beyond all doubt she should be free.

Mi.   For what?

De. For that.   Nay, take the sum, whate'er it be,
Of me.

Sy.   Now all the powers above grant all
Your wishes, Demea.

Mi.   You have thriv'd to-day
Most rarely, Syrus.

De.   And besides this, Micio,
It would be handsome to advance him something,
To try his fortune with.   He'll soon return it.

Mi. Not that.   (*Snapping his fingers.*)

Æ.   He 's honest.

Sy.   Faith, I will return it.
  Do but advance it.
Æ.   Do, sir.
Mi.   Well, I'll think on 't.
De. (*To Syrus.*) I'll see that he shall do 't.
Sy.   Thou best of men!
Æ. My most indulgent father!
Mi.   What means this?
  Whence comes this hasty change of manners, brother?
  Whence flows all this extravagance? and whence
  This sudden prodigality?
De.   I'll tell you:
  To show you that the reason why our sons
  Think you so pleasant and agreeable,
  Is not from your deserts, or truth, or justice,
  But your compliance, bounty, and indulgence.
  —Now, therefore, if I'm odious to you, son,
  Because I'm not subservient to your humor,
  In all things, right or wrong: away with care!
  Spend, squander, and do what you will—but if,
  In those affairs where youth has made you blind,
  Eager, and thoughtless, you will suffer me
  To counsel and correct—and in due season
  Indulge you—I am at your service.
Æ.   Father,
  In all things we submit ourselves to you.
  What 's fit and proper, you know best.—But what
  Shall come of my poor brother!
De.   I consent
  That he shall have her: let him finish there.
Æ. All now is as it should be. (*To the audience*) Clap your
    hands.

In this play of Terence's a considerable advance from Plautus
toward the modern type of comedy will readily be found.

The glimpses that, through Roman adaptations, we catch of
the New Comedy of Athens, make us feel how much we lost
in losing the originals. As it is, modern comedy, best, no
doubt, in the French language, has been not a little indebted
to inspiration and example derived, through Plautus and
Terence, from Menander and his peers. Ancient Greece
reaches long hands in many directions, to mold for us the
forms, and to dictate to us the spirit, of our literature and art.

CHAPTER X.

An Epicurean, but an Epicurean very different in motive and in tone from merry-making Terence, was the grave, earnest, intent poet Lu-cre'tius. Dramatist, and scarce poet at all, though he wrote in verse, was Terence. Philosopher principally (or expounder of philosophy), but true poet, too—incidentally and as it were involuntarily—was Lucretius. The Lucretian philosophy—science call it rather, or attempted science—has perished utterly ; the Lucretian poetry survives, to perish never. Such sport are we mortals of a power not ourselves, a power greater than we ! What Lucretius mainly meant, has come to naught. What he at times hardly seems to have meant at all, is his chief title to living human praise. A great poet he was, wrecked in seeking to be a great expounder of philosophy—a great poet, let us shortly say, who did not write a great poem.

Titus Lucretius Carus was a contemporary of Cæsar and of Cicero. But, except this bare fact of date, we know almost nothing of the man. He scarcely belonged to the age in which he lived. His sympathies were all with an earlier time. He felt the existing political order crumbling about him ; but, though of knightly blood, he took no part in shaping the new political order that should succeed. Roman in character, he seems somehow not to have been Roman in aim and scheme of life. He made philosophy—that is, science—his chief motive. This was not Roman. The Roman course would have been to choose politics for the chief thing, and let philosophy take its chance as a thing incidental.

But nobody can separate himself completely from his times. And Lucretius, though insular, was yet in the sea. The sea around Lucretius was irreligion, skepticism, atheism. Olympianism was, indeed, still a ritual; but it was no longer a creed. The prevailing unbelief involved Lucretius. Nay, unbelief is not the word to describe the state of this man's mind. He was not an unbeliever, he was a disbeliever. He was a vehement disbeliever. What in others was an apathy, in him was a passion. He disbelieved in the gods so intensely, that he almost rehabilitated the gods, that he might hate them the better.

The title of Lucretius's poem is De Rerum Natura, Concerning the Nature of Things. The scheme of the poem is as large as the vagueness of the title would seem to imply. The poet, as just said, attempts nothing less than to explain the universe. His motive ostensibly is didactic, not poetic. He will establish atheism upon an impregnable basis of strict science. His subject is not for the sake of a poem. His poem is severely for the sake of his subject; as, finally, his subject itself is for the sake of his object.

It is constantly to be understood that, like his Roman literary brethren all, Lucretius was a copious borrower from the Greek. He does not pretend to be the inventor of the cosmical system that he expounds. He derives all from Epicurus, and he attributes all to Epicurus. For our knowledge in detail of what Epicurus taught, we are largely indebted to Lucretius. The great master's own works, multifarious as these were, have nearly all perished.

Lucretius begins his poem rather curiously, for an atheist. He begins it with an ostensibly dutiful invocation of Venus. We are, of course, to suppose that he meant his Venus to be simply a poetical personification of the principle of fecundity and grace. This invocation is one of the most celebrated passages in Latin poetry. Mr. Lowell speaks, strongly, thus of it:

"The invocation of Venus, as the genetic force of nature, by Lucretius, seems to me the one sunburst of purely poetic inspiration which the Latin language can show."

So famous a passage must be shown our readers. Here it is, first in the consummately fine prose version of Mr. Munro, acknowledged the best English translator of Lucretius:

Mother of the Aeneadae, darling of men and gods, increase-giving Venus, who beneath the gliding signs of heaven fillest with thy presence the ship-carrying sea, the corn-bearing lands, since through thee every kind of living things is conceived, rises up and beholds the light of the sun. Before thee, goddess, flee the winds, the clouds of heaven, before thee and thy advent; for thee earth manifold in works puts forth sweet-smelling flowers; for thee the levels of the sea do laugh and heaven propitiated shines with outspread light. For soon as the vernal aspect of day is disclosed, and the birth-favoring breeze of favonius unbarred is blowing fresh, first the fowls of the air, o lady, show signs of thee and thy entering in, throughly smitten in heart by thy power. Next the wild herds bound over the glad pastures and swim the rapid rivers: in such wise each made prisoner by thy charm follows thee with desire, whither thou goest to lead it on. Yes throughout seas and mountains and sweeping rivers and leafy homes of birds and grassy plains, striking fond love into the breasts of all thou constrainest them each after its kind to continue their races with desire. Since thou then art sole mistress of the nature of things, and without thee nothing rises up into the divine borders of light, nothing grows to be glad or lovely, I would have thee for a helpmate in writing the verses which I essay to pen on the nature of things for our own son of the Memmii, whom thou, goddess, hast willed to have no peer, rich as he ever is in every grace. Wherefore all the more, o lady, lend my lays an overliving charm. Cause meanwhile the savage works of war to be lulled to rest throughout all seas and lands; for thou alone canst bless mankind with calm peace, seeing that Mavors lord of battle controls the savage works of war, Mavors who often flings himself into thy lap quite vanquished by the never-healing wound of love. . . . While, then, lady, he is reposing . . . shed thyself about him and above, and pour from thy lips sweet discourse, asking, glorious dame, gentle peace for the Romans. For neither can we in our country's day of trouble with untroubled mind think only of our work, nor can the illustrious offset of Memmius in times like these be wanting to the general weal.

In printing the preceding extract, we have followed exactly the somewhat peculiar typography adopted by Mr. Munro for his translation of Lucretius.

The rest of our citations we shall take where we can from Mr. W. H. Mallock's metrical rendering.

The following is the fashion in which Lucretius at the same time acknowledges his discipleship to Epicurus, and vents his hatred of religion, as religion was understood by the Romans:

> When human life, a shame to human eyes,
>   Lay sprawling in the mire in foul estate,
> A cowering thing without the strength to rise,
>   Held down by fell religion's heavy weight—
> Religion scowling downward from the skies,
>   With hideous head, and vigilant eyes of hate—
> First did a man of Greece presume to raise
> His brows, and give the monster gaze for gaze.
>
> Him not the tales of all the gods in heaven,
>   Nor the heaven's lightnings, nor the menacing roar
> Of thunder daunted. He was only driven,
>   By these vain vauntings, to desire the more
> To burst through Nature's gates, and rive the unriven
>   Bars. And he gained the day ; and, conqueror,
> His spirit broke beyond our world, and past
> Its flaming walls, and fathomed all the vast.
>
> And back returning, crowned with victory, he
>   Divulged of things the hidden mysteries,
> Laying quite bare what can and cannot be,
>   How to each force is set strong boundaries,
> How no power raves unchained, and nought is free.
>   So the times change ; and now religion lies
> Trampled by us ; and unto us 'tis given
> Fearless with level gaze to scan the heaven.

Lucretius lays it down as his great first principle, that "no object is ever divinely produced out of nothing." This might seem only to mean that there must have been matter, prior to any creative act of a divine being. But Lucretius means more than that. For he speaks presently of being able also to show "the manner in which all things are done without the hand of the gods." "The hand of the gods" being thus out of the question, the universe, since it now exists, must always have existed. Always, but not always in its present state. There was a first state different from the present. That first state consisted of particles, particles moving, particles moving in a vacuum. Such was the universe in the beginning. Imagine a universal snow-storm. The spectacle of those falling flakes of snow will very well represent the spectacle of the universe in its Lucretian primordial condition. How the infinitesimal ultimate atoms, supposed by Lucretius, came first to exist, he does not explain ; as no more does he explain how those atoms came to be in motion. That such, however, was the primal state of things, he is quite sure. And he makes nothing of telling how, from the chaos of atoms moving in void, the present cosmos sprang into being. It is simply on this wise : One moving atom had some slight, very slight, deflection—whence received, does not appear—from its straight course, and so, impinging on a fellow atom, adhered thereto—why adhered, is left unsaid—or else, bounding off repelled, attached itself to its neighbor on the other side. Thus at length by chance the infinite multitude of individual atoms arranged themselves into the existing order of the universe. " A fortuitous concourse of atoms," and no god, did the whole business for Lucretius then ; as the great principle of " evolution," and no God, does the whole business now—for some. And of these two attempts to solve the problem of the universe, one perhaps is as truly philosophical as the other.

That characteristically Roman sentiment, desire of deathless literary fame, is acknowledged by Lucretius, in the following strain of genuine, nay, of exquisite, poetry. The poet has been avowing his sense of the difficulty of his subject ; "yet," he says :

Yet my heart, smarting with desire for praise,
   Me urges on to sing of themes like these,
And that great longing to pour forth my lays
   Constrains me, and the loved Pierides,
Whose pathless mountain-haunts I now explore,
And glades where no man's foot has fallen before.

Ah sweet, ah sweet, to approach the untainted springs,
   And quaff the virgin waters cool and clear,
And cull the flowers that have been unknown things
   To all men heretofore! and yet more dear
When mine shall be the adventurous hand that brings
   A crown for mine own brows, from places where
The Muse has deigned to grant a crown for none,
Save for my favored brows, and mine alone.

Such a passage as that, presenting the writer in the character of conscious and confessed poetical aspirant—"garland and singing robes about him"—almost makes one give up holding that Lucretius was in aim and ambition preeminently philosopher. That passage at least reads quite like the authentic outburst of a distinctively and predominantly poetic aspiration pent up in the breast of the man.

Toward the end of book first, Lucretius reaches, in a kind of resumption of his argument, the following statement of his theory of atoms and void:

For blindly, blindly, and without design,
   Did these first atoms their first meetings try;
No ordering thought was there, no will divine
   To guide them; but through infinite time gone by
Tossed and tormented they essayed to join,
   And clashed through the void space tempestuously,
Until at last that certain whirl began,
Which slowly formed the earth and heaven and man.

The second book opens with a celebrated passage:

'Tis sweet when tempests roar upon the sea
   To watch from land another's deep distress
Amongst the waves—his toil and misery:
   Not that his sorrow makes our happiness,
But that some sweetness there must ever be
   Watching what sorrows we do not possess:

So, too, 'tis sweet to safely view from far
Gleam o'er the plains the savage ways of war.

But sweeter far to look with purgéd eyes
   Down from the battlements and topmost towers
Of learning, those high bastions of the wise,
   And far below us see this world of ours,
The vain crowds wandering blindly, led by lies,
   Spending in pride and wrangling all their powers.
So far below—the pigmy toil and strife,
The pain and piteous rivalries of life.

O peoples miserable! O fools and blind!
   What night you cast o'er all the days of man!
And in that night before you and behind
   What perils prowl! But you nor will nor can
See that the treasure of a tranquil mind
   Is all that Nature pleads for, for this span,
So that between our birth and grave we gain
Some quiet pleasures, and a pause from pain.

In the following stanza, removed from those just quoted by
only a short interval, a genuine feeling for the beauty of
nature will be recognized, feeling such as was not common
in the literary world before Lucretius—in fact, a modern-
seeming sentiment, a quality almost Wordsworthian:

The grass is ours, and sweeter sounds than these,
   As down we couch us by the babbling spring,
And overhead we hear the branching trees
   That shade us, whisper; and for food we bring
Only the country's simple luxuries.
   Ah, sweet is this, and sweetest in the spring,
When the sun goes through all the balmy hours,
And all the green earth's lap is filled with flowers!

The love of nature thus exemplified from Lucretius may be
said to constitute in him almost a characteristic trait. Virgil
might conceivably have written his descriptions from pictures
of what he describes. Lucretius could not have written his
descriptions otherwise than directly from nature herself. Not
sentiment, however, and not fancy, not indeed poetry in any
form, but scientific discussions and explanations compose the
main tissue of Lucretius's work.

Our poet-philosopher applies his atomic theory to explain the origin and reason of different tastes to the palate. The different tastes are due to the different shapes of the atoms of which the sapid substances consist. Lucretius (according to Mr. Munro) :

The liquids honey and milk excite a pleasant sensation of tongue when held in the mouth ; but, on the other hand, the nauseous nature of wormwood and of harsh centaury writhes the mouth with a noisome flavor; so that you may easily see that the things which are able to affect the senses pleasantly, consist of smooth and round elements ; while all those, on the other hand, which are found to be bitter and harsh, are held in connexion by particles that are more hooked and for this reason are wont to tear open passages into our senses, and in entering in to break through the body.

Lucretius blithely undertakes to tell a great secret of the universe. "Let us now sing," he says—we make a long skip forward to the fifth book, to find this extract—"Let us now sing what causes the motions of the stars :"

In the first place, if the great sphere of heaven revolves, we must say that an air presses on the pole at each end and confines it on the outside and closes it in at both ends; and then that a third air streams above and moves in the same direction in which roll on as they shine the stars of the eternal world ; or else that this third air streams below in order to carry up the sphere in the contrary direction ; just as we see rivers turn wheels and water-scoops.   It is likewise quite possible too that all the heaven remains at rest, while at the same time the glittering signs are carried on ; either because rapid heats of ether are shut in and whirl round while seeking a way out and roll their fires in all directions through heaven's vast quarters; or else an air streaming from some part from another source outside drives and whirls the fires ; or else they may glide on of themselves going whithersoever the food of each calls and invites them, feeding their flamy bodies everywhere throughout heaven.   For which of these causes is in operation in this world, it is not easy to affirm for certain ; but what can be and is done throughout the universe in various worlds formed on various plans, this I teach, and I go on to set forth several causes which may exist throughout the universe for the motions of stars ; one of which however must in this world also be the cause that imparts lively motion to the signs ; but to dictate which of them it is, is by no means the duty of the man who advances step by step.

Memmius, that friend of the poet to whom the poem is inscribed and addressed, must have felt embarrassingly free to choose, among so many proffered alternatives of explanation—all about equally good. If he was of a poetical turn, as there is grave reason to fear he was not, he probably preferred—we do, we confess—among the various conjectures proposed by Lucretius, the pleasing bucolic view of the case, the idea, namely, that the stars are at large in a kind of celestial pasture, that they "glide on of themselves, going whithersoever the food of each calls and invites them, feeding their flamy bodies everywhere throughout heaven."

The intrepid poet does not shrink from attacking, in the sixth book, the problem of thunder and lightning. He proceeds on an easier plan than that adopted so long after by Franklin. Instead of going out in a thunder-storm, to try, as Franklin did, a dangerous experiment with the clouds, Lucretius retires into the safe recesses of his own mind and evolves his explanation on *a priori* principles. If the facts of nature chanced not to correspond with the theory, why, so much the worse for the facts. In the case, however, of Lucretius, the poet's eye, in a fine frenzy rolling, must have seen things in the sky that perhaps escaped the ken of the more practical American philosopher. Otherwise, how could the poet have described, with such power as is displayed in the passage we are about to quote? (It is uniformly the incomparable prose translation of Munro, whenever the form is prose in which we present Lucretius.) One imagines Memmius "burning with high hope" of true enlightenment at last, as he reads the fair and fine promise of explanation, and no mistake this time, with which his poet-friend committed himself in the prefatory words now following:

And now in what way these [thunderbolts] are begotten and are formed with a force so resistless as to be able with their stroke to burst asunder towers, throw down houses, wrench away beams and rafters, and cast down and burn up the monuments of men, to strike men dead, prostrate cattle far and near, by what force they can do all this and the like, I will make clear and will not longer detain you with mere professions.

Thunderbolts we must suppose to be begotten out of dense clouds piled up high; for they are never sent forth at all when the sky is clear or when the clouds are of a slight density. . . .

I have shown above [in a passage not here reproduced] that hollow clouds have very many seeds of heat, and they must also take many in from the sun's rays and their heat.   On this account when the same wind which happens to collect them into any one place, has forced out many seeds of heat and has mixed itself up with that fire, then the eddy of wind forces a way in and whirls about in the straitened room and points the thunderbolt in the fiery furnaces within; for it is kindled in two ways at once; it is heated by its own velocity and from the contact of fire. After that, when the force of the wind has been thoroughly heated and the impetuous power of the fire has entered in, then the thunderbolt fully forged, as it were, suddenly rends the cloud, and their heat put in motion is carried on traversing all places with flashing lights.   Close upon it follows so heavy a clap that it seems to crush down from above the quarters of heaven which have all at once sprung asunder.   Then a trembling violently seizes the earth and rumblings run through high heaven; for the whole body of the storm then without exception quakes with the shock and loud roarings are aroused.   After this shock follows so heavy and copious a rain that the whole ether seems to be turning into rain and then to be tumbling down and returning to a deluge; so great a flood of it is discharged by the bursting of the cloud and the storm of wind, when the sound flies forth from the burning stroke.   At times too the force of the wind aroused from without falls on a cloud hot with a fully forged thunderbolt; and when it has burst it, forthwith there falls down yon fiery eddying whirl which in our native speech we call a thunderbolt. . . .

The velocity of thunderbolts is great and their stroke powerful, and they run through their course with a rapid descent, because their force when aroused first in all cases collects itself in the clouds and gathers itself up for a great effort at starting; then when the cloud is no longer able to hold the increased moving power, their force is pressed out and therefore flies with a marvellous moving power, like to that with which missiles are carried when discharged from powerful engines.   Then too the thunderbolt consists of small and smooth elements, and such a nature it is not easy for anything to withstand; for it flies between and passes in through the porous passages; therefore it is not checked and delayed by many collisions, and for this reason it glides and flies on with a swift moving power. . . .

It passes too through things without injuring them, and leaves many things quite whole after it has gone through, because the clear bright fire flies through by the pores. And it breaks to pieces many things, when the first bodies of the thunderbolt have fallen exactly on the first bodies of these things, at the points where they are intertwined and held together. Again it easily melts brass and fuses gold in an instant, because its force is formed of bodies minutely small and of smooth elements, which easily make their way in and when they are in, in a moment break up all the knots and untie the bonds of union.

Lucretius certainly had a genius for description more magnificent than Virgil could boast—more magnificent, perhaps, than any other ancient poet whatever. It must, we think, be evident to every reader, that the poet tends often to get the better of the philosopher, with Lucretius. The complacency, however, with which Lucretius regarded his treatment of the present matter considered as pure science, is unmistakable:

This is the way to see into the true nature of the thunderbolt and to understand by what force it produces each effect.

Through a page or so following, Lucretius laughs mercilessly at the idea of Jupiter's being launcher of thunderbolts—Jupiter, and his fellow-Olympians. "Why aim they at solitary places," he asks, "and spend their labor in vain? Or are they then practicing their arms and strengthening their sinews?" It reads not unlike Elijah chaffing the prophets of Baal. We wish we had room to give here the raking and riddling fire of sarcastic interrogation with which, at his leisure, Lucretius pursues and persecutes his afflicted theme. He triumphs and glories in jubilant atheism—more exactly, in rioting anti-Olympianism. It is to "the gods," rather than to God, that Lucretius opposes himself so fiercely.

Atheist though he was, the gods whom he denied were the gods of Olympus. He hated religion; but the religion that he hated was the hateful religion of Greece and of Rome.

Who can say how Lucretius might have borne himself toward the unknown God, had there, in his time, been the apostle Paul to declare to him that God; how Lucretius might have borne himself toward Christianity, could he have met, in Christianity, a system of doctrine not less intensely,—and so much more effectively!—hostile to Olympianism than was the Lucretian philosophy itself?

It is needless to say that Lucretius was a thorough-paced materialist. Death with him ended all. Powerful, and drearily powerful, not untouched with pathos, is the strain in which he announces and reasons this dreadful creed—as will amply show the following stanzas of translation by Mr. Mallock :

> Death is for us then but a noise and name,
>   Since the mind dies, and hurts us not a jot;
> And as in bygone times when Carthage came
>   To battle, we and ours were troubled not,
> Nor heeded though the whole earth's shuddering frame
>   Reeled with the stamp of armies, and the lot
> Of things was doubtful, to which lords should fall
> The land and seas and all the rule of all;
>
> So, too, when we and ours shall be no more,
>   And there has come the eternal separation
> Of flesh and spirit, which, conjoined before,
>   Made us ourselves, there will be no sensation;
> We should not hear were all the world at war;
>   Nor shall we, in its last dilapidation,
> When the heavens fall, and earth's foundations flee:
> We shall nor feel, nor hear, nor know, nor see.

That indestructible instinct in man, by virtue of which he divinely "doubts against the sense," and, in spite of appearance, still dreams of "soul surviving breath," Lucretius recognizes, and deals with, as follows :

> Perplexed he argues, from the fallacy
>   Of that surviving self not wholly freed.
> Hence he bewails his bitter doom—to die;
>   Nor does he see that when he dies indeed,
> No second he will still remain to cry,

> Watching its own cold body burn or bleed.
> O fool! to fear the wild-beast's ravening claw,.
> Or that torn burial of its mouth and maw.
>
> For lo! if this be fearful, let me learn
>   Is it more fearful than if friends should place
> Thy decent limbs upon the pyre and burn
>   Sweet frankincense? or smother up thy face
> With honey in the balm-containing urn?
>   Or if you merely lay beneath the rays
> Of heaven on some cold rock? or damp and cold
> If on thine eyelids lay a load of mold?
>
> 'Thou not again shalt see thy dear home's door,
>   Nor thy dear wife and children come to throw
> Their arms round thee, and ask for kisses more,
>   And through thy heart make quiet comfort go:
> Out of thy hands hath slipped the precious store
>   Thou hoardedst for thine own,' men say, 'and lo,
> All thou desired is gone!' but never say,
> 'All the desire as well hath passed away.'
>
> Ah, could they only see this, and could borrow
>   True words, to tell what things in death abide thee!·
> 'Thou shalt lie soothed in sleep that knows no morrow,
>   Nor ever cark nor care again betide thee:
> Friend, thou wilt say thy long good-bye to sorrow,
>   And ours will be the pangs, who weep beside thee,
> And watch thy dear familiar body burn,
> And leave us but the ashes and the urn.'

With emphasis, in dismissing the subject of this chapter, we call attention to the remarkable poem, entitled "Lucretius," of Tennyson. For the full understanding of that poem, one needs to remember the tradition transmitted by St. Jerome, the Latin Christian father (the sole tradition extant concerning Lucretius's end), to the effect that his wife, jealous of him, for whatever reason—perhaps only because he made himself too much the bridegroom of his vocation as philosopher and poet—resorted to a professor of magic arts and procured a potion supposed of power to win for herself her husband's love. This love-philter, administered without the poet's knowledge, worked a madness in his brain, under the influence of which, in the prime of manhood, at forty-seven years of age, he committed suicide.

Lucretius and Tennyson seem almost to be brethren in genius and temperament. Tennyson is perhaps the one English mind of our day who could, by exchange of time and place, conceivably have mingled poetry and philosophy, in a production like the De Rerum Natura of Lucretius.

CHAPTER XI.

HORACE.

HORACE is not one of the great poets of the world. But he is, emphatically, one of the best known. He does not overawe us with a vastness in his genius. But he satisfies us with far-sought perfection in his workmanship. If Homer, if Virgil, if Dante, if Milton, are each like a great statue, like a Phidian Jove—Horace is like an exquisite cameo, delighting us, not with mass, but with fineness, not with majesty, but with grace. His lines are not large, but they are clean and clear. You may use the microscope and discover no flaw. One must not look for the great thought that "strikes along the brain and flushes all the cheek." To this height Horace does not aspire. One must not even look for plenitude and variety of wisdom. Horace is wise, but he is narrowly, he is, as it were, penuriously, wise. He is worldly-wise. His reflections cling faithfully to the ground. Occasionally there is a bold stretch of wing, and a rising as if to try the eagle's flight. But the poet soon recollects himself, and descends, with conscious grace of self-control, to the safe lower level that he loves.

Horace's odes are, many of them, perhaps the most of them, occasional poems. Few escape the quality that thus naturally belongs to them as being done to order. They are works of labor, quite as much as works of love. But then Horace's genius was so well trained, so obedient to its owner's will, that there is no revolt at task-work apparent. Deliberateness almost becomes spontaneousness. The artist's delight in execution almost becomes equivalent to the poet's delight in conception. Art, in short, is nature, with Horace.

It follows from this character in Horace, that he suffers more than most other poets from translation. There is not, and there cannot be, any adequate transcript, in another language, of his verse. Thought, image, you can translate, but you cannot translate form. And form is more, than is any thing besides form, in Horace's odes. There is considerable monotony of topic and sentiment. And the sentiments that keep recurring are not very numerous, not very profound, not very novel. They are in truth the obvious, the commonplace itself, of pagan life. 'Life is short, is uncertain. Death ends all. It is not best to fret. Take things as they come. Be contented. Moderation is wisdom. Keep the golden mean. Wealth will not make you happy.' These ideas revolve constantly into view, as you read the odes of Horace. But you do not see them in this bareness and baldness. As in a kaleidoscope, they undergo various permutation of arrangement and they take on beauty, when Horace sings them for you in his verse. This magician in metre could go on repeating himself forever, and the repetition should never weary you. You would scarcely think of its being repetition—this continuous flow from form to form of the same ideas, in the shaken kaleidoscope of Horace's verse.

The experience we describe belongs, however, exclusively to the man reading the original Latin itself. No art of translation can make an equivalent experience possible to the reader of Horace in English. The Latin scholar finds the very aspect of the Horatian verse a refection to the eye. It is like looking at the fine lines of a perfect medallion, or a gem exquisitely engraved. Not in the whole round of ancient classic literature have we encountered any author from whom a greater proportion of his individual quality is lost, than is lost from Horace, in an English translation. A discouraging statement, do you say? Perhaps, say we in reply ; but one obtains a truer impression of Horace by knowing this, to begin with, about him, than would be possible with any illusion in the mind of the contrary. What we have said applies, however, to the properly lyrical productions of Horace. His satires and his epistles are capable of being translated with less loss.

Horace is chiefly his own biographer. We know little, and there is little that we need to know, of his life, beyond what his writings reveal. Horace is a perfectly frank egotist, the best-bred and the most agreeable of the tribe. He does not scruple to write himself, anywhere it may happen, into his verse. His audience were almost all of them personally known to the poet. He met them familiarly, at the court of Augustus, or on the streets, and in the baths, of Rome. He held a well-established and a universally recognized position, as the laureate of the empire and the lyrist and the satirist of Roman society. His natural complaisance was well supported by an unperturbed complacency. He went smiling through his easy and fortunate experience of life, the happiest, or the least unhappy, of Romans. He was a courtier ; but never was courtier compelled to pay less for what he enjoyed, than was Horace. To Horace's honor let it be also recorded, that never perhaps was successful courtier less inclined to pay any thing that could justly be judged misbecoming to himself. With apparently faultless suavity in manner, he maintained an entire manliness of bearing toward his patron Mæcenas and his emperor Augustus. It reflects credit, almost equally, both upon patronizer and patronized, this admirable relation, steadfastly sustained on the one side, and scrupulously respected on the other, between the freedman bachelor poet and those two high-placed formidable friends of his.

Freedman, we say, but Horace was removed by one generation from the freedman's condition. It was his father that had once been a slave and from being a slave had been raised to a freedman. Horace praised his father with reason. The son owed much to the father. Freedman though he was, the elder Horace had ideas that became a Roman citizen. He gave his boy the best chance that Rome could supply. He tasked his own resources to situate him well and to educate him as if he were the son of a Roman knight. According to the easy ethical standard that prevailed at Rome, possibly above that standard, Horace's father and, after him, Horace, seem to have been both of them true and good men. This does not mean that bachelor Horace kept himself unspotted, either in life, or in his verse. No, he did things, and he wrote things, that only to mention would now be an offense. The world is already somewhat better, when it is under sense of compulsion to seem to be better. And Christianity, since Horace's time, has at least enforced on vice a heavy fine in the form of fair pretense. Vice must now put on, however loth, a mask of virtue.

Horace, as a young man, was not incapable of enthusiasm. He experienced an attack of such emotion, at the time when, Cæsar having been slain, there was a moment of promise that the Republic would be restored. He joined the republicans and fought on their side at Philippi. In one of his odes, he alludes, with not unthrifty humor, to his conduct on the occasion. He threw away his shield, he says, and ran for dear life. In such frank raillery at his own expense, he had perhaps his purpose. His republicanism, he would have it understood, was not serious enough to be either dangerous or offensive to the conquerors. Horace left the ardor of enthusiasm behind him with his youth. Never, so far as we know, after that affair at Philippi, did he do any thing out of the safely moderate and regular. He did not cravenly fling away his spirit, but he kept his spirit in good training. He was, we say, a prosperous courtier; still he remained a man you could respect. If Mæcenas hinted to him that he did not show himself enough at Rome, Horace replied, with perfect temper, that he had his reasons, and that he would rather resign the bounty that he owed to the grace of the great minister, than leave the country for the city when those reasons forbade. Mæcenas had given him a modest estate of land in the Sabine country, for which Horace—he having, as republican, lost his all through confiscation—was properly grateful to his patron. He addressed Mæcenas in many appreciative and laudatory odes. He paid similar tribute to Augustus; but not through any gracious imperial condescension, did Augustus prevail to beguile the wary poet into one moment's perilous parting with the subject's safe and proper distance from the sovereign. Horace basked continuously and blessedly in the sunshine of court favor, never once pushed off for discipline into the outward cold, but also never once tempted too near into the scorching heat. The remaining incidents and relations of his life will sufficiently come out, by occasion, in connection with the pieces that we shall bring forward to illustrate his genius.

Horace's poems are classified as odes, epodes (odes, simply, under an arbitrary alternative name), satires, and epistles.

The odes are most of them very short. The stanza in them is prevailingly either Sapphic or Alcaic. Horace was like Roman writers generally in being open debtor to the Greek. He subdued the difficult metres he borrowed, with signal success, to his use.

The first ode is inscribed to Mæcenas. It is not boldly eulogistic, though, all the more agreeably, eulogy is implied. It simply says, 'Every man to his taste; I, for my part, like to make verses. Rank me thou, Mæcenas, among thy lyric bards, and I shall be supremely proud and happy.'

The second ode is a tribute to Cæsar Augustus. In it occurs

the famous phrase, so familiar in quotation, *Serus in cœlum redeas!* ('Late return thou to the skies!') The emperor is begged by the poet indulgently to cherish a fondness for being styled father and prince to his people.

The third ode is addressed to the ship that was to have Virgil for passenger to Athens. The wind is charged to bear him safely on his way. It takes but two stanzas out of the ten composing the ode, to express adequately this sentiment of the poet's. The other eight stanzas are occupied with the suggested idea of the daring of man in attempting navigation of the dreadful sea. There is no return to what, from the title of the ode, should seem the proper controlling motive to the poem. We venture to think the ode wanting in unity and consistency of interest. It breathes perhaps of Pindar, in its bold following of far suggestion. Here are the two opening stanzas, those in which alone there is allusion to Virgil. We give them in the version of Dr. Philip Francis, an admirable, and formerly a very popular, work :

> So may the Cyprian queen divine,
> And the twin stars with saving lustre shine ;
>   So may the father of the wind
> All others, but the western breezes, bind,
>   As you, dear vessel, safe restore
> Th' intrusted pledge to the Athenian shore,
>   And of my soul the partner save,
> My much-loved Virgil, from the raging wave.

The fourth ode furnishes one of those familiar quotations of which Horace is a famously abundant source of supply to literature. There is a solemn roll, as of muffled drums, a solemn beat, as of slow footsteps keeping time, in the rhythm of the original verse, which no translation reproduces. We are not sure but plain prose translation, closely literal, will here be the best reflex of Horace's sense and sound : "Pale death, with equal foot, knocks at the cottages of the poor and at the palaces of kings." The sentiment indeed is commonplace, but the Horatian expression seems to the Latinist inimitable.

The next ode is one of Horace's amatory pieces. These, in general, are justly not very pleasing to the modern taste. Horace seemed to know nothing of women, except by the less favorable specimens of their sex. The fifth ode, however, is a comparatively innocent erotic effusion. It enjoys exceptional English fame from having been translated by Milton. Milton's Puritan conscience and imagination have unconsciously almost moralized the ode in rendering it. No English translator of Horace can ever pass this ode of his poet, without dipping his colors to Milton as he goes by. In his earlier editions, Professor Conington simply adopted Milton's rendering, without attempting any independent version of his own. Sir Theodore Martin, incidentally in a note, calls Milton's rendering an "overrated" piece of work—a judgment, on his part, rather bold than wise. Here is Milton's version—a little difficult perhaps, but not more difficult than the original :

> What slender youth, bedew'd with liquid odours
> Courts thee on roses in some pleasant cave,
> > Pyrrha? For whom bind'st thou
> > > In wreaths thy golden hair,
> Plain in thy neatness? O, how oft shall he
> On faith and changéd gods complain, and seas
> > Rough with black winds, and storms
> > Unwonted, shall admire !
> Who now enjoys thee credulous, all gold,
> Who always vacant, always amiable
> > Hopes thee, of flattering gales
> > Unmindful. Hapless they
> To whom thou untried seem'st fair! Me in my vow'd
> Picture, the sacred wall declares to have hung
> > My dank and drooping weeds
> > To the stern god of sea.

A parallel, interesting for coincidence as well as for contrast, is that between odes of invitation, like the ninth of Horace, first book (also the twelfth, fourth book), and the sonnets of invitation by Milton, inscribed respectively, "To Mr. Laurence" and "To Cyriack Skinner." Horace (according to Mr. Martin again):

> .   .   .   .   .
>
> Pile up fresh logs upon the hearth,
>   To thaw the nipping cold,
> And forth from Sabine jar, to wing
> Our mirth, the ruddy vine-juice bring
>   Four mellowing summers old.
>
> .   .   .   .   .
>
> Let not to-morrow's change or chance
>   Perplex thee, but as gain
> Count each new day!   Let beauty's glance
> Engage thee, and the merry dance,
>   Nor deem such pleasures vain!
>
> .   .   .   .   .

The other ode of invitation just mentioned is additionally interesting as being addressed to Virgil. Virgil and Horace were fast friends. Tennyson's epistolary poem to his friend, F. D. Maurice, may also be compared. Horace half-playfully, half in good earnest, conditions his invitation to Virgil. Virgil must bring some rare perfume, to pay for the rich wine that will be broached on the occasion at Horace's expense. The Romans were as fond of fragrance, as of flavor, at their feasts. Horace now (translated by Sir Theodore Martin):

> .   .   .   .   .   .
>
> Yes, a small box of nard from the stores of Sulpicius
>   A cask shall elicit, of potency rare
> To endow with fresh hopes, dewy-bright and delicious,
>   And wash from our hearts every cobweb of care.
>
> If you'd dip in such joys, come—the better the quicker!—
>   But remember the fee—for it suits not my ends,
> To let you make havoc, scot-free, with my liquor,
>   As though I were one of your heavy-pursed friends.
>
> To the winds with base lucre and pale melancholy!—
>   In the flames of the pyre these, alas! will be vain,
> Mix your sage ruminations with glimpses of folly,—
>   'Tis delightful at times to be somewhat insane!

Milton unbends in a manner very different from the fore-going. His conscience never lets up even in his most relaxed literary moods. Horace did not keep a conscience. He was simply a man of honor, as the world went, the world of his day and place.

Another poem to Virgil, very different from the one last quoted, is the famous twenty-fourth ode of the first book—a lyric of sorrow and consolation on occasion of the death of a common beloved friend. There is not, there cannot be, any adequate rendering of this fine ode. "What shame should there be, or limit, to the sense of loss indulged for so dear a head?"—thus Horace begins. "So then Quinctilius the perpetual slumber plies!" "Quinctilius—to him, ah, when will Purity, and—sister she to Justice—inviolate Faith, and Truth unclad, find ever any equal?" How bald, how harsh, the literal English of the consummate Latin looks! The charm dwells in the first perfect form. It is felt there by the scholar, but it is not, we suppose, transferable thence to any other than he. We have known an inimitably fine effect to be produced by apt quotation of the first two stanzas, untranslated, of this ode, for an occasion, the academic atmosphere of which made the classic Latin itself appropriate.

A very vengeful allusion to Cleopatra—vengeful, but re-lenting at last into Roman admiration of the spirit she dis-played in her disaster, in daring suicidal death as preferable to the disgrace of being driven in triumph through the streets of Rome—occurs in the thirty-seventh of the first book of odes. It will remind our readers of Tennyson's stanzas on the same subject, in his Dream of Fair Women. Here are the conclud-ing stanzas (according to Dr. Francis):

> With fearless hand she dared to grasp
> The writhings of the wrathful asp,
> And suck the poison through her veins,
> Resolved on death, and fiercer from its pains.
> Then scorning to be led the boast

> Of mighty Cæsar's naval host,
> And arm'd with more than mortal spleen,
> Defrauds a triumph, and expires a queen.

The tenth of the second book is too characteristic of the writer, too good in itself, too celebrated, and it has been by the poet Cowper too happily translated, not to be given by us here entire. It is a eulogy of the "golden mean":

> Receive, dear friends, the truths I teach,
> So shalt thou live beyond the reach
>   Of adverse Fortune's power;
> Not always tempt the distant deep,
> Nor always timorously creep
>   Along the treacherous shore.
>
> He that holds fast the golden mean
> And lives contentedly between
>   The little and the great,
> Feels not the wants that pinch the poor,
> Nor plagues that haunt the rich man's door,
>   Imbittering all his state.
>
> The tallest pines feel most the power
> Of wintry blasts; the loftiest tower
>   Comes heaviest to the ground;
> The bolts that spare the mountain's side
> His cloud-capt eminence divide,
>   And spread the ruin round.
>
> The well-informed philosopher
> Rejoices with a wholesome fear,
>   And hopes in spite of pain;
> If winter bellow from the north
> Soon the sweet spring comes dancing forth,
>   And Nature laughs again.
>
> What if thine heaven be overcast?
> The dark appearance will not last;
>   Expect a brighter sky.
> The god that strings a silver bow
> Awakes sometimes the Muses too,
>   And lays his arrows by.
>
> If hindrances obstruct thy way,
> Thy magnanimity display,

> And let thy strength be seen :
> But O ! if Fortune fill thy sail
> With more than a propitious gale,
> Take half thy canvas in.

Christian Cowper was unable to translate so earth-bound a poetic philosophy of life as the foregoing, without being moved to monitory reflection. He moralizes, in a rhymed sequel, as follows :

> And is this all ? Can Reason do no more
> Than bid me shun the deep and dread the shore ?
> Sweet moralist ! afloat on life's rough sea,
> The Christian has an art unknown to thee :
> He holds no parley with unmanly fears ;
> Where duty bids he confidently steers,
> Faces a thousand dangers at her call,
> And, trusting in his God, surmounts them all.

In the eleventh of the second book of odes, appears a touch, a mere touch, on the topic of advancing old age, that reminds one, by subtle association, of our own half-Horatian American poet of occasions, Oliver Wendell Holmes. We all know the humorous-pathetic fondness of Dr. Holmes's verse for this theme. And then, besides, the convivial spirit here conjoined is not alien to the parallel. Horace (according to Sir Theodore Martin) :

> .   .   .   .   .   .
>
> Say, why should we not, flung at ease 'neath this pine,
>   Or a plane-tree's broad umbrage, quaff gayly our wine,
> While the odours of Syrian nard and the rose
>   Breathe sweet from locks tipp'd, and just tipp'd, with Time's
>   snows.

It was one of the fortunes of Horace's life to escape death, on a certain occasion, very narrowly, from the accidental falling of a tree. He makes the occurrence the subject of an ode, the thirteenth of the second book. The opening stanzas are maledictory. He thinks the planter of that tree must have been a man of many crimes, actual or potential. After an imaginary list of such, he says (Martin) :

> All this he must have done—or could—
>   I'm sure—the wretch, that stuck thee down,
> Thou miserable stump of wood,
>   To topple on thy master's crown,
> Who ne'er designed thee any harm,
> Here on my own, my favorite farm.

A strain follows, of higher mood :

> How nearly in her realms of gloom
>   I dusky Proserpine had seen,
> Seen Æacus dispensing doom,
>   And the Elysian fields serene,
> Heard Sappho to her lute complain
> Of unrequited passion's pain :
>
> Heard thee, too, O Alcæus, tell,
>   Striking the while thy golden lyre,
> With fuller note and statelier swell,
>   The sorrows and disasters dire
> Of warfare and the ocean deep,
> And those that far in exile weep.
>
> While shades round either singer throng,
>   And the deservéd tribute pay
> Of sacred silence to their song,
>   Yet chiefly crowd to hear the lay
> Of battles old to story known,
> And haughty tyrants overthrown.
>
> What wonder they, their ears to feast,
>   Should thickly throng, when by these lays
> Entranced, the hundred-headed beast
>   Drops his black ears in sweet amaze,
> And even the snakes are charmed, as they
> Among the Furies' tresses play.
>
> Nay even Prometheus, and the sire
>   Of Pelops, cheated of their pains,
> Forget awhile their doom of ire
>   In listening to the wondrous strains ;
> Nor doth Orion longer care
> To hunt the lynx or lion there.

Allusion to this nigh-fatal tree recurs often throughout the odes.

In the fifteenth of the second book of odes, Horace appears

as upbraider of his own degenerate times. He inveighs against the growing luxury of private landscape gardening and architecture. Sir Theodore Martin renders:

> .   .   .   .   .
>
> It was not so when Romulus
>   Our greatness fostered in its prime,
> Nor did our great forefathers thus,
>   In unshorn Cato's simple time.
>
> Men's private fortunes then were low,
>   The public income great; in these
> Good times no long-drawn portico
>   Caught for its lord the northern breeze.
>
> Nor did the laws our sires permit
>   Sods dug at random to despise
> As for their daily homes unfit;
>   And yet they bade our cities rise
>
> More stately at the public charge,
>   And did, to their religion true,
> The temples of the gods enlarge,
>   And with fair-sculptured stone renew.

There is a note struck here that rings in the sense like that querulous line of Wordsworth,

> Plain living and high thinking are no more!

The first ode of the third book, entitled "In Praise of Contentment," is in part a very fine variation of this. But the motive of the poem last alluded to—it is a motive familiar with Horace—is different. See the following extracts from Martin's rendering:

> Ye rabble rout, avaunt!
>   Your vulgar din give o'er,
> Whilst I the Muses' own hierophant,
> To the pure ears of youths and virgins chant
>   In strains unheard before!
>
> .   .   .   .   .
>
> The fish are conscious that a narrower bound
> Is drawn the seas around
> By masses huge hurl'd down into the deep;

> There at the bidding of a lord, for whom
> Not all the land he owns is ample room,
> Do the contractor and his laborers heap
> Vast piles of stone, the ocean back to sweep.
>   But let him climb in pride,
>   That lord of halls unblest,
>   Up to his lordly nest,
>   Yet ever by his side
>   Climb Terror and Unrest;
>   Within the brazen galley's sides
>   Care, ever wakeful, flits,
>   And at his back, when forth in state he rides,
>   Her withering shadow sits.
>
>   If thus it fare with all;
> If neither marbles from the Phrygian mine
> Nor star-bright robes of purple and of pall
>   Nor the Falernian vine,
> Nor costliest balsams, fetch'd from farthest Ind,
>   Can soothe the restless mind;
>   Why should I choose
> To rear on high, as modern spendthrifts use,
>   A lofty hall, might be the home for kings,
> With portals vast, for Malice to abuse,
> Or Envy make her theme to point a tale;
>   Or why for wealth, which new-born trouble brings,
>   Exchange my Sabine vale?

One of the happiest bits of Sir Theodore Martin's workmanship chances to coincide with one of the most characteristic,
and one of the best, felicities of the original master himself.
We take a few stanzas out of the sixteenth of the second book
of odes :   .   .   .   .   .

> He lives on little, and is blest,
>   On whose plain board the bright
>   Salt-cellar shines, which was his sires' delight,
> Nor terrors, nor cupidity's unrest,
>   Disturb his slumbers light.
>
> Why should we still project and plan,
>   We creatures of an hour?
>   Why fly from clime to clime, new regions scour?
> Where is the exile, who, since time began,
>   To fly from self had power?

Fell care climbs brazen galleys' sides;
  Nor troops of horse can fly
  Her foot, which than the stag's is swifter, ay,
Swifter than Eurus, when he madly rides
  The clouds along the sky.

Careless what lies beyond to know,
  And turning to the best
  The present, meet life's bitters with a jest,
And smile them down; since nothing here below
  Is altogether blest.

In manhood's prime Achilles died,
  Tithonus by the slow
  Decay of age was wasted to a show,
And Time may what it hath to thee denied
  On me perchance bestow.

    .   .   .   .   .

To me a farm of modest size,
  And slender vein of song,
  Such as in Greece flowed vigorous and strong,
Kind fate has given, and spirit to despise
  The base, malignant throng.

There is Horace's philosophy of life, summed up in an ode.

With the epicurean's optimistic pessimism, exemplified in the foregoing ode, Horace united the Roman's thirst for posthumous fame. And of posthumous fame, an immortality of it, Horace was, in his own mind, not less sure than was contemporary Ovid. The twentieth of the second book, inscribed "To Mæcenas," deals with this topic, expressing boldly the poet's confidence of his own future renown. We take, however, a shorter variation on the same theme, the thirtieth of the third book, a still more celebrated ode of Horace's, which is well rendered by Sir Theodore Martin:

I've reared a monument, my own,
  More durable than brass,
Yea, kingly pyramids of stone
  In height it doth surpass.

Rain shall not sap, nor driving blast
  Disturb its settled base,

Nor countless ages rolling past
  Its symmetry deface.

I shall not wholly die. Some part,
  Nor that a little, shall
Escape the dark destroyer's dart,
  And his grim festival.

For long as with his Vestals mute
  Rome's Pontifex shall climb
The Capitol, my fame shall shoot
  Fresh buds through future time.

Where brawls loud Aufidus, and came
  Parch'd Daunus erst, a horde
Of rustic boors to sway, my name
  Shall be a household word;

As one who rose from mean estate,
  The first with poet fire
Æolic song to modulate
  To the Italian lyre.

Then, grant, Melpomene, thy son
  Thy guerdon proud to wear,
And Delphic laurels duly won
  Bind thou upon my hair!

The *Dulce et decorum est pro patria mori,* so familiar a quotation of patriotism, is a sentiment and expression of Horace's, occurring in the second of the third book of odes. The whole ode is very fine.

There is no loftier moral height touched anywhere by the wing of the Horatian muse, than that of the opening of the third ode of the third book. *Justum et tenacem propositi virum,* is the lordly first line.   How it fills the mouth that utters it ! The sound is almost enough to convey the sense, even to English ears unskilled of Latin. Here is Martin's resonant rendering of the first two stanzas :

He that is just, and firm of will
  Doth not before the fury quake
Of mobs that instigate to ill,
Nor hath the tyrant's menace skill
  His fixed resolve to shake;

> Nor Auster, at whose wild command
>   The Adriatic billows dash,
> Nor Jove's dread thunder-launching hand.
> Yea, if the globe should fall, he'll stand
>   Serene amidst the crash.

("Auster" is the name of a wind.)

Like, in the lofty Roman spirit of it, is the fifth of book third, which sings Regulus. Livy, become lyrist, might have written such an ode. The story of Regulus will be recalled by our readers. Taken prisoner by the Carthaginians in the First Punic War, he was, after years of captivity, despatched to Rome (under his promise to return, if unsuccessful in his embassy) charged from his captors to recommend peace on conditions humiliating to his country. He stoutly advised his countrymen to reject the terms proposed. Returning to Carthage, he was, with cruel torture, put to death. This latter part of the story of Regulus is now not generally credited. Horace makes fine use of the proud, if in part doubtful, tradition. We again let Sir Theodore translate for us. He certainly does upon occasion take fire from his original, and kindle into true poet's flame. Horace has just bemoaned the poltroon degeneracy of his countrymen:

> .   .   .   .   .
>
> Ah, well he feared such shame for us,
> The brave, far-seeing Regulus,
> When he the vile conditions spurn'd,
> That might to precedent be turn'd,
> With ruin and disaster fraught
> To after times, should they bo taught
> Another creed than this,—" They die
> Unwept, who brook captivity !"
>
> "I've seen," he cried, "our standards hung
> In Punic fanes, our weapons wrung
> From Roman hands without a blow ;
> Our citizens, I've seen them go
> With arms behind their free backs tied,
> Gates I have seen flung open wide,

Ay, Roman troops I've seen disgraced
To till the plains they had laid waste!

" Will he return more brave and bold,
The soldier you redeem with gold?
You add but loss unto disgrace.
Its native whiteness once efface
With curious dyes; you can no more
That whiteness to the wool restore;
Nor is true valor, once debased,
In souls corrupt to be replaced!

" If from the tangled meshes freed,
The stag will battle, then indeed
May he conspicuous valor show,
Who trusted the perfidious foe,—
He smite upon some future field
The Carthaginian, who could yield
In fear of death his arms to be
Bound up with thongs submissively!
Content to draw his caitiff breath,
Nor feel such life is worse than death!
O shame! O mighty Carthage, thou
On Rome's fallen glories towerest now! "

From his chaste wife's embrace, they say,
And babes, he tore himself away,
As he had forfeited the right
To clasp them as a freeman might;
Then sternly on the ground he bent
His manly brow; and so he lent
Decision to the senate's voice,
That paused and waver'd in its choice,
And forth the noble exile strode,
Whilst friends in anguish lined the road.

Noble indeed! for, though he knew
What tortures that barbarian crew
Had ripe for him, he waved aside
The kin that did his purpose chide,
The thronging crowds, that strove to stay
His passage, with an air as gay,
As though at close of some decree
Upon a client's lawsuit he
Its dreary coil were leaving there,
To green Venafrum to repair

> Or to Tarentum's breezy shore
> Where Spartans built their town of yore.

We shall supply a lively contrast to the tense high strain
of the preceding odes, by introducing here the ninth of the
third book. This is an Am-œ-be'an ode, so-called—one, that
is, composed of alternately responsive stanzas. It is a very
famous little piece. It will indicate the variety of genius and
character that Horace has, in every age, attracted to illustrate
his verse—at the same time exhibiting our ode in a really fine
version of it—if we take Bishop Atterbury's rendering, not
obsolete, though executed so long ago as 1700 :

Horace. While I was fond, and you were kind,
Nor any dearer youth, reclined
On your soft bosom, sought to rest,
Phraätes was not half so bless'd.

Lydia. While you ador'd no other face,
Nor loved me in the second place,
My happy celebrated fame
Outshone e'en Ilia's envied flame.

H. Me Chloë now possesses whole,
Her voice and lyre command my soul ;
Nor would I death itself decline,
Could her life ransom'd be with mine.

L. For me young lovely Calais burns,
And warmth for warmth my heart returns,
Twice would I life with ease resign,
Could his be ransom'd once with mine.

H. What if sweet love, whose bands we broke,
Again should tame us to the yoke ;
Should banished Chloë cease to reign,
And Lydia her lost power regain ?

L. Though Hesperus be less fair than he,
Thou wilder than the raging sea,
Lighter than down ; yet gladly I
With thee would live, with thee would die.

We have now done with the odes of Horace. In thus dismissing them, let us keep ourselves in countenance with our
readers by quoting, from the preface to his English Horace,

an expression of Mr. Conington's to confirm our own at once disparaging and admiring appreciation of these celebrated Latin lyrics :

" It is only the attractiveness of the Latin, half real, half perhaps arising from association and the romance of a language not one's own, that makes us feel this 'lyrical commonplace' more supportable than commonplace is usually found to be."

The satires proper of Horace—his satires, we mean, expressly so named—for the Horatian satiric vein runs also through the poetical epistles of this author—we shall have room, as in fact we shall have need, to detain but very briefly under notice. Of the epistles we shall perforce content ourselves with the merest mention. We simply now, for insertion here, detach from the sixth satire, second book, of Horace, the fable of The Town and Country Mouse. This is well rendered in rattling octosyllabics by Martin ; but we present instead a version which, besides being more exactly literal than that, is conformed in metre to the hexameter Latin original. (We ought to explain that, at one point in the story, Horace humorously incorporates, for mock-heroic effect, a Virgilian assemblage of words to mark the hour of midnight. By way of exception to our own literal exactness in rendering, we have ventured to reproduce (in English) this stroke of Horatian humor, by making conscript a slow-moving spondaic line of Milton's " Paradise Lost," to serve the same purpose.)

The fable translated is playfully introduced by Horace, as a threadbare story told by a guest, at a banquet imagined to take place in the country, where high themes are discussed. Cervus, a neighbor of Horace's, is one of those men whose idea of helping on conversation is to contribute a story. Some one has remarked on the anxious wealth of Arellius, when Cervus snuffs his chance and begins :

> Once, runs the story, a mouse of the country within his poor cavern

Welcomed a mouse of the city—old cronies they each of the other—
Manners uncouth, sharp eye to his hoard, yet disposed notwith-
standing,
Acting the host, his close heart to unbind.   Why multiply words?
He
Neither the stored-away chick-pea grudged, nor his longest oat-
kernel.
Forth in his mouth he, bringing the dry plum, also his nibbled
Bacon-bits, gave them, eager with various banquet to vanquish
Niceness of guest scarce touching with tooth of disdain any viand:
While, stretched on fresh litter of straw, he, lord of the household,
Ate him a spelt-grain or darnel, the choicer provisions not sharing.

Finally, city-bred says to the other: " What is it, companion,
Tempts you, enduring, to live on the ridge abrupt of the forest?
You, too—will you prefer men and town to the fierce savage wild-
wood?
Up and away—trust, comrade, to me; since creatures terrestrial
Live allotted a mortal portion of breath, nor is any
Refuge from death to great or to small: so, my excellent fellow,
While it is granted you, live in agreeable wise, well-conditioned;
Live recollecting of span how brief you are!"
                                        Soon as these speeches
Wrought on the swain, he out of his dwelling lightly leaps forth:
thence
Press they, the pair, on the journey proposed, being keenly desirous
Under the walls of the city to creep as night-farers. And night now
'Half-way up hill this vast sublunar vault' clomb, when
Each of the mice set foot in a palace resplendent, where drapings
Tinctured crimson in grain were glowing on ivory couches.
Numberless dishes remaining from yesterday's sumptuous supper
There at remove stood in panniers loftily built like a turret.

So when now he has placed at his ease on a couch-spread of purple
Countryman mouse, obsequious host he runs hither and thither,
Course after course the supper prolongs, and, with flourish of
service,
Does all the honors in form, whatever he offers foretasting.
He, reclining, rejoices in altered estate, and in plenty
Plays you the part of jolly good fellow—when, sudden, a mighty
Rumble of doors rolling open both of them shook from their
couches:
Helter-skelter scampering went they, stricken with terror—
Growingly breathless with panic they quake, while rings the great
mansion

Loud to the baying of mastiffs Molossian.
>   Then countryman mouse said:
" Life such as this I've no use for ; good-bye to you : me, with the
   lowly
Vetch, shall the woods, and a cave secure from surprises, make
   happy."

It is the contrast of the leisurely and remote conversation conceived thus as passing at the supposed banquet in the country—the contrast of this with the hurried and exciting scenes and occasions of life in the city, that affords the mild flavor of satire discoverable in this composition of Horace's.

Among the Epistles of Horace, there are two decidedly more interesting and more valuable for modern readers than any of the others. These are the Epistle to Augustus and that to the Pisos. The latter is generally called " The Art of Poetry," such being in fact the didactic subject of the epistle. Horace's " Ars Poetica " enjoys a high repute for the soundness of its inculcation on the subject which it treats. We cannot do more than thus ceremoniously salute this piece in passing it. We may, however, suggest to our readers that if they will study Pope's " Essay on Criticism," they will find that a lively and agreeable way of getting at the spirit, and at no small part also of the wisdom, of the ancient production.

The facility with which Horace lends himself to such adaptations as Pope's, may serve to remind one how fundamentally the same from age to age, and from race to race, our common human nature remains. It may serve also to show that Horace was in this at least a poet for all time. He took hold of what is permanent in the constitution of our human frame.

Both as man, and as man of letters, Horace was of the world, eminently so, and the world will always love its own. His fame will easily last as long as the world lasts— or as the fashion of the world lasts. And no one will grudge so accomplished and so agreeable a man his merited reward.

CHAPTER XII.

JUVENAL.

IF Tacitus had been a poet, he would have been a poet like Ju'-ve-nal. If Juvenal had been an historian, he would have been an historian like Tacitus. Both alike were satirists. The difference is that Tacitus satirized incidentally, and in prose, while Juvenal satirized expressly, and in verse.

It was noted by the Romans themselves that satire was a literary form—the only one—of their own origination. Juvenal was by no means the first in time, though he is so far the first in power, among Roman satirists. Horace was a satirist before Juvenal, as Lucilius was a satirist before Horace. Of Lucilius, true founder of Roman satire, only fragments remain. Between Horace and Juvenal came Persius, but those two are for us the representative satirists of Rome.

Horace's satires have the character of amateur performances, in comparison with the satires of Juvenal. Horace had not depth enough of nature, had not strength enough of conviction, to make him a really powerful satirist. He experimented, he toyed, with the satiric vein. Juvenal satirized in dead earnest. He did not play at his task. He wrought at it with might and main. His whole soul was in it, and his soul was large and strong. Satire, in his hands, was less a lash, even a Roman lash, than a sword. It did not sting. It cut. It did not cut simply the skin. It cut the flesh. It cut the flesh to the bone. It clove the bone to the marrow. Hardly ever, in the history of literature, has such a weapon been wielded by any writer.

Who was Juvenal? No one knows. He was this satirist. That is all we know of him. As a man, he is nothing but a name. Not that there are not traditions about Juvenal. But there are no traditions that we can trust. When he lived, is uncertain. We know only that it was about the close of the first century after Christ. He had seen the empire under several emperors. Some think that, having written earlier, he finally published under Trajan—a ruler great enough, and strong enough, and wise, as well as generous, enough, to let the satirist say his say, unhindered and unharmed. Not quite to the end, however, unharmed—if we are to trust the legend which relates that Juvenal was honorably, and as it were satirically, punished for the freedom of his pen, by being sent to Egypt at eighty years of age to command a cohort stationed in that province. He there soon died of his vexation and chagrin. Such is the story; but the story has no voucher. Juvenal is personally a great unknown. But can the man justly be called unknown who has written what Juvenal has written? The incidents of his life, the traits of his personal appearance, we are ignorant of—but do we not know Juvenal by what is far more central and essential in his character?

The answer to that question depends upon whether we take Juvenal's satires to shadow forth the real sentiments of the satirist, or to have been written by him in mere wanton play of wit, "without a conscience or an aim." Opposite views have been contended for on this point, but the present writer is sure he feels the pulse of personal sincerity beating strong in Juvenal's satires. It was the morals, much more than it was the manners, of the Roman empire, that engaged the genius of Juvenal. That the satirist himself remained a model of virtue, amid the general corruption that rotted around him, we should be far from maintaining. But Juvenal's conscience was on the side of virtue—his conscience, or at least his Roman pride and scorn. He truly despised vice, if he did not truly reprobate vice. Scorn edged the blade, and scorn urged the blow.

It is a pity, but for reasons of propriety, we cannot show our readers the one satire in particular which staggers, for many, their faith in Juvenal, but by which, we confess, our own faith in Juvenal is confirmed. Vice was so flagrant in imperial Rome, that only to name what was done there would now be an intolerable offense. But Juvenal named it, and never flinched. He painted it with colors dipped in hell. You look at the picture aghast. No wonder if for a moment you feel such a picture to be as wicked as that itself was, of which this is a picture. The picture breathes and burns. It is not like life—it is life. The artist has not depicted sin—he has committed sin.

But look again. There is no enticement here. You are not allured. You are revolted. It was not because he secretly loved them, that this man dwelt on images of evil. He dwelt on them because he hated, or at least despised, them, and would do his utmost to make them everywhere hateful or despicable. So at least we read Juvenal. But we will speak no more of what we must not show.

Happily what we can show of Juvenal is one of the best of his satires—one of the best, and, on the whole, perhaps quite the most celebrated. There are sixteen satires in all, and this is the tenth of the series. Dr. Samuel Johnson has given it added fame for English readers by his powerful imitative poem, "The Vanity of Human Wishes." It will be interesting to study the original and the imitation together.

It is wise always in the reader to remember that satires, like comedies, necessarily depend for their interest so much on that atmosphere of incident and event in which they were produced, as to be sadly deprived of color and tone through lapse of time and change of place. The full text of Juvenal's Tenth Satire would thus, we fear, notwithstanding the extraordinary merit of the poem, prove but dull reading to many. We shall need to be select and to be short.

The motive of the piece is tolerably well expressed in Johnson's title, "The Vanity of Human Wishes." That expression, however, is ambiguous. It might be understood to convey the idea that human wishes are vain, as impotent to bring about their own fulfillment. The satirist's true thought is rather, not that human wishes are weak, but that human wishes are blind and unwise. We wish at foolish cross-purposes. We desire our own bane, we dread our own blessing.

There is a recent prose translation, published by Macmillan & Co., very good, and interesting the more because coming to us from our antipodes. The translators are English scholars who date their work from the University of Melbourne, in Australia. We resist the temptation to seem fresh by using this version, and go back to the pentameter couplets of Gifford. The relief of verse and of rhyme will be found grateful. Juvenal's point will seem sharper, than it would do sheathed in scholarlike, but not literary, prose.

> Let Observation, with extensive view,
> Survey mankind from China to Peru,

is Johnson's familiar beginning. The tautologous verbosity of this has often been pointed out. It is an extreme specimen of Johnson at his worst. Juvenal gave Johnson the hint, but Johnson is himself responsible for suffering the hint to carry him so far. What Juvenal says is (as our Australian translators give it), "In all the world—from Gades [Cadiz] to the land of the Morning and its Ganges." Gifford rhymes it :

> In every clime, from Ganges' distant stream
> To Gades, gilded by the western beam.

Juvenal says that "in every clime" from West to East, the rule is for men to wish what, if granted, will probably injure them. For example, the universal craving is for wealth, but how often has wealth been the ruin of its possessor ! The rich, under bad emperors, became the prey of those emperors, while the poor escaped by their own obscurity. The satirist recalls historic instances (Gifford's translation) :

> For this, in other times, at Nero's word,
> The ruffian bands unsheathed the murderous sword,
> Rushed to the swelling coffers of the great,
> Chased Lat-e-ra′nus from his lordly seat,
> Besieged too-wealthy Seneca's wide walls,
> And closed, terrific, round Lon-gi′nus' halls:
> While sweetly in their cocklofts slept the poor,
> And heard no soldier thundering at their door.
>   The traveller, freighted with a little wealth
> Sets forth at night, and wins his way by stealth :
> Even then, he fears the bludgeon and the blade,
> And starts and trembles at a rush's shade ;
> While, void of care, the beggar trips along,
> And, in the spoiler's presence, trolls his song.

Juvenal thinks that if, in their own times, De-moc′ri-tus could laugh incessantly, and Her-a-cli′tus could incessantly weep, over the follies of their fellow-creatures, those philosophers would find much more food for laughter and for tears, were they to enjoy a resurrection under the Roman empire as he himself saw the Roman empire. The laughter of Democritus, by the way, Juvenal says, was intelligible—anybody could laugh ; but where could anybody get brine enough to keep him going in tears? This is the fashion in which Juvenal derided the pomp of civic processions and military triumphs in Rome :

> Democritus, at every step he took,
> His sides with unextinguished laughter shook,
> Though, in his days, Abdera's simple towns
> No fasces knew, chairs, litters, purple gowns.
> What! had he seen, in his triumphal car,
> Amid the dusty Cirque, conspicuous far,
> The Prætor perched aloft, superbly dress'd
> In Jove's proud tunic, with a trailing vest
> Of Tyrian tapestry, and o'er him spread
> A crown, too bulky for a mortal head,
> Borne by a sweating slave, maintained to ride

In the same car, and mortify his pride!
Add now the bird, that, with expanded wing,
From the raised sceptre seems prepared to spring;
And trumpets here; and there the long parade
Of duteous friends, who head the cavalcade;
Add, too, the zeal of clients robed in white,
Who hang upon his reins, and grace the sight,
Unbribed, unbought—save by the dole, at night!

Juvenal alludes at some length to the striking fate of Seja′-
nus. Sejanus, an imperial favorite under Tiberius, became a
pretender to the throne, and so a conspirator against his sovereign. He was found out, was strangled, and the populace rent
his dead body into fragments, which they flung into the Tiber.
The statues of the fallen man were tumbled down and melted
up in fierce fires, kindled on the street. The rabble meantime
ignorantly exchanged gibes, in their street talk, at the very
man whom, had he but succeeded, they would have hailed emperor with uproarious cheers. Now Juvenal, from the point at
which the fire is kindled for melting up the bronze Sejanus:

Then roar the fires! the sooty artist blows,
And all Sejanus in the furnace glows;
Sejanus, once so honored, so adored,
And only second to the world's great lord,
Runs glittering from the mould, in cups and cans,
Basins and ewers, plates, pitchers, pots, and pans.
  " Crown all your doors with bay, triumphant bay,
Sacred to Jove, the milk-white victim slay;
For lo! where great Sejanus by the throng,
A joyful spectacle! is dragged along.
What lips! what cheeks! ha, traitor!—for my part,
I never loved the fellow—in my heart."
" But tell me; Why was he adjudged to bleed?
And who discovered? and who proved the deed?"
" Proved!—a huge, wordy letter came to-day
From Capreæ." Good! what think the people? They!
They follow fortune, as of old, and hate,
With their whole souls, the victim of the state.
Yet would the herd, thus zealous, thus on fire,
Had Nurscia met the Tuscan's fond desire,
And crushed the unwary prince, have all combined,
And hailed Sejanus, MASTER OF MANKIND!

At this point occurs one of the most memorable of all Juvenal's satirical strokes. The satirist contrasts former popular freedom with present popular servitude. The same Roman people, he says, that once proudly by its votes conferred every privilege and every distinction, now confines its aspiration to the one cry for bread to stop its mouth, and for the games of the circus to set its eyes agape. *Panem et circenses !* Food and fun at the public expense, were, in Juvenal's time, sufficient to content the degenerate citizens of the empire. " Panem et circenses," is a famous phrase of quotation. 'Say,' exclaims Juvenal, suddenly—as would seem—bethinking himself that he had introduced Sejanus for a purpose, ' say, would you like Sejanus's power, bought at Sejanus's price ? '

From Sejanus, Juvenal goes back farther for historic instances, to Crassus, to Pompey, to Cæsar :

> What wrought the Crassi, what the Pompeys' doom,
> And his, who bowed the stubborn neck of Rome?
> What but the wild, the unbounded wish to rise,
> Heard, in malignant kindness, by the skies.
> Few kings, few tyrants, find a bloodless end,
> Or to the grave, without a wound, descend.

Wealth and power are not the only objects foolishly craved by men. The ambition and the prayer to be eloquent are also disguised and unconscious invocations of doom—witness the examples of Demosthenes and Cicero :

> The child, with whom a trusty slave is sent,
> Charged with his little scrip, has scarcely spent
> His mite at school, ere all his bosom glows
> With the fond hope he nevermore foregoes,
> To reach Demosthenes' or Tully's name,
> Rival of both in eloquence and fame!—
> Yet, by this eloquence, alas ! expired
> Each orator, so envied, so admired !
> Yet, by the rapid and resistless sway
> Of torrent genius, each was swept away !
> Genius, for that, the baneful potion sped,
> And lopped, from this, the hands and gory head:

> While meaner pleaders unmolested stood,
> Nor stained the rostrum with their wretched blood.

In the gibe, now to follow, of Juvenal, at Cicero's jingling braggadocio verse, our readers will note how ingeniously the effect on the ear, of the Latin line laughed at by the satirist, is imitated by Mr. Gifford in his translation. Juvenal avers that, for Cicero's own happiness, it would have been better for him to write nothing but such stuff as even that ludicrous line of poetry, than it was to launch at Antony the flaming bolt of eloquence which cost the orator his life :

> " *How fortu*NATE A NATAL *day was thine,*
> *In that* LATE *consu*LATE, *O Rome, of mine !*"
> Oh, soul of eloquence! had all been found
> An empty vaunt, like this, a jingling sound,
> Thou might'st, in peace, thy humble fame have borne,
> And laughed the swords of Antony to scorn!
> Yet this would I prefer—the common jest—
> To that which fired the fierce triumvir's breast,
> That second scroll, where eloquence divine
> Burst on the ear from every glowing line.
> And he too fell, whom Athens, wondering, saw
> Her fierce democracy, at will, o'erawe,
> And "fulmine over Greece!" Some angry Power
> Scowled, with dire influence, on his natal hour.
> Bleared with the glowing mass, the ambitious sire,
> From anvils, sledges, bellows, tongs, and fire,
> From temp'ring swords, his own more safe employ,
> To study RHETORIC, sent his hopeful boy.

Macaulay thinks that Johnson's passage, parallel to the foregoing—a passage descriptive of the disappointments that dog the literary life—is finer than the original which it imitates.

The topics successively treated by Juvenal are Wealth, Power, Eloquence, Military Fame, Long Life, Personal Beauty, as objects of human desire likely, even if gained, to involve the gainer in special disappointment and misery. Hannibal, Alexander, Xerxes, are the historical examples adduced, of thirst for the vain delight of warlike renown. A wild desire, Juvenal declares it, and says (Gifford's translation) :

> Yet has this wild desire, in other days,
> This boundless avarice of a few for praise,
> This frantic rage for names to grace a tomb,
> Involved whole countries in one general doom;
> Vain "rage!" the roots of the wild fig-tree rise,
> Strike through the marble, and their memory dies!

The "wild fig-tree" of Juvenal is, no doubt, the allusion intended in Tennyson's "Princess":

> "though the rough kex break
> The starred mosaic, and the wild goat hang
> Upon the pillar, and the wild fig-tree split
> Their monstrous idols."

Juvenal's passage about Hannibal is one of the finest in the satire. The words, "Expende Hannibalem" meaning "Weigh Hannibal"—that is, weigh the inurned ashes, or the buried dust, that alone remain as relic of the living man—these two words have become a not infrequent literary quotation used to set forth the "little measure" to which the mightiest dead are shrunk. Hodgson dilutes, but dilutes rather successfully, as follows:

> How are the mighty changed to dust! How small
> The urn that holds what once was Hannibal!

Now Gifford's version of Juvenal's satirical homily on Hannibal:

> Produce the urn that Hannibal contains,
> And weigh the mighty dust, which yet remains:
> AND IS THIS ALL? Yet THIS was once the bold,
> The aspiring chief, whom Afric could not hold,
> Though stretched in breadth from where the Atlantic roars,
> To distant Nilus, and his sun-burnt shores;
> In length, from Carthage to the burning zone,
> Where other Moors, and elephants are known.
> —Spain conquered, o'er the Pyrenees he bounds:
> Nature opposed her everlasting mounds,
> Her Alps, and snows; o'er these, with torrent force,
> He pours and rends through rocks his dreadful course.
> Already at his feet Italia lies;—
> Yet thundering on, "Think nothing done," he cries,
> "Till Rome, proud Rome, beneath my fury falls,

And Afric's standards float along her walls!"
Big words!—but view his figure!—view his face!
O, for some master-hand the lines to trace,
As through the Etrurian swamps, by floods increased,
The one-eyed chief urged his Getulian beast!
　　But what ensued?　Illusive Glory, say.
Subdued on Zama's memorable day,
He flies in exile to a petty state,
With headlong haste! and, at a despot's gate,
Sits, mighty suppliant! of his life in doubt,
Till the Bithynian's morning nap be out.
　　No swords, nor spears, nor stones from engines hurled,
Shall quell the man whose frown alarmed the world:
The vengeance due to Cannæ's fatal field,
And floods of human gore, a ring shall yield!
Fly, madman, fly! at toil and danger mock,
Pierce the deep snow, and scale the eternal rock,
To please the rhetoricians, and become
A DECLAMATION for the boys of Rome!

Charles XII. of Sweden serves Johnson for his modern
instance, matched against the Roman's Hannibal.　On Charles
for text, Johnson is fired to preach in sonorous rhymes his
very best sermon.　"Juvenal's Hannibal must yield to Johnson's Charles," says Macaulay.　But let our readers judge.
Here is Johnson :

On what foundation stands the warrior's pride,
How just his hopes, let Swedish Charles decide.
A frame of adamant, a soul of fire,
No dangers fright him, and no labors tire;
O'er love, o'er fear, extends his wide domain,
Unconquer'd lord of pleasure and of pain;
No joys to him pacific sceptres yield,
War sounds the trump, he rushes to the field.
Behold surrounding kings their pow'rs combine,
And one capitulate, and one resign :
Peace courts his hand, but spreads her charms in vain;
'Think nothing gain'd,' he cries, 'till naught remain,
On Moscow's walls till Gothic standards fly,
And all be mine beneath the polar sky.'
The march begins, in military state,
And nations on his eye suspended wait;
Stern Famine guards the solitary coast,

And Winter barricades the realms of Frost;
He comes, nor want nor cold his course delay!—
Hide, blushing glory, hide Pultowa's day:
The vanquish'd hero leaves his broken bands,
And shows his miseries in distant lands;
Condemn'd a needy supplicant to wait,
While ladies interpose, and slaves debate.
But did not Chance at length her error mend?
Did not subverted empire mark his end?
Did rival monarchs give the fatal wound?
Or hostile millions press him to the ground?
His fall was destin'd to a barren strand,
A petty fortress, and a dubious hand;
He left the name at which the world grew pale,
To point a moral, or adorn a tale.

So much perhaps will do in the way of paralleling Johnson with Juvenal. In what remains, from this point onward to the end, of the two poems, both poets are at their best in fecund conception and in felicitous execution. We, however, will refrain from Johnson and confine ourselves to Juvenal. At the same time, we cordially commend to readers that have the taste and the leisure for the purpose, a continued comparison of the modern with the ancient poem.

Juvenal's satiric genius fairly revels in describing the wretchedness of old age. The desire of long life, he says, entails, if gratified, unnumbered ills. These ills certainly were never more powerfully portrayed than they are here portrayed by Juvenal:

Strength, beauty, and a thousand charms beside,
With sweet distinction, youth from youth divide;
While age presents one universal face;
A faltering voice, a weak and trembling pace,
An ever-dropping nose, a forehead bare,
And toothless gums to mumble o'er its fare.
Poor wretch! behold him, tottering to his fall,
So loathsome to himself, wife, children, all,
That those who hoped the legacy to share,
And flattered long—disgusted, disappear.
The sluggish palate dulled, the feast no more
Excites the same sensations as of yore;

> Taste, feeling, all, a universal blot,
> The dearest joys of sense remembered not.
>
>   .   .   .   .   .
>
> Another loss!—no joy can song inspire,
> Though famed Seleucus lead the warbling quire:
> The sweetest airs escape him; and the lute,
> Which thrills the general ear, to him is mute.
> He sits, perhaps, too distant: bring him near;
> Alas! 'tis still the same: he scarce can hear
> The deep-toned horn, the trumpet's clanging sound,
> And the loud blast which shakes the benches round.
> Even at his ear, his slave must bawl the hour,
> And shout the comer's name, with all his power!
>
>   .   .   .   .   .
>
> These their shrunk shoulders, those their hams bemoan;
> This hath no eyes, and envies that with one:
> This takes, as helpless at the board he stands,
> His food, with bloodless lips, from others' hands;
> While that, whose eager jaws, instinctive, spread
> At every feast, gapes feebly to be fed,
> Like Progne's brood, when, laden with supplies,
> From bill to bill the fasting mother flies.
> But other ills, and worse, succeed to those:
> His limbs long since were gone; his memory goes.
> Poor driveler! he forgets his servants quite,
> Forgets, at morn, with whom he supped at night;
> Forgets the children he begot and bred;
> And makes a strumpet heiress in their stead.

The allusion to Prog'ne is the translator's, not Juvenal's own. Progne was one of Ovid's women, changed to a swallow.

Two or three lines of Johnson's imitation are too good not, after all, to be quoted here:

> Superfluous lags the veteran on the stage.

> From Marlborough's eyes the tears of dotage flow,
> And Swift expires a driveler and a show.

Juvenal prolongs his detail of the miseries unconsciously invoked in prayers for longevity, through a hundred lines or so additional to those which we have given. Out of Homer, Nestor is cited as a witness, and Ulysses's father, Laërtes, and Pe'leus, father to Achilles—all living to deplore their children dead or lost; Priam, too, surviving the glory of Troy, and Hec'uba transformed to a barking bitch. Mithrida'tes, then, is summoned, and Crœsus with the legend of Solon admonishing him; and aged Marius bereft of everything but life; and Pompey recovering from a Campanian fever, only to encounter in Egypt a worse doom of death. By the mocking irony of fate, conspirators Len'tu-lus, Ceth-e'gus, Cat'i-line escaped at least the indignity of bodily mutilation in dying. Readers depressed by all this remorseless realism of the satirist describing old age, may turn the pages of the present volume and, from Cicero's store, refresh themselves as they can, with the suave consolations of the philosopher treating the same subject.

The last topic treated in the satire is that of Personal Beauty. Juvenal, with great power, exhibits the spectacle, so familiar in history, of

> Beauty and anguish walking hand in hand
> The downward slope to death.

We shall not follow the satirist in this part of his poem. Some of the strongest strokes in it are of a nature that unfits them to be reproduced in these pages. And we need to say that the dotted lines in previous extracts, have, more than once, marked the omission of verses which we could not properly show. In barely a single instance foregoing—where, for completion of thought, it seemed necessary to retain the line—we even ventured on a silent change of half a dozen words, in order so to make the frankness of Juvenal less intolerable to modern taste.

Here is a couplet of Gifford's, translating with spirit a sentence of Juvenal's, in the latter part of his satire, that well deserves its fame:

> A woman scorned is pitiless as fate,
> For there the dread of shame adds stings to hate.

Every student of history is qualified, but a Roman under

the empire was peculiarly qualified, to appreciate the justness of the sentiment. Congreve's couplet will naturally occur to some minds:

> Heaven has no rage like love to hatred turned,
> Nor hell a fury like a woman scorned.

The conclusion of all is well-nigh Christian—in spirit, though at points the form is pagan enough. We present it in the prose translation, which is very readable, furnished in Bohn's Classical Library:

Is there then nothing for which men shall pray? If you will take advice, you will allow the deities themselves to determine what may be expedient for us, and suitable to our condition. For instead of pleasant things, the gods will give us all that is most fitting. Man is dearer to them than to himself. We, led on by the impulse of our minds, by blind and headstrong passions, pray for wedlock, and issue by our wives; but it is known to them what our children will prove; of what character our wife will be! Still, that you may have somewhat to pray for, and vow to their shrines the entrails and consecrated mincemeat of the white porker, your prayer must be that you may have a sound mind in a sound body. Pray for a bold spirit, free from all dread of death; that reckons the closing scene of life among nature's kindly boons; that can endure labor, whatever it be; that knows not the passion of anger; that covets nothing; that deems the gnawing cares of Hercules, and all his cruel toils, far preferable to the joys of Venus, rich banquets, and the downy couch of Sar-dan-a-pa'lus. I show thee what thou canst confer upon thyself. The only path that surely leads to a life of peace lies through virtue. If *we* have wise foresight, *thou*, Fortune, hast no divinity. It is we that make thee a deity, and place thy throne in heaven!

As might, from the foregoing, be guessed, the well-worn phrase, *mens sana in corpore sano*, "a sound mind in a sound body," is Juvenal's. In proposing the combination thus named, as a good of life proper to be prayed for, Juvenal makes the impression of being himself a well-attempered mind judging as soundly as a pagan could, of the chief earthly human need.

There is a note struck in the conclusion to Juvenal's great

masterpiece of satire, not far out of chord with the closing lines of Bryant's Thanatopsis.   One word alone in the American's strain distinguishes it in tone from the Roman's.   That word is "trust."   But trust, in prospect of death, is a Christian idea, and Juvenal was no Christian.   To face death without fear, but also without trust,—that was Roman ; and Roman of Romans was Juvenal.   How one sighs, and vainly sighs, with desire to have sweetened the bravery and the scorn of many of those majestic men of Rome with the meekness of trust and obedience toward Jesus !

CHAPTER XIII.

THIS chapter will somewhat resemble the inscription on a cenotaph. If we had left ourselves room for the purpose, we should have been glad to go far enough beyond the limit fixed in our choice of title for this volume, to provide, from the admirable post-classic writer Quintilian, such retrospective commentary on Latin literature taken in its entirety as would constitute a true epilogue to the present work. As it is, we must content ourselves with simply directing our readers to the place where what may be considered at least a kind of epilogue may be found. That place is in the CLASSIC FRENCH COURSE IN ENGLISH, a book of the same series with this, devoted to the exhibition of one, the chief one, of those great modern literatures which have used for their vehicle of expression various languages modified from the ancient Latin, as their common original.

The Roman Empire in giving a language to the literature which was finally to be in the largest and most important section of the imperial province of Gaul, gave also in some sense a law and a spirit to that literature. This relation it is of French letters to Latin that warrants us in suggesting, by way of present farewell to our readers, that in the abovementioned volume they may find, not indeed a formal, but a virtual, epilogue to what has been submitted for their consideration in the foregoing pages.

INDEX.

ADDISON, Joseph, 22, 88.

Æschines, 10.

Alexander the Great, 288.

Antony, Mark, 55, 56, 70 ff., 94.

Aristophanes, 217.

Aristotle, 82.

Atterbury, Bishop, 277.

Augustus, Cæsar, 11, 12, 21, 56, 92, 93, 94, 96, 98, 136, 175, 261, 263.

Bryant, William Cullen, 295.

Burke, Edmund, 57.

CÆSAR, Julius, 9, 11, 13, 14, 20, 27, 28–50, 54, 68, 69, 75, 83, 85, 86, 90, 143, 245.

Carlyle, Thomas, 10.

Catiline, 13, 31, 53, 58ff.

Cato (the Censor), 9, 10, 11, 88, 89.

Charles XII. (of Sweden), 290.

Choate, Rufus, 55, 76, 77.

Church and Brodribb, 165.

CICERO (Tully), 8, 10, 51–90, 106, 245, 287, 288, 293.

Cicero, Quintus, 43, 44, 48.

Columbus, Christopher, 49.

Congreve, William, 294.

Conington, John, 95 ff., 278.

Cortes, 49.

Dante, 259.

Democritus, 285.

Demosthenes, 10, 57, 70, 287.

DeQuincey, Thomas, 50.

Dryden, John, 97, 102, 124.

Ennius, 8, 10, 84.

Epicurus, 246.

Francis, Dr. Philip, 264, 267.

Gifford, William, 284–293 freq.

Gracchi, The, 11.

Hannibal, 146 ff., 288, 289, 290.

Havelock, Sir Henry, 44.

Heraclitus, 285.

Hesiod, 97.

Hirtius, 49.

Hodgson, 289.

Holmes, Oliver Wendell, 269.

Homer, 11, 27, 56, 91, 97, 102, 103, 112, 140, 141, 142, 259, 292.

HORACE, 8, 9, 12, 21, 259–280, 281.

Hortensius, 10, 11.

Jerome, Saint, 257.

Johnson, Dr. Samuel, 283–292.

Jugurtha, 13ff.

JUVENAL, 9, 89, 281–295.

Livius, Andronicus, 8.

LIVY, 11, 21, 143–174, 175.

Lowell, J. R., 12.

Lucan, 212.

Lucilius, 79, 281.

LUCRETIUS, 8, 111, 245–258.

Luther, Martin, 82.

Macaulay (Lord), 177, 204, 215, 288, 290.

Mæcenas, 12, 21, 261, 263.

Mallock, W. H., 248, 256.

Marie Antoinette, 200.

Marius, 13 ff., 30, 51, 144.

Martin, Sir Theodore, 265, 266, 269, 271, 278.

Maurice, F. D., 266.

Menander, 9, 217, 244.

Milton, John, 22, 93, 259, 265, 266, 267, 278.

Mommsen, Theodor, 31.

Munro (translator of Lucretius), 247, 248, 252, 253.

Nævius, 8, 9.

Napoleon (the Great), 149.

Napoleon III., 32.

Nepos, 11.

Nero, 48, 179ff.
OVID, 12, 13, 21-27, 292.
Paul (the Apostle), 84, 86, 256.
Persius, 281.
Philip (of Macedon), 70.
Pindar, 264.
PLAUTUS, 9, 217-234, 244.
Pliny, 55, 176.
Plutarch, 40.
Pompey, the Great, 54, 55, 59, 143.
Pope, Alexander, 21, 96, 139, 142, 280.
Quintilian, 12.
SALLUST, 11, 13-20, 21.
Scipio (Africanus Major), 150.
Scipio (Africanus Minor), 151, 171-174.
Scott, Sir Walter, 101.
Seneca, 143, 180, 197, 208ff.

Suetonius, 11, 48.
Sulpicius, 79, 80.
Sylla, 13ff., 144.
TACITUS, 8, 11, 165, 175-216, 281.
Tennyson, Lord, 257, 258, 266, 267, 289.
TERENCE, 9, 217-244, 245.
Theocritus, 94, 95.
Thomson, James, 101.
Thucydides, 176.
VIRGIL, 8, 11, 12, 13, 16, 21, 27, 91-142,
    255, 259, 266, 267.
Wellington, Duke of, 204.
William (of Orange), 215.
Wordsworth, William, 271.
Xenophon, 151.
Xerxes, 288.